# LEGAL ETHICS AND PROFESSIONAL RESPONSIBILITY

Other books in *Essentials of Canadian Law* Series

Criminal Law

The Law of Evidence

Statutory Interpretation

Media Law

The Law of Trusts

Intellectual Property Law

Income Tax Law

The Law of Partnerships and Corporations

Constitutional Law

Immigration Law

Environmental Law

Young Offenders Law

International Trade Law

Computer Law

The Charter of Rights and Freedoms

Family Law

ESSENTIALS OF
CANADIAN LAW

# LEGAL ETHICS AND PROFESSIONAL RESPONSIBILITY

## ALLAN C. HUTCHINSON
### Osgoode Hall Law School

IRWIN
LAW

Published in 1999 by
Irwin Law
325 Humber College Blvd.
Toronto, Ontario
M9W 7C3

ISBN: 1-55221-030-8


**Canadian Cataloguing in Publication Data**

Hutchinson, Allan C.
  Legal ethics and professional responsibility

(Essentials of Canadian law)
Includes bibliographical references and index.
ISBN 1-55221-030-8

1. Legal ethics – Canada.   I. Title.   II. Series.

KE339.H87 1999        174.3′0971        C98-930583-X
KF306.H87 1999


Printed and bound in Canada.

1   2   3   4   5     03   02   01   00   99

# SUMMARY
# TABLE OF CONTENTS

# DETAILED
# TABLE OF CONTENTS

# FOREWORD

What a twist of fate! No sooner do I appear in print deploring the lack of reflective and critical Canadian scholarship in the field of legal ethics[1] than I am asked to write an introduction to just such a book on that very subject. Not that I ought to have been surprised. Allan Hutchinson's enquiring mind and encyclopedic interests have taken him across a wide spectrum of legal subjects. He has written in a variety of styles and for academic, professional, and lay readers; and he is virtually incapable of writing something that is *not* reflective and critical. I would have predicted, however, that in turning his attention to legal ethics and professional conduct, he just might have tackled one subject too many. But I would have been wrong.

This field is a particularly daunting one for any serious scholar: in fact, when it comes to legal ethics, the more serious the scholar, the more daunted she or he might be. After all, scholars need a body of materials to work with, but in Canada at least, decisional material, commentary, and sociological analysis are all in scarce supply in this field. Take the Canadian Bar Association's Code of Professional Conduct as a case in point. Although this was supposedly the template for professional discipline across the country, for fifty years after its adoption in 1920, the CBA code was a well-kept secret — never litigated, virtually unremarked upon in the secondary literature, already obsolete at its inception, and positively anachronistic by the time it was replaced. Then, in 1974, the CBA adopted a totally new code. It seemed destined for more active life: it was a more ambitious work; it backed up its prescriptive

---

1    "Why Canadian Law Schools Do Not Teach Legal Ethics" in K. Economides, ed., *Ethical Challenges to Legal Education and Conduct* (Oxford: Hart Publishing, 1998) 105.

provisions with commentary and citations to the pertinent literature in Canada and abroad; some of its more controversial provisions generated debate when it was adopted by the CBA and by governing bodies; and it triggered a wholesale redrafting of ethical codes across the country. Mysteriously, however, this 1974 version of the CBA code seemed to suffer the same fate as its progenitor: it was only occasionally cited in published decisional material or mentioned in commentaries; and it did not seem to make much impression "on the ground." Nonetheless, perhaps sustained by a determination to reinvigorate debate and improve the profession's public image and actual behaviour, in 1987 the CBA revised and republished the 1974 Code, albeit with only modest changes.

What is the lesson of this short and trivial history of Canada's most important legal-professional charter? Legal ethics, it seems, is not a field such as criminal law or *Charter* law or commercial law, where the fundamental principles are constantly being tested in practice, and where practical experience in turn stimulates reformulation of the principles. The absence of intellectual or practical engagement with the CBA codes and their provincial counterparts has been a problem for both commentators and critical scholars. In effect, there has been nothing to comment upon or criticize, nothing to stimulate or sustain a body of Canadian academic and professional scholarship in the field of legal ethics.

By default, in times past, we relied nostalgically and unthinkingly on English tradition and ideology; more recently, the United States has been an important point of reference; but while the experiences of both foreign systems is informative, neither necessarily speaks directly to the situation of Canadian lawyers. Moreover, not enough is known about the Canadian legal profession — whom it serves, what it does, how its formal and informal normative systems operate — to permit us to compare our experience of professional discipline with that of these two cognate systems. To what extent, for example, does the still-persisting differentiation of advocacy and advice-giving functions in England make inappropriate the content and practical application of professional conduct rules dealing with the treatment of witnesses or relationships with the bench? To what extent should differences between Canada and the United States in areas such as legal aid, lay advocacy, and title insurance make us wary of adopting American approaches to legal ethics? Or for that matter, is it really appropriate for general practitioners in, say, Prince Edward Island, or defence counsel in Saskatchewan to take the same approach to conflict of interest rules as corporate lawyers in Vancouver or Toronto?

As it happens, the administration of professional discipline is the one pertinent area where a modest corpus of Canadian scholarship has developed.[2] But what that scholarship reveals is rather unsettling for those of us who preach, teach, or dispense professional discipline. Essentially, word and deed seem to bear little resemblance to each other. Most provisions of the CBA's code of professional conduct, and of provincial codes of ethics, are simply ignored by professional disciplinary bodies (perhaps rightly so). And the provisions applied most frequently and vigorously — those dealing with abuse of trust, theft of client funds, or failure to pay fees and file forms — tend to be applied against demographically well-defined target groups at the margins of the profession. Thus, there is a real question as to what constitutes the "living law" of legal ethics. This causes considerable problems for any author trying to understand the philosophical and socio-economic underpinnings of the existing norms of professional conduct, to critically evaluate their content and interpretation, to accurately inform readers about their content and administration, and to propose how (in Allan Hutchinson's words) one might develop "an ethically satisfying and professionally responsible approach to legal practice."

All that said, there are some signs that the practice and theory of professional responsibility and legal ethics may be on the verge of profound change. Decisions of professional disciplinary bodies have recently become available for the first time thanks to Quicklaw, and Gavin MacKenzie's comprehensive book[3] provides a framework for collecting and analysing this growing Canadian jurisprudence of professional conduct. Several provincial law societies seem to be on the verge of seriously addressing competence for the first time as an issue of professional responsibility, which should lead to a rethinking of what the profession, clients, and society can expect of practitioners. Others — notably the Law Society of Upper Canada — are in the midst of a major overhaul of their professional conduct codes and of their disciplinary structures. The emergence of new modalities of practice — multidisciplinary partnerships, global law firms, and credentialed specialists — is

2    S. Arthurs, "Discipline in the Legal Profession in Ontario" (1970) 7 Osgoode Hall L.J. 235; B. Reiter, *Discipline as a Means of Assuring Continuing Competence* (Unpublished Study for the Professional Organizations Committee, Ontario, 1978); J. Brockman & C. McEwen, "Self-Regulation in the Legal Profession: Funnel In, Funnel Out, or Funnel Away?" (1990) Can. J. Law & Soc. 1; B. Arnold and J. Hagan, "Careers of Misconduct: The Structure of Prosecuted Professional Deviance Among Lawyers" (1992) Am. Soc. Rev. 771; B. Arnold & J. Hagan, "Self-Regulatory Response to Professional Misconduct within the Legal Profession" (1994) 31 Can. Rev. Soc. & Anthrop. 168; H. Arthurs, above note 1.

3    G. MacKenzie, *Lawyers and Ethics: Professional Responsibility and Discipline* (Scarborough, Ont.: Carswell, 1993).

clearly going to force governing bodies to think long and hard about what, if anything, differentiates lawyers from other professionals and for that matter, from each other. The rapidly changing demographics, market conditions, sources of intellectual capital, and professional ideologies among Canadian lawyers have created crises of professional governance, which to some extent manifest themselves in a critique of the whole apparatus of professional discipline. And, of course, changes in Canada's political economy, and in public attitudes towards élites and regulatory institutions, are bound to generate pressures for a change in how lawyers behave individually and collectively. It would be surprising indeed if these and other important developments did not soon lead to a top-to-bottom rethinking of the style, content, and practice of professional ethics in Canada.

These developments, however, underline the need for a new Canadian literature on legal professionalism. Law without context, without critique, is likely to be — and will be perceived to be — incoherent, which would not be an unfair way to describe much of the scant Canadian literature on professional responsibility. Only when we begin to move towards coherence, only when we are able to locate our emerging jurisprudence of legal ethics in a theoretical, psychological, social, political, and comparative context will that jurisprudence be taken seriously as a guide to the behaviour of lawyers and as a subject fit for study by aspiring lawyers. Happily, Allan Hutchinson has taken a first significant step towards laying the foundations of a scholarly Canadian literature on legal-professional ethics. He offers a thoughtful critique of "the traditional approach" and presents his own "alternative vision," grounded in sociological data, framed up by his own well-developed work on theories of adjudication, and informed by current scholarly discourse in the field of practical and professional ethics. In this sense his book can be called an introduction to legal ethics: it marks the beginning of a new literature on the subject.

At the same time, Hutchinson's alternative vision is, as he claims, a "contextual and pragmatic approach to legal ethics." While he begins with what many observers see as a serious crisis of legal ethics, he directly addresses the practical, everyday problems that all practitioners must either resolve or suffer the consequences. In this second and more conventional sense, then, the book is also an introduction: it is easily accessible to readers — scholars, students, and practitioners — who may be considering issues of professional responsibility for the first time. Indeed, as with all of Allan Hutchinson's writing, it is more than accessible: it is always engaging and often compelling. And finally, because it is also provocative, this book is almost certain to cause thoughtful rank-

and-file lawyers — as well as benchers, discipline staff, legal academics, and managing partners — to treat issues of professional conduct and legal ethics more thoughtfully, more professionally, more critically than they have up to now.

H.W. Arthurs
Osgoode Hall Law School
York University

# PREFACE

To write a book on legal ethics and professional responsibility is quite a challenge — particularly for someone who has not spent a great deal of time in the hurly-burly of legal practice. I have tried to use this disadvantage to my advantage. Rather than fall into the familiar trap of reproducing prevailing wisdom on the ethics and etiquette of current practitioners, I have been more reflective and critical. My ambition has been to unearth the foundations of present thinking and practice and subject them to a searching critique. Having reassessed and reworked those underlying assumptions, I have sought to suggest a slightly different and more challenging approach to legal ethics and professional responsibility. Throughout, my emphasis has been on the practical context and real pressures of contemporary lawyering, particularly for the neophyte lawyer. My approach is premised on the view that, as a profession, lawyers are motivated by the desire not only to make a good living but to act in an ethical manner and to lead a good professional life. Accordingly, this book offers itself as both a critical guide to present dogma and doctrine as well as a call to ethical arms. The unifying theme — the development of an ethically satisfying and professionally responsible approach to legal practice — is, I hope, a sensible contribution to an important task that should be appreciated and shared by all lawyers.

One point about the text's format is in order. I have included fifty or so problems throughout the book. They are intended to provoke discussion and focus debate. However, I have resisted the temptation to offer my own suggestions about how to resolve them. This reticence is in keeping with the overall message of the book — ethics is all about private decision making and draws on knowledge, experience, and serious commitment: there are no easy or set answers, only hard choices and constant reassessment.

In writing this book, I am grateful to a number of people. In particular, Gavin MacKenzie's large and original tome, *Lawyers and Ethics: Professional Responsibility and Discipline*, has been a major source of guidance, research, and help. Harry Arthurs proved again that he is the sternest of critics and the best of academic friends. Jennifer Blitz provided excellent research assistance; her attention to detail complements her more general skills. Also, I am most grateful to Lincoln's Inn and the Institute for Advanced Legal Studies in London, England, where I spent the summer of 1997 as the Inns of Court Fellow in the Legal Profession: their warm support and stimulating collegiality offered a welcome setting for researching and planning this book. Finally, Lisa and Aaron kept the home fires stoked and burning. Thanks to one and all.

# CHAPTER 1

# INTRODUCTION: OF CRISIS AND CODES

The lawyer is always in a hurry. He has become keen and shrewd . . . but his soul is small and righteous.

—Plato

A couple of years ago, I taught a class on legal ethics. In typical fashion, I began by throwing out a crude hypothetical. It went something along the lines that, as a young lawyer, your client tells you that he has discovered he is HIV-positive from a botched injection by his doctor. He requests you to negotiate a settlement on his behalf. Negotiations proceed quickly and the doctor's lawyers seem willing to settle for a sizeable amount. Shortly before you finalize the settlement, the client informs you that he has had a second medical examination, which has revealed conclusively that he is not HIV-positive. He insists, however, that he still wants you to continue the negotiations on the basis that he is HIV-positive and to take the settlement on offer. What should you do? To my considerable surprise, a significant number of students insisted that they should follow their client's instructions: it was for the doctor's lawyers to ascertain whether your client is telling the truth. Moreover, in doing so, most contended they would not be acting unethically, but would actually be fulfilling the special moral obligations of lawyers to put their clients ahead of all others. After some discussion, most students were reassured that such a course of action would be not only unethical but tantamount to fraud. Still, a few persisted in protesting the moral innocence of the lawyer, whatever the ethical impropriety of the client's instructions.

1

This incident galvanized me in my belief that the need to take legal ethics and professional responsibility seriously was never more urgent. The fault in the situation was less that of the students and more that of the legal community, including lawyers, professors, judges, and administrators. However wrong-headed the students were, their response reflected a common misunderstanding — that lawyers are simply glib actors who do the bidding of their directorial clients. Accordingly, this book is a preliminary attempt to challenge many of the misunderstandings that pervade discussions of legal ethics and to make good on present shortcomings in professional responsibility. It is intended to be both a critical primer on the current approaches to professional responsibility and also a call to ethical arms. The driving ambition is to redeem the ethical standards that the legal profession presently seems to honour more in the breach than the observance. Heeding Lord Bolingbroke's caution that "the profession of law, in its nature the noblest and most beneficial to mankind, is in its abuse an abasement of the most sordid and pernicious kind," I want to advise young (and old) lawyers against the temptation to professional abasement in the belief that it is done for the most noble and beneficial of professional causes. Legal ethics and professional responsibility can be most beneficial to mankind when lawyers take them seriously as issues of personal as well as professional good character.

## A.  A CRISIS OF ETHICAL PROPORTIONS?

Law and lawyering seem full of oxymorons. In the popular imagination, the most prominent is the notion of *legal ethics*. For many, it is a contradiction in terms to talk about lawyering and ethical standards of behaviour in the same breath: lawyers are on a par with pariahs, not paragons. Indeed, some go so far as to suggest that to be a lawyer is to vacate the ordinary domain of ethical judgment and to inhabit a perverse world of normative disingenuity. By and large, society tends to view lawyers as a rich and élite profession that is more interested in its own pocketbook than the public interest. The number of savage jokes about lawyers would be funny if they did not touch a raw nerve: after all, humour is not so much an escape from reality as from despair. In receipt of a professional monopoly, lawyers are considered self-interested and undeserving of their privileged right to govern themselves. Indeed, the contemporary legal profession is seen to epitomize George Bernard Shaw's quip that "every profession is a conspiracy against the laity."

Of course, the legal profession has never been much loved. From Plato through Shakespeare and Charles Dickens to Tom Wolfe, literature attests eloquently to its impugned status. As much envied as reviled, the reputation and prestige of lawyers are now considered by many to be at an all-time low. Law's image as a noble and honourable profession is in tatters. As far as contemporary lawyers are concerned, professional responsibility and legal ethics have not recovered from the hammering they took in the 1970s. This debasement is symbolized by the Watergate fiasco in which, of the twenty or so culprits, only three were not lawyers. Already in disgrace, President Richard Nixon resigned from the California bar rather than face disbarment proceedings. Indeed, recent shenanigans in the American courts, of which the O.J. Simpson trial is only the most notorious, have done little to rehabilitate the profession's reputation for ethical integrity. Furthermore, there seems to be a growing sense, both within and outside the profession, that it is less a problem of a few bad apples needing to be plucked out than of the overall professional barrel being rotten.[1]

Many Canadian observers of the legal scene maintain that this sense of malaise and disaffection is an American phenomenon. There is some force to this observation, but it would be far too complacent and, dare I say, Canadian to slough off such concerns as being an American problem and, therefore, one that should not concern Canadian lawyers and society too much. I disagree. While the American situation is more extreme and evident, there are still fundamental and serious difficulties in the state of legal ethics and professional responsibility as practised in Canada. This might not warrant the declaration of a crisis, but there is sufficient immediacy and pervasiveness to the problem to deserve greater attention and action; there is little reason to allow the difficulties to become endemic and disabling before remedial action is taken. The fact that many people believe there is a crisis ought to be enough to oblige the Canadian legal profession to take a hard look at its professional practices and ethical standards. Public perception is not everything, but it is vitally important in such matters. While many lawyers lead ethical lives and carry much of that over into their professional lives, there is still a depressing indifference among lawyers to issues of legal ethics and a lamentable ignorance about how to identify and deal with situations that raise ethical queries and challenges. The challenge is both a collective and a personal one for lawyers.

---

1   For a strong view on the extent of the crisis, see M.A. Glendon, *A Nation under Lawyers: How the Crisis in the Legal Profession Is Transforming American Society* (New York: Farrar, Straus and Giroux, 1994).

Lawyers have been collectively long on righteous celebration of the importance of maintaining strong ethical standards, but short on any serious action and debate. One indication of the failure to take legal ethics and professional responsibility seriously is the lack of institutional vigour in disciplining lawyers: law societies tend to take a reactive stance, and the enforcement of the various ethical responsibilities under codes of conduct is selective and seldom. Another sign of this lack of seriousness is the half-hearted effort by law schools and bar admission courses to include a sizeable and sustained component in their curricula on legal ethics and professional responsibility: only four Canadian law schools have compulsory courses. A further indication of the profession's lack of commitment is the dearth of available literature. While most areas of legal doctrine and professional practice are well served by treatises and commentaries, until recently there has been a marked gap on library shelves in the area reserved for legal ethics and professional responsibility. In Canada, the seminal contribution of Gavin MacKenzie is the contemporary exception that proves the historical rule. Moreover, while scholars such as Harry Arthurs have long tried to keep the profession intellectually honest, the range and depth of critical scholarship has been very thin and unsystematic. Nevertheless, the existence of a steady stream of American literature on the topic demonstrates that there is no necessary connection between the amount and sophistication of academic commentary and the ethical performance of the legal profession.[2]

There are various reasons why the legal community — practitioners, teachers, and administrators — has only recently begun to take legal ethics and professional responsibility as matters of scholarly study and critical interest. Some of the explanations count as significant reasons and demand sober attention; others are more convenient rationalizations and can be ignored as such:

- In the past, professional etiquette has been passed off for legal ethics. Instead of engaging in robust debate over the style and substance of what counts as ethical lawyering and how to develop such a professional practice, established lawyers have been content to reduce their mentoring to inculcating young students in the protocols, manners, and customs of the bar.

---

2    See G. MacKenzie, *Lawyers and Ethics: Professional Responsibility and Discipline* (Scarborough, Ont.: Carswell, 1993), and H.W. Arthurs, "The Dead Parrot: Does Professional Self-Regulation Exhibit Vital Signs?" (1995) 33 Alta. L. Rev. 800. For a collection of the best of available Canadian literature, see D. Buckingham et al., *Legal Ethics in Canada: Theory and Practice* (Toronto: Harcourt Brace Canada, 1996).

- In Canada (and the United Kingdom), there has been no defining cultural moment, as with Watergate in the United States, in which lawyers were placed under national scrutiny and obliged to reconsider the legitimacy of their professional practices and norms of conduct. It has always been possible to deal with delinquent lawyers as isolated and occasional misfits.
- There has been a generational transformation of lawyering. While lawyering remains very much an élite profession, it has also become one more business in the marketplace. Whether by necessity or design, many lawyers now see themselves as being just as concerned with the bottom line as with broader issues of social justice. This shift (at least of perception, if not reality) has resulted in a reworking of professional conventions and customs to meet the changing expectations and economy of legal practice. (See chapter 3.)
- Within the last decade, the demographics of those entering law school and the legal profession has begun to diversify considerably. More people from groups that were traditionally absent from the ranks of legal practice are now bringing a different set of social customs and moral attitudes to issues of professional responsibility. While this diversification has not brought about major changes in institutional arrangements or standards, the pressure to change is growing. (See chapter 3.)

While the more progressive sectors of the established profession struggle to respond to these forces of change, crises are commonly attributed to the fact that the profession has lost the shared sense of legal ethics and professional responsibility it once had. As the legal profession becomes more a corporate business than a public vocation, lawyers are urged to revert to this traditional *esprit de corps* if they are to regain their respectability and stature. They must reclaim the ethical legacy of noble lawyers past, and neophyte lawyers must be schooled in that wisdom and professional justification. Although this characterization of the perceived crisis and its proffered solution, like most expressions of nostalgia, has some grounding in reality, it is as much a pious pretence as a genuine remedy for institutional ills. The profession has indeed become more businesslike in operation and more corporate in attitude; legal services are treated as one more commodity to be bought and sold in the marketplace. This tendency has been facilitated by the traditional view of legal ethics that puts service — the belief that lawyers do not have responsibility for the law and its development, but only for the satisfaction of their clients' wishes — before justice.[3]

---

3    See D. Coquillette, *Lawyers and Fundamental Moral Responsibility* (Cincinatti: Anderson Publishing Co., 1995).

The cure for the perceived professional blight is not a return to the values and standards of yesteryear. On the contrary, these old standards are part of the problem. What is required is the development of a fresh approach to legal ethics that is sensitive to the changing shape and style of modern legal practice, one that demands that lawyers aspire to a more diverse and critical self-image. Accordingly, mindful that the homogeneity of lawyers is beginning to be replaced by more diversity in personnel, the unifying theme of this book will be the challenge that a fragmented society and legal profession holds for the development of a transformed practice of professional responsibility. Most important, I am conscious that any non-traditional approach must be realistic and specific; I do not intend to offer an approach that is so precious and self-righteous as to be ineffectual, nor do I succumb to a that's-the-way-it-is approach, in which the only rule is "kill or be killed." My proposals will, I hope, combine to illuminate the choices that lawyers must make and accept in their daily efforts to create their own ethical way in the world of professional responsibility. To emphasize this contextual and practical dimension, I have included a series of problems that are intended to encourage readers to (re)discover and work through their ethical sensibilities.

After sketching the different demands and design of a fragmented society, I will concentrate on how the legal profession itself is beginning to fragment, and what that means for existing accounts of legal ethics. In particular, my focus will be on how it is vital to rethink present understandings of lawyers' ethical personae and to canvass future possibilities for a more compelling vision of a professional *modus vivendi*. Emphasizing the Canadian predicament, I will argue that a fragmented society deserves a fragmented legal profession, which, in turn, warrants a more fragmented conception and implementation of legal ethics. There must be a shift of emphasis from professional regulation to personal responsibility. As well as indicating the shape and direction such a revised ethical stance might take, I explore the more substantive and concrete consequences for legal education and professional practice. My ambition is not to promote a particular set of ethical outcomes or inculcate a specific mode of professional responsibility; rather, it is to challenge students and lawyers to develop a professional *modus vivendi* of their own that constructs as it constantly challenges and reworks an appropriate professional attitude and practice. In the same way that there is no one or unchanging way to be a good person, so it is with being a good lawyer. Each and every lawyer must be capable of developing a style and substance of lawyering that incorporates a continuing dialogue — with oneself, clients, other lawyers, other professionals, and the community at large — about what counts as good lawyering. The central question is whether it is ever acceptable that lawyers might, can, or should act in a professional capacity in a way that would be contrary to their own moral values.[4]

# B. PROFESSIONAL TIES

In examining present and future efforts by lawyers to regulate legal ethics, much is made of the fact that legal practice is a profession. Ultimately, lawyers do not operate as individuals, but as part of teams, as part of a profession. As professionals, the moral obligations of lawyers are seen to extend beyond concern with their own individual actions and to encompass a responsibility to monitor the actions of other lawyers and contribute to the moral health of the profession as a whole. In this way, professional responsibility is as much a collective as a personal undertaking; lawyers have the privilege and the duty to regulate the ethical activities and professional practices of other lawyers. Accordingly, it is important to clarify what constitutes the legal profession and what follows from that designation. The arguments for professional self-regulation by lawyers can be summarized in three points: the regulation of lawyers is too complex and technical to be understood by non-lawyers; lawyers, by virtue of their training and experience, possess such knowledge and insight; and there is an admirable history of effective regulation in the public interest. In an over-the-top endorsement of the need for professional independence, Justice Estey of the Supreme Court of Canada stated:

> The independence of the Bar from the state in all its pervasive manifestations is one of the hallmarks of a free society. Consequently, regulation of these members of the law profession by the state must, so far as by human ingenuity it can be so designed, be free from state interference, in the political sense, with the delivery of services to the individual citizens in the state, particularly in fields of public and criminal law. The public interest in a free society knows no area more sensitive than the independence, impartiality and availability to the general public of the members of the Bar and through those members, legal advice and services generally.[5]

---

4   See R. Cranston, *Legal Ethics and Professional Responsibility* (Oxford: Clarendon Press, 1995).

5   *Canada (A.G.) v. Law Society (British Columbia)*, [1982] 2 S.C.R. 307 at 335–36.

Bolstered by a considerable body of sociological literature, the traditional claim is that there are three ideas that are essential to a profession: a sophisticated structure of organization, a formal learning process, and the spirit of public service. Gaining a livelihood and making money are not thought to be important. Indeed, some insist that they are incidental and superfluous. After all, they claim, an organized profession is not the same as "a retail grocers' association."[6] On this basis, lawyers clearly qualify to be members of a profession. However, much of the theorizing has not established that, because law is a profession, it should regulate itself; rather, the assumption is made that, because lawyers regulate themselves, they must be a profession. Most of the literature is given over to justifying the self-governing and autonomous functioning of the profession, the claim being that, as a body of experts who served the public interest, it was legitimate and indeed necessary to allow the profession to ensure its own integrity. A typical line of defence is made by Justice Iacobucci of the Supreme Court of Canada.[7] He outlines the distinguishing features of a profession: that its practice requires substantial intellectual training and the use of complex judgments; that clients, because they cannot adequately evaluate the quality of the service, must trust those whom they consult; that the client's trust presupposes that the practitioner's self-interest is overbalanced by devotion to serving both the client's interest and the public good; and that the occupation is self-regulating (i.e., organized in such a way as to assure both the public and the courts that its members are competent, do not violate the client's trust, and transcend their own interests).

It is this third feature of public-spiritedness that causes the problems, in that its disputed existence is a vital link in the reasoning chain that leads to the fourth feature of self-regulation. According to Iacobucci, law's distinguishing feature from other callings is that lawyers, unlike cabinetmakers, have "great power to influence the private lives and public affairs and, correspondingly, great responsibility to [their] clients and community." However, he is unclear about why that

---

6   R. Pound, *The Lawyer from Antiquity to Modern Times: With Particular Reference to the Development of Bar Associations in the United States* (St. Paul, Minn.: West Pub. Co., 1953) at 5, 89. For sociological accounts along similar lines, see E. Durkheim, *Professional Ethics and Civic Morals*, trans. C. Brookfield (London: Routledge & Kegan Paul, 1957), and T. Parsons, "A Sociologist Looks at the Legal Profession" in T. Parsons, *Essays in Sociological Theory* (Glencoe, Ill.: Free Press, 1958). For an excellent survey of the present literature, see D.L. Rhode, "The Professionalism Problem" (1998) 39 W. & M. L. Rev. 283.

7   F. Iacobucci, "Striking a Balance: Trying to Find the Happy and Good Life within and beyond the Legal Profession" (1992) 26 L.S.U.C. Gazette 205.

fact should mean that, whereas cabinetmakers are "disciplined by the adjudicative apparatus of the community," lawyers are to be "judged and disciplined by a community of [their] peers." It is surely the case that lawyers, precisely because of their distinctive powers, should be subject to more, not less, regulation than cabinetmakers. Exactly why is it that lawyers should be (or are thought to be) better judges of lawyers and their responsibilities than laypersons? While some matters do require considerable expert knowledge, many do not; the technical component is a relevant factor, but not an exclusive or dominant one. There is a strong argument that, at a minimum, laypersons have a major role to play in the regulation of lawyers. Although most law societies have introduced a dimension of lay participation into their operation, it remains a minor and unconvincing part of their regulatory process.

The traditional notion of the profession as a trade that is given professional and independent status because it is devoted to serving the public interest has come under strong criticism. Some have gone so far as to suggest that, like other professionals, lawyers "differ from trade unions only in their sanctimoniousness."[8] There are three main parts to this critique:

- Historical and sociological research confirms that the profession has often paid only lip-service to its moral mandate: it has operated as much as a business as any other trade and has frequently placed the interests of its members ahead of those of the public. A cynical view of lawyers is that they are more members of a state-backed cartel than an independent and self-regulated profession; rules exist as much to restrict competition and impress the public as anything else.[9]
- The traditional ideal of professionalism has been critiqued politically. Whereas it has been argued from the right that the rejection of a free-market approach has rendered the delivery of legal services both inefficient and democratically unaccountable, it is argued from the left that traditional professionalism entrenches bureaucratic hierarchies and threatens democratic institutions.
- Most important for this book's purposes, critics have assailed the moral mandate that lies at the heart of the traditional model: the adversarial client-is-all mentality is condemned as more a fudging of public responsibility than a realization of it. Legal ethics has become

8    E. Friedson, *Profession of Medicine: A Study of the Sociology of Applied Knowledge* (New York: Dodd, Mead, 1970) at 369.

9    See J.E. Bickenbach, "The Redemption of the Moral Mandate of the Profession of Law" (1996) 9 Can. J. of L. & J. 51.

synonymous with gamesmanship and with a sense, particularly among the criminal bar, that it is permissible to do everything and anything that the letter of the law or the Code of Professional Conduct allow.

Indeed, the overall tenor of recent work on the profession is that there must be a concerted effort to reclaim and rethink the moral high ground that is essential if lawyers are to retain the privileges and independence they presently claim, but only infrequently deserve. The argument that there is a strongly differentiated role morality that lawyers are to interpose between their personal and their professional lives can only be justified by reference to the overall and deeper moral worth of the profession's work generally. In short, it is incumbent on the profession to ensure that the interests of justice are placed squarely and regularly at the forefront of professional concerns. Of course, what counts as "justice" and what lawyers can do to serve it are by no means obvious and will always remain a matter of contestation. However, lawyers, either individually or collectively, cannot rely on that fact to justify the amoralism that permeates their profession and its work.

Notwithstanding the arguments against lawyers having the professional privilege of regulating themselves, this remains the central device for framing and controlling matters of legal ethics and professional responsibility. The power of provincial law societies to regulate the admission, conduct, and disbarment of lawyers is established under provincial statutes. Accordingly, the introduction of professional rules is part of their regulatory function within their delegated authority from the provincial legislatures. As such, they are subject and must conform to the dictates of the *Charter of Rights and Freedoms*.[10] Nevertheless, apart from the enacted professional rules, there are other ways in which the legal profession as a whole, and society in general, seek to ensure that lawyers act ethically and responsibly both in the fulfillment of their duties and in the exercise of the considerable power bestowed upon them. The three main methods are set out below:

- *Legal control*. These controls include the general norms of criminal law that apply to everyone, and the civil rules of law, such as tort and contract, that impose obligations on all relations between people. Also, the courts discipline lawyers under their inherent jurisdiction

---

10   *Klein v. Law Society of Upper Canada* (1985), 50 O.R. (2d) 118 (Div. Ct.).

and the provincial Rules of Civil Procedure. Indeed, in recent years, the courts have reasserted their authority to use costs provisions to discipline lawyers who engage in unwarranted delay and disregard of litigation principles. Nevertheless, this power is exercised only rarely. As the Supreme Court of Canada has recently stated:

> The basic principle on which costs are awarded is as *compensation* for the successful party, not in order to punish a barrister. Any member of the legal profession might be subject to a compensatory order for costs if it is shown that repetitive and irrelevant material, and excessive motions and applications, characterized the proceedings in which they were involved, and that the lawyer acted in bad faith in encouraging this abuse and delay. It is clear that the courts possess jurisdiction to make such an award, often under statute and, in any event, as part of their inherent jurisdiction to control abuse of process and contempt of court. . . . Moreover, courts must be extremely cautious in awarding costs personally against a lawyer, given the duties upon a lawyer to guard confidentiality of instructions and to bring forward with courage even unpopular causes. A lawyer should not be placed in a situation where his or her fear of an adverse order of costs may conflict with these fundamental duties of his or her calling.[11]

- *Professional regulation.* Under various statutory provisions, law societies are entrusted with the task of regulating the legal profession and, because law societies are almost entirely made up of lawyers, the legal profession is largely self-regulated. As well as overseeing membership in the profession and licensing their activities, law societies impose rules of professional conduct on their members which are intended to govern and guide lawyers in their daily routines and practices. They also assume responsibility for discipline and enforcement.
- *Professional culture.* This complex of shared norms, values, and expectations has developed (and continues to develop) to determine those types of behaviour that are inimical to the practice of a profession. It gives rise to a set of traditions, customs, and conventions (such as style of dress, manner of speech, and rules of etiquette) that begins to discipline and shape the routines and rites of the legal profession. A network of informal sanction is then enforced by the practising profession (e.g., disapproval, bad-mouthing, ostracism, lack of cooperation, and economic exile).

---

11  *Young v. Young*, [1993] 4 S.C.R. 3 at 135–36, McLachlin J.

## C. CODES AND DISCIPLINE

The key device that is used to establish the framework for legal ethics and to ground the process for disciplining lawyers is the Code of Professional Conduct. The reasons for having codes are fairly obvious: to educate lawyers on communal expectations; to affect behaviour; and to offer a basis for discipline. Codes are developed by lawyers themselves and without the general input of society. Lawyers believe that the content and reach of such codes and their ethical obligations can only be defined by those with special expertise and experience in law and its practice. What counts and does not count as ethically appropriate behaviour is to be decided by the profession itself. As such, the professional codes function in a variety of capacities:

- They represent the *ethos* of the profession: they are intended to capture and codify the beliefs, customs, and conventions of the majority and are intended to guide the conduct of members.
- They operate as a quasi-legal set of rules: compliance with codes is not optional, but is demanded by the profession and is used as the basis for disciplining and sanctioning its members.
- They establish role-specific requirements: they impose a special set of ethical obligations on lawyers which arise as a result of the special role and nature of lawyering in society.

A key question for any critical introduction to legal ethics and professional responsibility is to determine whether the need for a separate and professional code of conduct can be justified and what the relationship is between such codes and general ethical principles that are thought to govern society at large. Some have insisted that such codes are little more than ethical window-dressing; they serve to legitimate what lawyers do and impose control over economic competition. Codes are no more effective in themselves than the *Criminal Code* or the *Charter*; there is no necessary link between a statement of what is and is not permitted, and whether people do or do not act accordingly. What passes for talk of ethical standards is, at best, a stylized form of professional regulation and, at worst, a self-serving paean to professional prestige. Moreover, the codes seem to be premised on the assumption that lawyers are a homogeneous group who engage in broadly similar work. The truth is that they are a highly stratified and increasingly heterogeneous collection (see chapter 3).

The challenge in drafting any code of professional conduct is twofold. First, it must be sufficiently general to provide a principled framework within which lawyers can orient their general behaviour, but not so specific as to amount to a limited list of instructions. Second, it must be sufficiently specific to influence the nature of particular conduct, but not so general as to offer no real guidance in actual situations of moral soul-searching. If a code is too general and insufficiently specific, it will be little more than a vague statement of intent to which lawyers will occasionally nod when asked to justify a challenged action. However, if it is too specific and insufficiently general, it will amount to a limited list of do's-and-don'ts which will be of no value when it is most needed in those ethically grey areas of indecision and difficulty.

Each province has enacted its own code of professional conduct. However, throughout the book, I will use the Canadian Bar Association's Code of Professional Conduct as the source of professionally sanctioned standards and norms. The first effort to establish canons of legal ethics began in 1915, hard on the heels of the American Bar Association's adoption of a set of canons in 1908. In 1921 the CBA's Canons of Legal Ethics were accepted by the membership and largely adopted by the provincial law societies.[12] In 1969 the CBA struck a committee to review the original canons, and this review resulted in a new Code of Professional Conduct being introduced in 1974 which was again largely adopted and adapted by the provincial law societies. Another CBA committee was established in 1984 to review and reform the 1974 Code. As a result, a substantially amended Code was approved in 1987. In one form or another, this Code still provides the basis of almost all the provincial rules of professional conduct. Accordingly, rather than attempt to move between and among the only slightly different provincial codes, I will focus my discussion around the 1987 Code (the Rules). I have included a copy of that Code in Appendix A and will make frequent reference to it throughout the book.

Under the Rules, lawyers have a variety of duties, obligations, and responsibilities that can be divided into three main groups:

- *As a representative of clients.* Once lawyers have taken on clients and decided to act as their representatives, they assume a set of special obligations to those persons or organizations: they must advise their clients about their legal rights and responsibilities, the possible courses of action, and the likely consequences; they must advocate their clients' position and defend their interests in a vigorous and competent manner; they must negotiate on their clients' behalf so as to obtain the best possible result; and they must pursue litigation, as and when appropriate, in a prompt and diligent way.

---

12  See W.W. Pue, "Becoming 'Ethical': Lawyers' Professional Ethics in Early Twentieth Century Canada" (1991) 20 Man. L.J. 227.

- *As an officer of the legal system.* In ensuring that they act within the law, lawyers must act in such a way that they respect the law's personnel, including other lawyers; they must avail themselves of legal procedures in a legitimate and non-abusive way; they must uphold the legal process generally; and they must act at all times in a way that does not bring the administration of justice into disrepute.
- *As a public citizen.* Mindful of the special responsibility that lawyers have for the quality of justice in society, lawyers must keep themselves informed about the law. They must seek to ensure that access to the law is made available to as many people as possible, especially the poor and disadvantaged; they must contribute to the reform and improvement of the legal process; and they must support efforts to ensure that the legal profession fulfills its civic and public calling.

Of course, these responsibilities do not interpret themselves: their application might be unclear, their range might be vague, their direction might be mixed, and responsibilities might clash. For instance, the responsibilities to one's clients with respect to confidentiality might be unclear in themselves and might recommend a different course of action from those recommended by the responsibilities as an officer of the court. In some instances, the Rules demand that lawyers "must" make certain choices and give priority to certain actions. However, the Rules more often offer no definite resolution and simply provide a rudimentary framework within which lawyers can debate and develop an ethical practice of law. The Code is a mix of prohibitive and exhortative language: some rules emphasize the "shall not," whereas others stress the "are encouraged to." Consequently, it is important to remember that the Rules do not and cannot relieve lawyers of the continuing responsibility to exercise their own professional and moral judgment about the appropriate course to follow. Unthinking compliance with the specified Rules does not guarantee that lawyers will develop a sense of ethical judgment: professional morality is more than law-abiding conformity. The fact that most decisions and practices by lawyers allow for a variety of manoeuvres or results means that lawyers need to develop a professional facility to comprehend and handle such challenges. In many so-called hard cases, there is rarely an obvious or incontestable path to follow.

With this in mind, any attempt to elaborate the ethical duties and professional responsibilities of lawyers by exclusive reference to the Rules is misplaced. There is little to be gained by providing an elaborate and exhaustive annotation of the Rules, since this has already been done adequately, and it ignores the very real fact that the influence on lawyers' daily routines and rituals is small: the constant attention to and redrafting of the Rules is of decreasing and marginal utility. The

enforcement of the various ethical responsibilities is selective and seldom. This results in a hierarchy of collective ethical concerns, with
money-related offences, serious addiction, and lack of cooperation with
the law society at the top of the list. Those directives to act in the public
interest, to strive to reform the law, and to ensure that the administration of justice is available to all are almost entirely ignored by regulatory
agencies, even though they are consistently overlooked by many lawyers. Indeed, while a considerable number of disbarred lawyers have a
career of marginal performance and misfortune, there is substantial evidence to suggest that it is those lawyers outside the professional mainstream that are targeted for special scrutiny: "[T]he evidence supports a
labeling model of deviant careers in which inexperienced solo practitioners are placed at heightened risk of surveillance and sanctioning during a recessionary period . . . [and] it is regulatory attention more than
pre-existing behavioural differences that structures these deviant
careers."[13] While there are occasional high-profile cases involving élite
lawyers and law firms, the (small) bulk of disciplinary activity occurs at
the margins of the profession, even though there is no evidence that
lawyers who work for wealthy clients are any more (or less) ethical than
those who have disadvantaged clients.

Nevertheless, the Rules do have a place in any appreciation of legal
ethics and their improvement. They are an important resource in discussion and decision making, but they are not a decisive or determinate
play-book that relieves lawyers of the personal responsibility to develop
an ethical style and substance of legal practice. As I try to stress throughout this book, the Rules are only a starting point or resource in the
broader debate about appropriate ethical behaviour: they act as the outside limits within which debate can and must occur. They are intended
to operate as a didactic device as much as a disciplining tool: they serve
to inculcate a certain professional self-image and provide a rhetorical
front to the public. In many ways, the Rules are as much for the benefit
of the public as the profession. The actual legal ethics of the profession
are to be found in its cultural norms and routines. Indeed, according to
some commentators, the Rules do little to affect professional conduct or
to inform ethical debate among practising lawyers.

Lawyers who fall foul of the professional Rules are subject to potential discipline by their law society. The process is complaint-driven,

---

13   See H. Arthurs, "Climbing Kilimanjaro: Ethics for Postmodern Professionals"
     (1993) 6:1 Westminster Affairs 3, and B.L. Arnold and J. Hagen, "Careers of
     Misconduct: The Structure of Prosecuted Professional Deviance among Lawyers"
     (1992) 57 American Sociological Review 771 at 779.

though there are occasional random audits, and it can be triggered by clients or by other lawyers. Disciplinary hearings are a hybrid between criminal and civil proceedings. For instance, while the formal process from complaint through investigation and hearing to punishment resembles criminal proceedings, the rules of evidence tend to be civil in origin, especially in regard to the fact that accused lawyers are required to cooperate with any investigation and are compellable as witnesses. The panel that hears complaints consists almost exclusively of lawyers. Also, there is a general duty on the law society's counsel to disclose all relevant documents to the accused lawyers and, as a general rule, to make the disciplinary proceedings open to the public. Any tribunal that is empowered to discipline lawyers must act judicially and is required to conform with the traditional rules of natural justice on bias, conflict of interest, and the like. The penalties can range in severity from non-public reprimands to disbarment. However, the most common penalties are public reprimands, suspensions, and permission to resign. Depending on the outcome, lawyers and law societies can be required to pay the costs and expenses of the other. Finally, disciplinary proceedings are vulnerable to judicial review and can be set aside for a jurisdictional error, manifest wrong, and substantial miscarriage of justice.

# D.  CONCLUSION

In the chapters that follow, I attempt to offer a critical introduction to legal ethics and professional responsibility. Owing to common misunderstandings about the legal profession and its ethical responsibilities, it is imperative and urgent that the task of rethinking the ethics of lawyering be undertaken. As the legal profession's status continues to grow in terms of power and influence in public and private life, the need to construct a revision of ethical lawyering is paramount. Such a reconstruction must be consonant with the legal profession's contemporary socioeconomic organization and political responsibilities in a society that still, at least nominally, pays lip-service to the ideals of democratic governance and accountability. This book is devoted to such a task. It is about neither indoctrination nor ideology. What it does do is put each individual lawyer and student to the test by asking them to justify their sense of professional responsibility through their actions rather than to justify their actions by reference to the ideals of professional responsibility. If the legal profession is to live up to its own cherished ideals and to reclaim its reputation as an honourable undertaking, it must challenge each of its present and future members to take this task seriously.

# CHAPTER 2

# TRADITIONAL ACCOUNTS: CONTENTS AND CRITICISM

Most lawyers eschew the worth of legal theorizing; they prefer to think of themselves as practical men and women of the world who are guided by the traditional imperatives of their professional craft. However, in matters of legal ethics and professional responsibility, intellectual theory holds great sway over legal practice. John Maynard Keynes's comments on economists seem especially apposite to contemporary lawyers: they are "slaves of some defunct economist" and "madmen in authority, who hear voices in the air, are distilling their frenzy from some academic scribbler of a few years back."[1] Accordingly, although most practising lawyers give little thought to the informing theory, the practice of legal ethics and responsibility is based on definite theoretical models of what practising lawyers should do if they wish to act with legal and professional responsibility. These models are vitally important in providing lawyers with a self-image that can guide and justify what they do and what they might become. While they tend to surface only at times of ethical difficulty, the regnant models of lawyering work to inform and inspire the daily routines and regularized decision making of professional practitioners.

In this chapter, I will sketch and criticize the traditional image and defence of the ethical lawyer. The first section looks at the idea of lawyers

---

1   J.M. Keynes, *The General Theory of Employment Interest and Money* (London: Macmillan, 1936) at 383.

as hired hands and unpacks the various components of this model; particular attention is given to the importance of the adversary system and its implications for legal ethics and professional responsibility. In the second section, I criticize the traditional image because it is based on a flawed set of assumptions about the practice of law in contemporary Canada. The third section examines the critical efforts to ameliorate the deficiencies of the traditional model by suggesting an alternative model of the lawyer as civic campaigner. Unfortunately, this improved account of legal ethics and professional responsibility creates almost as many problems as it resolves. Finally, the fourth section responds to those progressive detractors who maintain that the image of an ethical lawyer or a radical lawyer is unavoidably perverse: lawyers are always part of the problem, never a component in the solution. Throughout the chapter, I seek to lay the foundations for my own more compelling and workable account of lawyering.[2]

## A.  HIRED HANDS

The traditional image of the ethical lawyer has remained largely static and unchanged for many decades. Although it has received considerable maintenance work by way of renovation and redecoration, the basic structure and foundations remain much the same. Caricatured as "hired guns," the more serious core of the traditional image is that of lawyers as hired hands. Although it has come in for considerable criticism, this image remains the operating model through which lawyers are trained, under which most lawyers function, and which is formally sanctioned by the provincial law societies in their codes of conduct. As would be expected in the common law, this traditional model of professional responsibility has its roots in the practical routines of daily lawyering rather than in any well-founded theoretical appreciation. Nevertheless, to grasp fully the appeal of such a model and the force of the criticism against it, it is important to understand the definite and partial assumptions, processes, and values about law, society, and ways of thinking about them that support the traditional model.

---

2   This chapter owes a great deal to the insightful and important work of Anthony Alfieri. In a series of articles, he has offered both a powerful critique of traditional lawyering and a constructive alternative for transformative lawyering. See A.V. Alfieri, "Impoverished Practices" (1993) 81 Georgetown L.J. 2567, and A.V. Alfieri, "Reconstructed Poverty Law Practice: Learning Lessons of Client Narrative" (1991) 100 Yale L.J. 2107.

The traditional image of lawyering is centred on the idea that lawyers are super-technocrats; they possess a special set of talents and techniques which they deploy for the advantage of the people who hire them. They regard themselves as being neutral on the substance and form of the law; their task is very much to apply the law, a little to criticize it, but most certainly not to make it. Their commitment is to the legal system which, even when they are working around and within it, must be accepted as given. If lawyers have a larger social calling, it is "to achieve the moral integration of [their] clients into the social order."[3] They might have misgivings about the merit of particular laws or decisions, but they are committed to the Rule of Law and its values. In their professional lives, ethical lawyers serve the legal process and, therefore, society at large. Within such an image, the clash between professional ethics and personal morality is seen to be more apparent than real.

While almost indifferent to who their clients are, lawyers think of themselves as more chosen than choosing. The relationship between lawyer and client is built upon trust and respect: clients are to trust lawyers to act in the clients' best interests and, in return, lawyers will respect the clients' autonomy. It is not for lawyers to impinge on the clients' autonomy, but to act on behalf of the clients to realize their interests and inspirations. Indeed, clients tend to be fungible. While it is recognized that richer and poorer clients will have different problems because of their wealth, and that the appropriate strategies to be followed will be tailored to the particular client's needs and demands, all are entitled to equal access to the legal process. The lawyer-as-hired-hand treats all clients exactly the same, in the sense that they are citizens who have had their rights infringed and want relief or vindication. Advocacy and action tend to be standardized and routinized. Insofar as lawyers and clients are from different cultures and classes, lawyers are expected to bridge the gap by personal empathy and professional solidarity.

At the institutional heart of this traditional model is the implicit commitment to the adversary system. Much has been written about it, and most law students or lawyers need little instruction in its basic format and rationale. However, a basic recap of its fundamental features seems in order. The adversary system is an ideal or model that lawyers use as a shorthand to describe the institutional setting for their work; it is intended to be contrasted to an inquisitorial system, which is more usual in civil law systems. However, like the common law generally, the adherence to such an approach is pragmatic and undogmatic. Several

---

3   "Impoverished Practices," *ibid.* at 2603.

features make up the adversary system: party initiation and control of both the issues and the presentation of evidence; a judge and jury that are neutral and passive; and results that tend to be either/or in nature. The rationale for such a system is very much like Churchill's defence of democracy — it is the worst form of proceeding except for all the others. The usual objectives of the adversary system are that it best facilitates the pursuit and discovery of truth; it facilitates the protection of basic rights and freedoms; and it ensures the satisfaction of litigants by giving them their day in court.

Each of these objectives of the adversary system is open to easy criticism: it obscures rather than illuminates truth; it allows the strong to triumph over the weak; and it adds further bitterness to the parties' lives. None of this should come as a surprise, as the adversary system has its historical origins in trials by ordeal and, later, by battle; the parties (or their champions) would compete in the belief that justice would be revealed to be on the side of the aggrieved. The modern defence of a continuing commitment to the adversary system is more subtle, but no less suspect. It is contended that the lasting attraction of the adversary system is the way it mirrors and reinforces the political values of a liberal democratic system in which individual initiative and limited state involvement are celebrated. Moreover, like the socioeconomic order that it reflects, the adversary system fails because of marked disparities in resources that people have in accessing and utilizing the legal process. In particular, insofar as there is some crude correlation between the cost of individual lawyers and their success rate, the financial capacity of clients might have a strong impact on their ability to gain "access to justice."[4]

Nevertheless, the existence of the adversary system is something to which any approach to legal ethics and professional responsibility must accommodate itself. For the foreseeable future, it is unlikely that any substantial changes will be made to this structural dynamic of litigation and lawyering. However, this does not mean that legal ethics must subordinate itself to the present understandings about the imperatives of the adversary system or that the adversary system cannot be softened or modified. It is not so much the adversary system that is to blame for many of the current practices and excesses in professional behaviour, but the fixed and unimaginative attitudes of lawyers that serve to energize it and stymie fresh interpretations of its demands and possibilities. As with so much else in matters of professional responsibility and legal ethics, it is

---

4   See N. Brooks, "The Judge and the Adversary System" in W.R. Lederman et al., *The Canadian Judiciary*, ed. A.M. Linden (Toronto: Osgoode Hall Law School, York University, 1976).

less that the formal structure and official rules create difficulties than that the values and norms of its personnel inhibit change. As MacKenzie puts it, "to describe the system as adversarial should not connote contrariness or contentiousness, but rather only that the parties, through their counsel, are responsible for leading evidence before a neutral adjudicator."[5]

The single most important implication of this traditional adversarial system for legal professional responsibility and ethics is that lawyers' primary obligation is to their clients. In prioritizing the different duties that lawyers owe, the one to their clients is treated as trumping all others in almost all situations. Except in the most egregious circumstances, lawyers are expected to be single-minded in their devotion to their clients' cause and to use whatever legal means are at their disposal to advance that cause. On a hard-line understanding of the traditional model, many potential ethical dilemmas disappear — lawyers are required to put their clients' interests ahead of all others, which tend to arise only by way of afterthought. Indeed, for some commentators, such as Charles Fried, this ethical model permits lawyers to do what they might otherwise condemn as unjust and abusive: "[A] lawyer is morally entitled to act in this formal, representative way even if the result is an injustice, because the legal system which authorises both the injustice . . . and the formal gesture for working it insulates him from personal moral responsibility."[6]

As attitudes have softened, the Rules insist that lawyers must temper their zealous advocacy of their clients' interests. Restraints on adversarial zeal on behalf of clients are mitigated not only by competing duties to the courts and the public but also by the basic duty to be honest and honourable (see, for example, Appendix A, III, c. 6; IX, c. 8; IX, c. 2a; XVI, c. 3; IX, c. 7; XVI, c. 4; and IX, c. 2h). However, while lawyers are admonished not to engage in "sharp practices" by taking advantage of "slips, irregularities or mistakes" by other lawyers, the Rules speak more in terms of etiquette and courtesy than anything else (see XVI, c. 4). Nevertheless, lawyers do owe special duties to their clients and are not only entitled but obliged to give their interest priority in the clash with others' interests. However, priority does not mean that lawyers must be oblivious to all other interests except their clients': it simply means that they can give their clients' interests more weight on the scales. Other interests still count, but for much less (see chapter 6).

---

5   G. MacKenzie, *Lawyers and Ethics: Professional Responsibility and Discipline* (Scarborough, Ont.: Carswell, 1993) at 2-20.

6   C. Fried, "The Lawyer as Friend: The Moral Foundations of the Lawyer-Client Relation" (1976) 85 Yale L.J. 1060 at 1084.

There is considerable justification for adhering to an uncompromising adversarial ethic in criminal matters. Here, the individual is pitted against the state, with all its resources and power at its disposal. Moreover, it is not for the lawyer to determine guilt, but the judge and jury. The accused's lawyers are simply committed to raising a "reasonable doubt" (see chapter 9). Nonetheless, apart from obvious restrictions on their partiality, even the defence lawyers might begin to feel certain ethical doubts in some situations: Do you use a "technicality" to help a dangerous and aggressive client escape a long prison term when you have strong reason to believe that this person is guilty of the offence charged and of other even more serious offences? There is much less reason for adopting a strict adversarial ethic in civil cases. Although the stakes can still be high, the legal circumstances are such that there is a different dynamic in play. Lawyers acting for the plaintiff in particular should have a greater sense of responsibility for the clients they choose to represent, the causes they lend their legal skills to, and the tactics they use. Indeed, mindful of the inequality in access to legal services, the need for civil lawyers to question what they do is acute.

The exchange of documents during the discovery process provides an example of how an unthinking and aggressive adherence to an adversarial ethic can take lawyers into dangerous territory. Taking to extremes the idea that it is for each party to make its own case, and not for the opposing party, lawyers can soon get into ethical difficulties — by hiding relevant documents among a stack of irrelevant documents, for example, or by reluctantly handing over documents. Apart from the legal requirements of the provincial Rules of Civil Procedure, the different codes and rules do not address such matters in any direct or helpful way. Although active deception is prohibited, there is a thin line between a commitment to deceive the other side and an unwillingness to help it make its own case. Nonetheless, lawyers who acquiesce in their clients' failure to produce relevant documents are open to being required personally to pay costs.[7]

PROBLEM 1: You represent the defendant in a claim for damages resulting from the plaintiff's physical injury. Before discovery, you receive information in a medical report that the plaintiff is more seriously injured than he or his lawyer realizes. Do you offer to settle immediately for a few thousand dollars when you know that the claim is worth much more than that? Would it make a difference to you if the plaintiff was represented by someone you thought to be an immature and bad lawyer?

---

7    *Myers v. Elman*, [1940] A.C. 282 (H.L.(E.)).

PROBLEM 2: Your client wants to get to trial as soon as possible. At her urging, you inform the opposing lawyer that all time limits will be strictly enforced, with no concessions. Consequently, you refuse all requests for extensions, even though most are reasonable and the kind that are normally indulged. However, you wait until the last possible minute to serve all documents, including lengthy and complex ones, on the opposing party, despite requests for early delivery. Is your conduct defensible and/or ethical?

The fact that this traditional adversarial image still has great currency in the legal profession has much to do with the equally traditional theory of law from which it draws its shape and justification. For better or for worse, the hallmark of good lawyers is found in their cultivation of rule-craft — the ability to identify the extant rules of the legal system and apply them to particular situations. The central article of faith of this traditional positivism is that rules are the basic currency of legal transactions and that their application can be performed in a professional and objective way. If not quite the "brooding omnipresence in the sky,"[8] law is an imposing and imposed structure that has considerable stability, that is operationally determinate in the guidance it extends to the trained lawyer, and that is institutionally distinct from the more open-minded disputations around ideological politics. As such, the image of the lawyer-as-hired-hand embraces the idea that the law has a life of its own and is not influenced by the lawyers or legal officials who engage in the system. In this sense, any legal practice that craves and expects professional recognition must be seen to take law seriously in the sense that it pursues clients' interests through the extant rules, procedures, and venues of law: overt politicization is severely frowned upon. It is a proud, unapologetic, and defiant defence of the Rule of Law.

## B. THE CRITIQUE

As attractive and as comforting as this image of lawyer-as-hired-hand may be to legal practitioners, its problems are manifest and manifold. It fails theoretically, empirically, and ideologically: it is based on a formalistic theory of law that is largely discredited and defunct as a serious attempt to understand law and its operation. It describes a version of legal practice that no longer has any empirical validity or historical accuracy, if it ever did have; and it defends both its informing theory and its governing practice of lawyering as apolitical in such a way that merely serves to underline its very definite ideological commitments.

---

8    *Southern Pacific Co. v. Jensen*, 244 U.S. 205 at 222 (1917), Holmes J.

While mainstream jurisprudence continues to recognize an important role for rules in a modern legal system, almost all jurists of any credibility or respectability accept that the law is not as objective, stable, or determinate as the image of lawyer-as-hired-hand maintains. It is not that they have abandoned a commitment to the Rule of Law and hold law to be irredeemably indeterminate, but they hold that "law . . . is deeply and thoroughly political . . . but not a matter of personal or partisan politics."[9] The coherence and intelligibility of law and lawyering is inextricably implicated in the contingent world of political values and ethical stances. The law never simply *is,* and lawyering is never completely the passive and technical involvement in that *is.* Choice and responsibility for those choices is part and parcel of lawyering. Moreover, there is a certain disingenuity to lawyers' claims about the given nature of law. Once out of their apologists' stance, it is hard to find lawyers who actually proceed on the basis that the law is fixed, certain, and determinate. Sophisticated (and unsophisticated) lawyers recognize that most cases have some chance of success that is attributable to more than the capacity of the opposing lawyer or the presiding judge to get the law wrong: it is as much about the arguments made and the surrounding circumstances as anything else. The fallout from the *Charter of Rights and Freedoms* and the trajectory of the resulting constitutional doctrine provide proof of that.

In light of the empowered role and the elevated status of lawyers in society, the hired-hand image is a humble representation of what lawyers do and what people experience in their dealings with lawyers. For instance, it is fairly obvious that lawyers pick their clients indirectly through the fees they charge. It is not that lawyers openly pick between competing clients for their services, but that only certain kinds of clients come in to certain kinds of law offices: Imasco is not shopping around at the local mall for an affordable or available lawyer. There is nothing necessarily wrong with charging substantial fees for services, but the reality of variable and high legal fees confounds the claims of the lawyer-as-hired-hand image. Of course, some lawyers will decide to represent particular groups of clients either indirectly by the kind of practice they decide to pursue or directly by the kind of issues they countenance. Again, it is an unreal assumption to imagine that many clients come to lawyers with a full and clear understanding of what they want done and what is in their best interests. Indeed, it is often for the reason of clari-

---

9    R. Dworkin, *A Matter of Principle* (Cambridge, Mass.: Harvard University Press, 1985) at 146.

fying what those interests and values might be that some clients come to lawyers in the first place.

A particular fallacy that is contained within the image of the lawyer-as-hired-hand is the belief that legal practice is much the same for those who serve disenfranchised people and for those who work for more privileged clients; it is simply a matter of following different rules. Not only is access to legal services obviously disparate but the needs of the poor require a very different kind of lawyering. Treating all clients the same will do little to alleviate the situation of poorer people. Unlike more privileged people, their problems are continuing and systemic rather than sporadic and particular; legal problems do not arise so much in the otherwise smooth course of their life, but constitute and define much of their life. Whereas advantaged clients want their lawyers to use the system to remedy a discrete conflict, disenfranchised clients want their lawyers to change the system so they can escape life's continual round of legal difficulties and bureaucratic hassles.[10] Apolitical engagement in social struggles through law is a luxury that poverty lawyers and their clients cannot afford.

Finally, the insistence that lawyering is a neutral exercise that does not implicate lawyers in any political process or demand a commitment to any particular ideology is as weak as it is wilful. Such an image is a profoundly conservative and crude understanding of what it is to engage in the business of courts, legislatures, and the like: it accepts and works within the bounds of the status quo. Lawyers tend to confuse legal justice with social fairness. Indeed, the power and prestige of lawyers flows from their professional allegiance to the state's official laws and existing institutions; lawyers are the enlisted custodians of the status quo. By pretending otherwise and renouncing responsibility for the system that their actions hold in place, lawyers are able to maintain their so-called independence and political authority. As well as being a very misleading account of lawyering, the image of lawyer-as-hired-hand is an impoverished vision of the part that lawyers can and do have in the establishment of a substantively just society.

---

10   See S. Wexler, "Practicing Law for Poor People" (1970) 79 Yale L.J. 1049.

## C. A MORE CIVIC PROPOSAL

Of course, dissatisfaction with the dubious assumptions and limited aspirations of the traditional image has led some lawyers and jurists to propose an alternative vision of lawyering. This option is inspired by the Realist critique of law. It seeks to provide a better theoretical framework within which the practice of law can attempt to redeem the ideal of lawyering as a noble profession that places the needs of popular justice above the demands of institutional allegiance. While there is much nostalgic thinking in this ambition, the belief that lawyers do more than simply seek to enforce the law, and, instead, that they might occasionally turn the law to just ends, is a worthwhile and obvious improvement on the traditional image of the lawyer-as-hired-hand. Consequently, the notion of the lawyer-as-civic-campaigner has gained a certain popularity and appeal among some lawyers.

The controlling idea behind this image is the acceptance that law is not nearly so determinate, objective, and stable as formalists maintain. Litigation and adjudication are much more value-laden and result-oriented than traditionalists suppose. Consequently, lawyers must take an appropriate share of the responsibility for those values and results. As players in the system, lawyers must be prepared not only to take credit for the good but also to take blame for the bad. At the very least, they must engage in the struggle to make the legal process the best that it can be for the benefit of those who live under its directives, particularly the disadvantaged and the disenfranchised. As much as lawyers are officers of the law, they are also agents of the people; they ought not to uphold the law for its own sake, but must commit themselves to achieving justice through law. Lawyers should represent only those clients and causes that contribute to the furtherance of the common good. In this sense, lawyers are entitled and expected to straddle the roles of private partisans and public regulators. This does not mean that they do (or do not do) entirely as they please: lawyers must still obey the general imperative to uphold the public purposes of legal rules at the same time that they constantly challenge or uphold those rules in line with their compatibility with the highest substantive ideals of a truly democratic polity.

Accordingly, rather than view lawyers as stoic mediators between the determinate, articulated interests of clients and the determinate, articulated requirements of the legal system, this Realist-inspired critique considers it better to view lawyers as creative constitutors who work the indeterminate relation between law and clients to progressive effect. In doing this, lawyers are entitled to retain their own sense of autonomy in their relations with clients and to exercise their own ethical judgment as to the best course to follow. While not acting against or in disregard of their wishes, clients represent an opportunity for lawyers to fulfill their own agenda of civic struggle; consequently, lawyers ought to take clients and adopt strategies that are compatible with that agenda. In a manner of speaking, the lawyer-as-civic-campaigner insists that lawyers and clients must be "at one" and form a team, with lawyers being prepared to treat the case as if it were their own and to put themselves on the line.

While the basis for this image of the lawyer-as-civic-campaigner is to move beyond the restricting confines of the lawyer-as-hired-hand and its formalistic underpinnings, it is a muted and only partial improvement. Although this Realist image of lawyering recognizes that there is considerable indeterminacy throughout the legal process and that political involvement is virtually unavoidable, it does so in what is ultimately a weak and moderate way. Fearing that anything stronger and more uncompromising might result in "argumentative nihilism,"[11] its proponents hedge on the ramifications of accepting the incorrigible indeterminacy of law. They remain committed to a fairly traditional law-centred approach to social change and political struggle in which it is generally thought to be important to respect law's procedures and "to forego actions that would reduce its efficacy."[12] Accordingly, for the lawyer-as-civic-campaigner, uncertainty and choice are marginal and manageable features of the legal craft rather than debilitating threats to the very core of continued practice: law is as much part of the solution as it is part of the problem. There is a sufficient degree of operational efficacy to satisfy the need for professional self-respect and to refute criticisms of ideological illegitimacy. Despite its intellectual protestations and critical tone, the lawyer-as-civic-campaigner is still a member of the Rule of Law family.

In their zeal to escape the cultivated false modesty and political indifference of the lawyer-as-hired-hand's image, the defenders of the lawyer-as-civic-campaigner's image seemed to have jumped out of the frying pan and into the fire. Eager to take more responsibility for what lawyers do, they have allowed the interests of lawyers to eclipse the needs of clients. Both the lawyer-as-hired-hand and the lawyer-as-civic-

---

11  D.B. Wilkins, "Legal Realism for Lawyers" (1990) 105 Harvard L. Rev. 468 at 484. See also D.B. Wilkins, "Who Should Regulate Lawyers?" (1992) 105 Harvard L. Rev. 799.

12  W.H. Simon, "Ethical Discretion in Lawyering" (1988) 101 Harvard L. Rev. 1083 at 1100. See also W.H. Simon, "Visions of Practice in Legal Thought" (1984) 36 Stanford L. Rev. 469.

campaigner fail to connect properly with clients. Whereas the former claims to accept their clients' values and agendas at face value, the latter submerges them under the lawyers' own values and agendas. Although defended in the name of the common good and democratic empowerment, the image of the lawyer-as-civic-campaigner makes clients captive to one more élite cult of expertise which claims to know what is best for clients and everyone else. On the road to civic redemption, lawyers are the drivers; clients can only take a back seat and enjoy the ride. Lawyers decide who is deserving of access to legal services and representation, what is best for those people taken on, and how their interests should be furthered. This is aristocratic rule masquerading as popular justice.

No matter how enlightened or well intentioned, this way of proceeding is paternalistic and patronizing: it glorifies lawyers individually at the expense of people generally. Lawyers move even more into centre-stage and impose their own moral or political agenda on society at large. Rather than demystify the allure of the legal system and reduce the power of lawyers, the image of lawyer-as-civic-campaigner actually increases law's prestige and lawyers' importance. For instance, the integrationist impetus of much American civil rights litigation of the 1960s and 1970s failed to respect the political demands of blacks for local schools over which black communities could exercise some control: the lawyers' visions overwhelmed and took precedence over the clients'.[13] While lawyers might well have a role to play in the struggle for greater social justice, it is a much more humble and much less presumptuous one. In an effort to remedy the shortcomings of the traditional accounts, the supporters of the lawyer-as-civic-campaigner model have introduced a new but equally inadequate account of ethical lawyering: what it makes up for in lawyers' ethical involvement and responsibility for what they do, it loses in the disregard it shows for people's ethical sensibilities.

Although this alternative proposal is flawed in its recommendations about the handling of cases and the resolution of ethical dilemmas, it does hold considerable promise and legitimacy in dealing with some of the recurrent issues around the selection of clients. Even (or especially) if it is conceded that once lawyers take on clients, they assume some obligation to put the clients' interests and values over those of others, including lawyers' own, there is no reason why lawyers cannot and should not give their own preferences a decisive role in determining which clients they will act for and what causes they will favour (see

---

13   See D.A. Bell Jr., "Serving Two Masters: Integration Ideals and Client Interests in School Desegregation Litigation" (1976) 85 Yale L.J. 470.

chapter 4). Although this is claimed to be contrary to the implicit logic of the traditional model, the fact is that most lawyers do exercise considerable control and discretion over the identity of the clients they choose to represent and the causes they choose to pursue. The lawyer-as-civic-campaigner simply gives ethical and overt approval to what is presently and traditionally done, albeit in an unacknowledged way. In Canada, there is no equivalent to the English cab-rank rule that requires barristers to accept any client at a reasonable fee in their area of expertise.[14] Indeed, client selection is one of the most important and most neglected issues for lawyers because, once clients are taken on, lawyers and clients are engaged in a special relationship that lawyers cannot simply abandon as and when they choose. Consequently, notwithstanding rhetoric to the contrary, lawyers can and do choose whatever clients and causes they wish and, as such, must take responsibility for those clients and causes.

Instead of succumbing to the urge to become authority figures and turn the lawyer-client relationship into an occasion for moral education, lawyers might attempt to nurture a political dialogue in which both lawyers and clients can share, learn, and change, and from which some mutually viable way of proceeding — not anything as pretentious or preposterous as *the* right thing to do — might emerge. In this vision of lawyering, lawyers would not be merely the mouthpieces for their clients' views, nor would they use their clients as soapboxes for their own preferred causes. The ambition is to establish the lawyer-client relationship as a conversational microcosm of democratic culture in which two citizens are able and entitled to contribute fully. This is the key to rethinking the shift from traditional images of lawyering to a more contextual approach to the role and possibilities of lawyers in modern society (see chapter 3).

## D.  A MORE RADICAL VISION

Before proceeding to adumbrate the shape and substance of my own account of professional responsibility and legal ethics, there is one other view of lawyering that has to be considered. I hesitate to call it an image of lawyering because it actually maintains that legal practice is almost always a lost cause by the lights of any truly progressive politics: it is not possible to be a lawyer *and* to be politically progressive. Radical lawyering

---

14   See *Saif Ali v. Sydney Mitchell & Co.*, [1978] 3 W.L.R. 849 (C.A.).

is an oxymoronic pursuit of the first order. This unmitigated critique of the legal profession takes its rhetorical lead from Shakespeare's Dick: "The first thing we do, let's kill all the lawyers."[15] Its basic insight is that the legal process and community are basically a corrupt enterprise in cahoots with all kinds of public and private interests to preserve the status quo. Lawyers are major subcontractors in the capitalist enterprise of maintaining class relations; their professional ideology and action helps to constitute and hold in place social relations and official institutions. The real bargain between lawyers and clients is not one of trust and autonomy, but one in which many lawyers are willing (and often enthusiastic) to sell themselves and their consciences to the highest bidder. For such critics, the very reasons that gave rise to law and rights' original appeal have become the source of its contemporary failing as a program for progressive change: its universalistic pretensions, unyielding individualism, social insensitivity, and pervasive ahistoricality.

On this radical account, involvement with the legal system is necessarily co-optive because any resort to the law or the legal process generally for political relief is simply to reinforce the legitimacy of the very system that holds in place much of the oppression in people's lives. Any victories are quickly neutralized by bureaucratic inertia, political intransigence, and judicial complacency: hard-won litigation victories have had only negligible effect on providing better health care, education, housing, employment, and other substantive changes in people's material lives. As Canada's relatively brief experience with the *Charter* shows, even the most progressively inspired and successful litigation is more likely to result in weapons for future struggles being handed to better-resourced enemies of radical change; the triumph of individuals' free speech is nothing compared to the enhancement of corporate communication. The history of social struggle suggests strongly that the prospect of significant social change through litigation is little more than a teasing prospect. Accordingly, from the radical viewpoint, whether as a categoric system of political practice or as a contingent strategy of radical intervention, law and lawyering can never be productive of real or lasting social and economic improvement.[16]

---

15   W. Shakespeare, *The Second Part of King Henry VI* (Cambridge: Cambridge University Press, 1991) at Act IV, Scene ii, line 75.
16   See M. Mandel, *The Charter of Rights and the Legalization of Politics in Canada*, 2d ed. (Toronto: Thompson Educational Publishing, 1994), and J. Fudge & H. Glasbeek, "The Politics of Rights: A Politics with Little Class" (1992) 1 Soc. & Legal St. 45.

Although this radical critique is overstated and unnecessarily doom-laden, there is much good sense to the suggestion that lawyers' routine resort to the courts is profoundly mistaken: it dissipates large amounts of scarce radical energy; it fails to involve citizens as democratic participants in the process of change; and it has a very limited and limiting effects on social change. Yet this line of argument has a tendency to be too polarized, too blunt, and too unrealistic in both its critical analysis and its political recommendations. In the same way that it is no longer possible to invoke "material interests" or "class analysis" as a decisive ploy in political argument, forswearing engagement in law or through lawyering at all is no longer (if it ever was) a viable or a responsible tactic. Like the abstract instincts and intimations of the traditional image of lawyering, the reductionist politics of class struggle fail to respect sufficiently differences of race, gender, and sexuality in its totalizing march to social justice. Such a radical campaign can too easily fall victim to the same kind of universalistic judgment that afflicts the lawyer-as-hired-hand in its all-or-nothing embrace of legal action as a political way of life.

On the jurisprudential front, the debilitating problem with this critique is that, ironically, it is based on a very formalistic understanding of law and society — stable, determinate, and objective — that shares much with the traditional image of the lawyer-as-hired-hand and its jurisprudential footings. The major difference, of course, is that radical critics reject the substantive values that such a legal process represents and enforces; what traditionalists treat as just, critics see as oppressive. The political danger of the old-style left is that, as well as overestimating the thereness of law, it tends to underestimate the transformative impact that individual agents and legal interventions might have in some circumstances.[17] Law is much more indeterminate and, therefore, manipulable than either traditionalists or their critics appreciate. While it is crucial not to exaggerate the contributions of the court, it is equally important not to deny entirely the possibility that legal forums could contribute to transformative struggle. Lawyers are not always and only the urbane and highly paid operatives of the ruling class.

Consequently, I accept that a blanket commitment to a Rule of Law mentality can actually betray the cause of democracy governance and egalitarian justice. However, I am firmly convinced that it is not possible

---

17    See R.L. Nelson & D.M. Trubeck, "New Problems and New Paradigms in Studies of the Legal Profession" in R.L. Nelson, D.M. Trubeck, & R.L. Solomon, eds., *Lawyers' Ideals/Lawyers' Practices: Transformations in the American Legal Profession* (Ithaca: Cornell University Press, 1992).

or desirable to ignore entirely the progressive or transformative potential that professional, ethical, and responsible lawyering can have in a society that is so thoroughly pervaded by law and lawyers. While both the wholesale adoption and rejection of the legal order as a schematic process for substantial social renovation are fundamental errors, the critical challenge is to move beyond such political stereotypes and their one-dimensional narratives for transformative action. The choice is *not* so stark or binary in the struggle for progressive change and social justice. Mindful that there is no "outside" from which to work, there may be occasional strategic advantage in making "inside" resort to the courts in the struggle to advance the project of progressive justice. It involves the precarious but unavoidable task of trying to tread a thin line between engaging with the system and being co-opted by that system. The only other choices are that you can withdraw entirely and wail in the wilderness, or you can go underground and foment bloody revolution. Neither of these seem attractive or tenable solutions in Canada today.

Nevertheless, for those committed to a more radical practice of law, it is possible to formulate a style of lawyering that works within the system as it challenges that system. Such a *modus vivendi* will not receive the approval of all, but it need not be dismissed out of hand as lacking in ethical purpose or professional responsibility. To be effective, any strategy to help poor people must not simply take (and leave) the legal system as it is, but should seek to challenge and transform the process itself; the courts and lawyers are as much part of the problem as the solution. As the government's hostility to legal aid increases and lawyers' willingness to engage in pro bono work decreases, the issue of what is an ethical approach to lawyering and professional responsibility deserves to be urgently revisited (see chapter 10).

# E.  CONCLUSION

So what have I got to offer in place of these discredited versions of lawyering? What vision can I offer that takes account of existing expectations and, at the same time, contributes to a more responsible and transformative practice of law? Although I hesitate to use labels, I want to offer an idea of what a *pragmatic* vision of lawyering might look like. In doing this, my aim is not simply to colonize the middle ground between the cultivated professional neutrality of the lawyer-as-hired-hand and the imposed political viewpoint of the lawyer-as-civic-campaigner. Instead, I want to get beyond this polarized and dichotomous way of proceeding. I want to offer an account of professional responsibility and legal ethics that is something of both and something of neither. Nor do I want to take off on a flight of juristic fantasy, in a misguided attempt to redeem the dubious ideal of "justice through law." I want to situate a vision of pragmatic lawyering in the here and now. The ambition is not mild reform or wild revolution, but a vigorous practice of transformation and transgression. In the familiar imagery of Neurath's nautical metaphor, the legal profession is already well launched on the historical sea: it is unable or unwilling to return to the dry-dock for a complete overhaul.[18] If change is to be effective, it must be done one plank at a time and while the ship is still at sea.

---

18   See O. Neurath, "Protocol Sentences" in A.J. Ayer, *Logical Positivism* (New York: Free Press, 1966).

# AN ALTERNATIVE VISION: A CONTEXTUAL AND PRAGMATIC APPROACH

While there have been some adjustments and tinkerings to the traditional model, there has been little effort to rethink the basic obligations and demands of professional responsibility and legal ethics. In this chapter, I offer such a reformulation. The first two sections pursue the two underlying premises of the traditional model which are most pertinent and most problematic: one is the notion of a reasonably homogeneous and uniform legal profession, and the other is the idea of a role-differentiated and rule-based morality. After highlighting these shortcomings, I explore in the third section the nature of moral responsibility generally; this overview involves a critical challenge to standard conceptions of ethics and their application. The fourth section introduces a pragmatic approach to legal ethics and professional responsibility that emphasizes the special relation between personal morality and professional expectations. In the fifth and final section, I develop the idea of ethical character and judgment as it applies to the practice of law. Throughout the chapter, I try to make it clear that by *pragmatic* I most certainly do not mean that lawyers should take an expedient or less-than-serious approach to issues of legal ethics and professional responsibility. On the contrary, I maintain that a pragmatic perspective implies a committed ethical stance and demands a genuine appreciation of what taking responsibility involves.

# A. A FRAGMENTED PROFESSION

An underlying premise of the traditional model of lawyering is that there is a reasonably homogeneous and uniform legal profession. This assumption cannot be justified as an empirical claim or as a prescriptive ideal. On closer inspection, the traditional image and professional codes are underpinned with the view of the white male lawyer as an independent professional who deals with a range of legal tasks and who is driven as much by civic pride as by commercial ambition; lawyers are a homogeneous group who engage in broadly similar work. This notion of the fungible lawyer who inhabits, with only slight variation and adaptation, all the offices and activities throughout society is a myth. The reality is that, while such anachronisms exist, they are the exception rather than the rule. Indeed, there is no longer one image of the lawyer; rather, lawyers are an increasingly heterogeneous and stratified bunch whose backgrounds, ambitions, and standards are much less uniform than was previously the case. However, while the legal profession is becoming more diversified, it remains a stratified profession in which white male lawyers still exercise the most control over the regulation and self-image of the profession.

Whether there ever has been one type of lawyer or one kind of legal practice is moot, but it is certain that Canada's legal profession at the end of the twentieth century comprises many types of lawyers and many kinds of legal practices. Although the Canadian literature is not as extensive or as thorough as that of the United Kingdom and the United States,[1] there is ample evidence to support the view that talk of one legal profession is becoming fanciful. There is such a horizontally and vertically differentiated set of people and organizations engaging in different sorts of legal practice that generalizations are as unfounded as they are misleading. The profession is differentiated into megafirms, smaller partnerships, and single practitioners, not to mention government lawyers and the like; there is little shared experience, little interaction among them, and each operates in line with different cultures and norms. Indeed, the idea that there is a unified legal profession not only is mythical but has an insidious bearing on legal ethics. From its élite status at Confederation, the legal profession has become increasingly fragmented, both in terms of diversity (different people and forms of organization) and stratification (a hierarchical order to such diversity). Unfortunately, there has been a marked tendency for the benefits of diversity to be neutralized by the imposition of stratification: the new

---

1   See R.L. Abel, *American Lawyers* (New York: Oxford University Press, 1989), and *The English Legal Profession* (Oxford: Blackwell, 1988).

and diverse personnel are relegated to the marginalized periphery of the legal profession. While the profession has diversified, the typical lawyer remains male, white, English-speaking, early middle-aged, and Christian; lawyers who deviate from this norm are greater in number, but still less powerful in prestige and influence.[2]

Legal practice is shaped by many factors, both external and internal. In recent decades, the Canadian legal profession has been strongly influenced by a variety of environmental forces over which it has little control: decreasing state regulation; the juridification of dispute resolution; the restructuring of the economy; the extent of globalization; and the spread of computerization and information technology. Not surprisingly, these external forces have been mediated through a set of internal filters that affect their impact on the workings of the legal profession.[3] The result is that there is no longer a Canadian legal profession; rather, there are many different ones, ranging from the solo practice to the large corporate bureaucracy to the small partnerships and government lawyers. The days of the fungible lawyer or legal practice are long gone. A wide range of lawyering types engage in a wide variety of practices. Who does law (men and women, young and old, black and white, etc.), where they do it (office towers, shopping malls, clinics, home basements, government offices, mobile vans, etc.), how they do it (with entrepreneurial flair, part-time, on a shoestring, as big business, etc.), who they do it for (Aboriginal people, rich individuals, international conglomerates, homeless, small businesses, etc.), and what they do it for (subsistence income, personal satisfaction, enormous income, political influence, etc.) have gone through a transformation. However, as well as a greater diversification of the legal profession, there has been a marked increase in stratification. Lawyers are distinguished not only by what they do but by the professional satisfaction, financial reward, public esteem, and political influence they experience.

The size of the Canadian legal profession increased by 430 percent from 1931 to 1986, and rose from 27,100 members in 1986 to 49,680 in 1996. These figures translated in Ontario into the lawyer/population ratio jumping from 1/1142 in 1960 to 1/574 in 1981. As tables 3.1 and 3.2 show, the proportion of different ethnicities, genders, nationalities, and religious affiliations has changed significantly: while the percentage of lawyers born in Canada has reduced slightly, the general diversity has improved significantly.

---

2   D.A.A. Stager & H.W. Arthurs, *Lawyers in Canada* (Toronto: Published in association with Statistics Canada by University of Toronto Press, 1990) at 159.

3   H.W. Arthurs, "Lawyering in Canada in the 21st Century" (1996) 15 Windsor Yearbook of Access to Justice 202.

**TABLE 3.1   Ethnic Background of Lawyers**

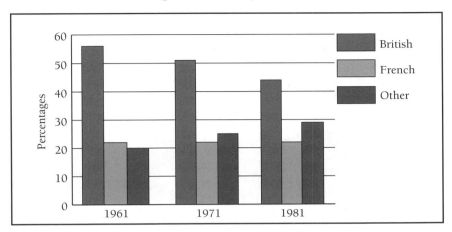

Source: Statistics Canada, *Census of Canada*, decennial publications.

**TABLE 3.2   Religion of Lawyers**

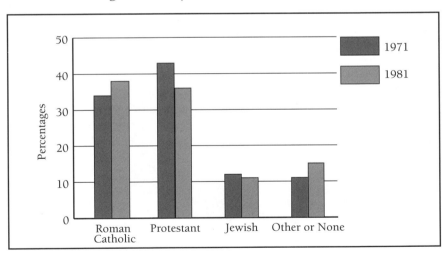

Source: Statistics Canada, *Census of Canada*, 1971 and 1981, special tabulations.
Note: There was no question about religion in the 1986 census.

With regard to the organization and hierarchy of legal practice, tables 3.3 and 3.4 reflect the increasing variety of ways in which lawyers practise law. However, certain forms of legal practice are much more prestigious than others, and certain differences have definite implications for legal ethics.

**TABLE 3.3**   Industrial Distribution of Lawyers

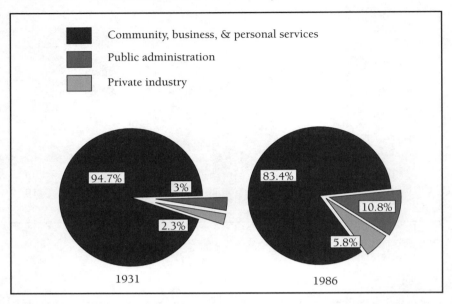

Source: Statistics Canada, *Census of Canada, Occupation by Industry*, decennial
publications; special tabulations for 1986.

**TABLE 3.4**   Distribution of Lawyers in Firms and Solo Practice

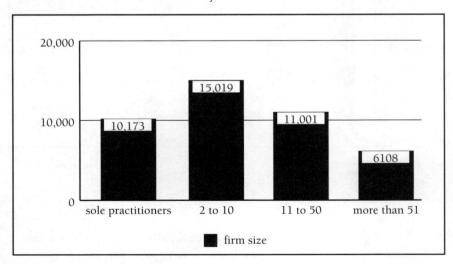

Source: Federation of Law Societies in Canada, 1996 statistics.

In particular, the élite firms have greater access to the law society bodies that develop the rules and culture of the profession, while the sole practitioner is much more likely to be subject to formal monitoring by the profession. In short, big-time lawyers establish the standards of good lawyering for the rest of the profession and, insofar as they are interested in enforcement, they focus attention on the activities of small-time lawyers. A refusal to abandon the assumption of a homogeneous profession, even in the face of a statistically diverse one, will not only be mismatched to the needs of the public and the profession but will exacerbate stratification and hierarchy in the profession.

These changes, brought about by the external forces operating on the structure and work of the legal profession and its internal reorganization and economy, have exerted a strong influence on the governance of the profession and the status of legal ethics. As well as important changes in the nature of law and legal education, the different kinds of legal practice mean that the effort to impose a unitary and uniform system of governance on the legal profession is coming under increasing pressure; the different constituencies agitate for very different initiatives and regimes of collective supervision. The debates over continuing legal accreditation, articling, diversity, and malpractice insurance pit one part of the profession squarely against another. At its most extreme, this unrest and division of interests will likely precipitate moves to remove or, at least, curtail the legal profession's monopoly. As for legal ethics, the consequences of these external and internal pressures are affecting both the establishment of shared common norms and their enforcement. A number of small subcultures have developed and standardized their own expectations for ethical behaviour: small-town family lawyers, for example, operate in a different milieu from metropolitan corporate deal-makers. In this kind of professional climate, it is even more difficult to sustain the idea that there is a common set of rules and expectations that can both educate and discipline the legal profession in matters of ethical practice.

## B. ROLES AND RULES

The second major difficulty with the traditional image of the ethical lawyer is that it asks lawyers to subordinate their personal morality and identity to the standardized requirements of a role-defined and rule-based morality. It assumes that legal professionals will appreciate and actualize the demands of a role-differentiated morality in which lawyers' duties are exclusively bound by the law and the professional code of conduct on one side and the clients' interests on the other. It assumes a two-dimensional moral universe in which lawyers are no more expected to intrude their own personal values than actors or butlers in the performance of their duties.[4] Such a notion allows persons to claim moral legitimacy for actions that might be considered illegitimate in other roles and contexts. Moreover, in this professional role, lawyers are required to treat morality in the same way that they deal with law — as an exhaustive body of rules that can be formally applied to resolve the most recalcitrant of difficulties and dilemmas. Consequently, in the traditional approach, there is little space for reflection or engagement; reference to the professional codes is intended to provide definitive and authoritative answers.

Traditional views and understandings about what it means to be an ethical lawyer are based on narrow and unrealistic assumptions about what ethical decisions address and involve, who lawyers are and what they do, what constitutes law, and the professional contexts in which these issues arise. To be a legal professional is to enter into an increasingly diverse community that pretends to have developed and sustained a shared set of normative practices and expectations that it is authorized or prepared to enforce in the face of recalcitrant behaviour. While several devices are used to curb and monitor lawyers' behaviour, codes of professional conduct lie at the heart of the profession's focus on legal ethics and responsibility. The reasons for having codes of professional conduct are fairly obvious: to educate lawyers on communal expectations; to affect behaviour; and to offer a basis for discipline. However, when they have shown any interest in revising their professional rules, law societies have tended to develop and adapt them in response to problems that arise: it has been a reactive and unambitious approach that lacks any underlying direction or purpose. The recent episode over the drafting and introduction of a new rule on discrimination is a prime example of this process (see XX). Some critics have insisted that such codes are little more than ethical window-dressing; they serve to legitimate what lawyers do and to impose control over economic competition. What passes for talk of ethical standards is, at best, a stylized form of professional regulation and, at worst, a self-serving paean to professional prestige.[5] In short, professional bodies are, through their codes

---

4    See A.H. Goldman, *The Moral Foundations of Professional Ethics* (Totowa, NJ: Rowman and Littlefield, 1982).

5    See R.L. Abel, "Why Does the ABA Promulgate Ethical Rules?" (1981) 59 Texas L. Rev. 639, and D.L. Rhode, "Why the ABA Bothers: A Functional Perspective on Professional Codes" (1981) 59 Texas L. Rev. 689.

and rules, often as interested in enforcing collegial conformity as in fostering a sense of ethical purpose; there is a lingering suspicion that the rules essentially promote professional self-interest and do little to affect ethical behaviour or debate among practising lawyers (see chapter 1).

To read any of the provincial codes of professional conduct is to encounter a series of pronouncements that are long on righteous aspiration and vague generalities but short on serious instruction and concrete guidance. It is a case of not seeing the ethical forest for the lawlike trees. Although lawyers are weighed down with discrete and detailed directives on particular matters, there is little to counsel the floundering or jaded lawyer in establishing an overall and professional *modus vivendi*. Like the formalist lawyering that many claim to embody and extol, ethics is reduced to a technical compliance with a set of simple do's and don'ts: it is more of a shopping list than a genuine effort to inculcate a style and substance of legal practice that addresses the whole lawyer, and not merely the occasional legal transaction. It is as much about conformity as conscience. Lawyers approach ethics in the same way that they approach law — as a set of rules to be mastered and manipulated to serve the purpose in hand. Indeed, under the sway of a legalistic mentality, the teaching of legal ethics and responsibility is more like a course on office management; it is as much about techniques in filing and organization as about thinking through dilemmas and difficulties.

Even assuming that the various codes are treated as representing a serious attempt at ethical instruction and control, an exclusive concentration on the rules is misplaced. There is little to be gained by providing an elaborate and exhaustive annotation of the rules of professional conduct: not only has it been done but it ignores the fact that its influence on lawyers' daily routines and rituals is small. The constant attention to and redrafting of the rules is of decreasing marginal utility.[6] Nevertheless, this does not mean that the codes have no place in any appreciation of legal ethics and their actual improvement; they are an important resource in discussion and decision making, but they are not a decisive or determinate play-book that relieves lawyers of the personal responsibility to develop an ethical style and substance of legal practice. The codes are a site at which ethical debate can be joined and developed. As with many catalogues of rights and responsibilities, there will be competing and occasionally contradictory imperatives; duties to clients might suggest a different course of action from those recommended by

---

6   See H. Arthurs, "Climbing Kilimanjaro: Ethics for Postmodern Professionals" (1993) 6:1 Westminster Affairs 3.

the lawyers' responsibilities as officers of the court. In some instances, the rules demand that lawyers *must* make certain choices and give priority to certain actions. However, the rules more often offer no definite resolution and simply provide a rudimentary framework within which lawyers can debate and develop an ethical practice of law. It is important to remember that the rules do not and cannot relieve lawyers of the continuing responsibility to exercise their own professional and moral judgment about the appropriate course to follow.

In many ways, therefore, the interpretation of the professional codes and rules resembles other modes of legal interpretation. In the same way that the meaning of constitutional or statutory law is not fixed or exhausted by its textual rendering, so the requirements of professional responsibility and legal ethics are not reducible to the four textual corners of the codes: both require reference to a wide range of interpretive aids and sources, including conventions, customs, tradition, cultural expectations, institutional norms, and social values. As with teaching legal doctrine generally, little is achieved by asking students to learn rotelike the rules of professional conduct; they must also be provided with a critical framework within which to understand how those particular rules came into being or what they are intended to do. It is the same with legal ethics. If students are taught only the rules of professional conduct, they will be ill-prepared to adapt those sweeping injunctions to changing circumstances or to respond to uncertainty in the rules' meaning or application. As so much contemporary jurisprudence insists, it is never possible simply to "follow the rules." The question of what the rules mean and what it means to follow them are never beyond dispute.[7] Legal interpretation is an ungrounded practice in that it cannot be engaged in without taking a stand on values or choices that are themselves always open to challenge; the distinction between "following the rules" and "following one's conscience" is neither as clear nor as uncontroversial as traditionalists suggest. The suggestion that a viable and satisfying legal ethics can be maintained by adopting the professional role of a rule-ordered mentality is sorely mistaken.

As presently practised, legal ethics is not reducible to an unthinking compliance with the prevailing rules of professional conduct in order to avoid discipline or disrepute. Indeed, the rules are rarely referenced, and it is more common for practitioners to resort to personal conscience

---

7   See A.C. Hutchinson, *It's All in the Game: A Non-Foundational Account of Law, Politics and Adjudication* (Durham, NC: Duke University Press, 1999).

to determine what is a professionally appropriate course of action.[8] Like general ethics, legal ethics is contextual, in the sense that it involves particular people in particular situations making difficult decisions, with particular time constraints and imperfect information, and with particular consequences for particular people. And, of course, there is no context that allows people to fix once and for all their obligations and actions when acting in personal or professional roles. There are few right answers that stand outside any context or debate. The traditional understandings and expectations are nothing more, or less, than the accumulated practices of lawyers which have been affixed with institutional authority. Lawyers can and should contribute to, as much as respond to, the developing culture of lawyering. In this way, they are in a better position to cultivate a *modus vivendi* that enables them to bring together the promptings of their personal conscience with the demands of their professional occupation. Legal ethics ought to be an active meditation on law and lawyering rather than a passive and neutral adherence to a professional code. Indeed, the rules are less a set of directives from which lawyers can draw clear guidance than a collection of practical wisdom with which lawyers can engage and contest.[9] Accordingly, compliance with law, in both its spirit and its letter, does not amount to acceptable ethical behaviour: professional morality is more than law-abiding conformity. The fact that most decisions and practices by lawyers allow for a variety of manoeuvres or results means that lawyers need to develop a professional facility to comprehend and handle such challenges. There is rarely an obvious or incontestable path to follow.

## C. MORALITY AND RESPONSIBILITY

Any society has a set of moral standards by which it requires its members to abide. Although those standards might be more or less exacting in the obligations they impose, and more or less observed in actual compliance, they do constitute an important dimension of social life. However, efforts to map the morality of any particular society are of limited value because they will reveal little about the important questions of

---

8   See W.H. Simon, "The Trouble with Legal Ethics" (1991) 41 J. Legal Ed. 65, and P.J. Schlitz, "Legal Ethics in Decline: The Elite Law Firm, the Elite Law School, and the Moral Formation of the Novice Attorney" (1998) 82 Minn. L. Rev. 705 at 713–18.

9   See generally, Symposium — Critical Theories and Legal Ethics (1993) 81 Georgetown L.J. 2457, and Symposium — Teaching Legal Ethics (1995) 58 Law and Contemporary Problems (vol. 3 and 4).

whether such morality is worthy of approval or adoption. Accordingly, it is necessary to develop a framework within which to evaluate conduct that is claimed to be morally defensible and also to confirm or deny its acceptability. This is the focus of ethical study.[10] At its broadest, ethics involves a meditation on what is wrong and right and, most important, on how such standards are arrived at and validated. Traditionally, the task was to elaborate and justify a set of ethical norms that provide an authoritative code that people could consult and follow in resolving difficult dilemmas. However, faith in the possibility of sketching such a body of enduring and universally valid rules has been waning. There is now the less absolutist and more sceptical acceptance that ethics is a situational practice that cannot claim objective or neutral justification.

Although it is often forgotten by most lawyers, the study of legal ethics is a branch of ethics generally; it is not a subject unto itself. As with general ethics, the prevailing standards of right and wrong do not exhaust ethical inquiry into legal professionals' behaviour; those standards must themselves be subject to scrutiny and challenge. The different ethical theories seek to examine critically the conventional moral judgments and practices that make up contemporary legal practice; they offer methods and devices through which to justify or condemn particular moral answers to controversies or dilemmas. There are almost as many ethical theories as there are ethical philosophers. Accordingly, the focus of this section is on the ways in which lawyers might consider the more general and theoretical reasons as to why they are obliged to act in one way or another: How can lawyers formulate a sense of ethical judgment? What principles might govern their dealings with clients on issues of confidentiality and conflicts of interests? How far can lawyers go in helping accused persons to avoid conviction? What are the responsibilities of lawyers to those who cannot afford their services?

It is difficult to talk about professional responsibility and legal ethics without first saying something about the broader notion and practice of moral responsibility. In much discussion about legal ethics, it is assumed that people bring with them a fully formed and critical capacity for moral engagement. This notion is simply mistaken. People, especially young students, do not have a well-established and personal sense of moral responsibility they can refine or adjust to the special demands of professional circumstances; they have an inadequate basis on which to build such an undertaking. In developing an ethic of professional

---

10   For good introductory and modern overviews, see P. Singer, ed., *A Companion to Ethics* (Oxford: Blackwell Reference, 1993), and R. Scruton, *Modern Philosophy* (London: Sinclair-Stevenson, 1994).

responsibility, the first task is to enable and encourage people to enhance and interrogate their own sense of moral judgment and responsibility. In particular, law students need to confront general ethical dilemmas in concrete circumstances to begin to discover (or construct), question, and articulate their own moral views before they struggle with the complex demands of a professional ethic. Without the opportunity for young lawyers to develop such a critical sense of moral responsibility, the teaching and learning of legal ethics will be a hollow and unsatisfying exercise.

The terrain of ethical study is diverse, but it can be reduced to two different thrusts. Each approach tends to break down into a series of subdivisions that emphasize rather than prefer one set of methods or factors exclusively over another:

- *Goal-based or consequentialist (teleological) ethics.* This approach gives priority to the outcomes and consequences of behaviour; it is less concerned with whether that conduct is based on duty or principle. The test of ethical conduct is based on a balancing of the adverse effects of behaviour against its positive benefits. Of course, there are many different kinds of teleological theory, the two main ones being egoism (what is good for individuals) and utilitarianism (what is good for society). Each combines in its attention to the forward-looking impact of conduct, not its originating motivation.

- *Rights-based or principled (deontological) ethics.* This approach rejects the claim that the consequences of behaviour determine whether that behaviour is morally acceptable. Instead, it places much greater importance on the reasons for undertaking such conduct; behaviour is more deserving of ethical approval if it is derived from a duty or general sense of moral obligation. The fact that someone acts out of cold brutality rather than reasoned principle is of considerable moral significance. Again, there are many different kinds of deontological theory: the two main ones are monism (one basic and overriding moral principle) and pluralism (a series of general principles). Each combines in its attention to the intrinsic motivation for action, not its consequences or intended goals.

In many instances, all ethical theories will converge on a similar set of generally accepted norms and standards of moral conduct. But, in particular circumstances, the different ethical theories will pull in different directions, and a commitment to one or the other theory might prove decisive. However, there is more to ethics than a dogmatic allegiance to an abstractly favoured theory of general application. For many ethicists, a moral approach to life requires a sense of moral virtue that involves the development of a moral character in the hurly-burly of actual living. It is surely the case that most people will balance both consequences and moral duty in evaluating what to do in specific contexts; there will be a willingness to resist hard-and-fast solutions that are supposed to work in all situations. Moreover, when people act immorally, it might be for one or another reason: they have not thought through the nature of their action, or they have thought it through, but disagree on principle with the views of others. In some circumstances, people will have a clear and reasoned conclusion about what is and is not the right thing to do, but they will proceed to act immorally anyway.

None of these ethical theories is exclusive in its focus; each gives greater or lesser emphasis to some factors over others. Real life is messy, and it is not always possible to separate the reasons for action and its consequences. While it might be thought ethical never to lie, it becomes increasingly difficult to adhere absolutely to such a worthy principle if it might result in the death of several people. Any practical ethical theory cannot be inured entirely to the consequences of action, and no ethical theory can be totally unconcerned with the reasons for action: why and when people act in certain ways will be of crucial significance in any assessment of ethical merit. For example, in criminal law, there is a complex balance between the focus on the reasons for acting and the consequences of any behaviour. While the accused person's state of mind is a dominant focus of inquiry, the gravity of any offence and the seriousness of moral sanction are heavily influenced by the consequences of the imputed conduct; inchoate crimes are distinguishable in principle and punishment from choate ones.

Across the ethical terrain, debate is joined over the prickly issue of whether the authority or source of ethical principles is objective or relative. In establishing particular principles as binding on members of a community, are they absolutely valid, in the sense that they are binding on all professionals at all times and in all societies? Or do they hold sway and have ethical significance for particular communities only at particular times? While this disagreement continues to plague ethical theories, it is a false dichotomy in practical terms because what matters more is the fact of binding moral obligations, not the source of their bindingness. Moreover, the objective or relative basis of ethical principles does not have much weight in discussions of legal ethics because the special circumstances under which lawyers operate in different societies necessarily result in different considerations being taken into account. Even under these special circumstances and structural constraints, lawyers are still left with considerable room for movement in their ethical decision making. Also, there is always the personal ethical challenge of determining whether, because the Rules allow certain conduct, the individual lawyer should reflect on and perhaps refuse to operate in certain ways. The fact that the Rules allow lawyers to ignore the interests of other parties entirely does not mean that it is a morally unimpeachable course to follow: *can* does not necessarily imply *must*.

As much modern ethical theorizing insists, what counts as acting ethically will always be a contextual question. It bears repeating that there is no universal context that allows people to fix once and for all the obligations and actions of the ethically aware lawyer. In a world of shifting contexts, there is an even greater need to develop a sense of moral judgment that can respond flexibly and firmly to the different challenges that lawyers face in their professional lives. None of these qualifications should be taken to mean that ethical behaviour and decision making are condemned to be irrational or arbitrary; rather, what counts and operates as reason is never outside its informing context. The alleged uncertainty of a contextual approach is no more or less inefficient than complying with any other legal standard; certainty is not a virtue in and of itself. In this way, legal ethics can be viewed less as a fixed and independent code of professional conduct and more as a continuing practice within which lawyers construct acceptable norms of behaviour as they struggle to comply with them.

To be an ethical lawyer involves more than learning and applying a set of rules; it also demands the cultivation of a critical reflection on the professional role and responsibilities of lawyers. In short, a fully ethical practice requires an independent sense of moral virtue that involves the lifelong development of personal moral character. Because there is no one answer to ethical dilemmas, it does not mean that reasoning can be abandoned or that "anything goes." A contextual approach simply insists that there is no final or objective answer to ethical problems, not that there are no answers. As philosopher Isaiah Berlin argues: "Since some values may conflict intrinsically, the very notion that a pattern must in principle be discoverable in which they are all rendered harmonious is founded on a false *a priori* view of what the world is like. . . . The need to choose, to sacrifice some ultimate values to others, turns out to be a permanent characteristic of the human predicament."[11]

In ethical debate, a wide range of answers and arguments can be supported by sophisticated chains of reasoning. Moral reasoning is not something that stands outside of or in judgment on moral decision making; it is made and remade in the situational process of moral

---

11   I. Berlin, *Four Essays on Liberty* (London: Oxford University Press, 1969) at *li*.

engagement and debate. As such, what counts as a good moral reason is a matter of justification and persuasion, not proof and authority. Accordingly, I do not offer a recommendation that is relativistic (or nihilistic), in which each person's conception of right and wrong is as good or as valid as any one else's. Although values are constructed with particular social and historical contexts, standards develop about what is and is not acceptable behaviour, even though those standards are never themselves outside debate and transformation. My approach has the merit of demanding that, if ethical issues are to be taken seriously, there must be an acceptance that debate and reflection on moral issues are useful and worthwhile, and that the upshot of such engagement might have an effect on or make a difference to a person's decisions and actions. Most important, it suggests that acting ethically is not about adherence to a code that is resorted to in occasional moments of indecision. Rather, it is about the development of a moral way of living and lawyering that encompasses an organic set of attitudes, dispositions, and values, and that can be incorporated into each lawyer's daily routines and regimen.

## D.  PERSONAL AND PROFESSIONAL

From a pragmatic perspective, legal ethics is not about perfecting universal and enduring codes of conduct. It is about developing a transformative and pluralistic practice that respects the contingent and the particular, and allows for diverse answers and appreciations. The traditional concepts and practices of honesty, confidentiality, and trust remain most pertinent, but are given meaning and bite as the context varies; they are fundamental, but not absolute values in the legal ethics vocabulary. As Lon Fuller points out, there is a vast difference between a professional duty that is based on "duty" as opposed to "aspiration."[12] Whereas the former focuses on compliance with a set of rules, and concentrates on what is not to be done rather than what ought to be done, the latter speaks in more positive terms and asks professionals to develop a style of practice that inspires ethical conduct. The traditional emphasis on code-based morality breeds a mentality that is concerned with delineating how far a lawyer can go without engaging in unethical conduct: it tends to privilege social conformity over efforts to build moral character. It is important that lawyers do not internalize the view

---

12  See L.L. Fuller, *The Morality of Law*, rev. ed. (New Haven: Yale University Press, 1969).

that it is ethical to do whatever is not prohibited by the professional rules; this is an impoverished and thin view of professional responsibility and legal ethics.

Legal ethics should not be satisfied by memorizing appropriate institutionalized responses to particular fact situations. Rather, it should develop a framework within which to understand and reflect on the inevitable ethical dilemmas that arise for a professional. As such, legal ethics should not be something that lawyers refer to in stereotypical situations, but should provide a vibrant and dynamic context that pervades legal professionals' whole way of thinking about law and acting as a lawyer. In developing such a notion and practice of professional ethics, the challenge is neither to abandon a sense of personal morality and defer all ethical responsibility to the unique role and status of the legal professional nor to adhere to the dictates of one's personal conscience and ignore the special responsibilities that attach to being a professional. It is a matter of creating a balance between the two so it is possible to bring together the professional and the personal in a legal ethics that satisfies the pushes of personal morality and the pulls of professional conduct. To do otherwise is to relinquish personal responsibility entirely to the self-interested norms of official codes of professional conduct or to ignore entirely the genuine framework of professional responsibilities that must influence and affect the dictates of personal conscience. It most definitely is not a choice between law and morality, such that the true professional must abandon all efforts to be a good person in being a good lawyer.

Instead of positing professional ethics and personal morality as being entirely separate and, at times, in direct conflict, it is much more useful to view lawyers' ethical responsibility as part of their personal morality. Having developed a personal sense of moral integrity, lawyers should have this sense reinforced rather than jeopardized by the need to subordinate personal values to professional goals.[13] To ask lawyers to forgo moral judgment is to reduce them to amoral technicians with significant drawbacks and limitations. The defence of a role-differentiated ethics is only sustainable if there is widespread confidence in the institutional processes of law — and this protection is surely suspect. In the absence of moral considerations, lawyers will be more competitive, less cooperative, more opportunistic, less principled, more self-regarding, and less committed. Moreover, on the basis that lawyers tend to identify

---

13   See S.G. Kupfer, "Authentic Legal Practices" (1996) 10 Georgetown J. of Legal Ethics 33.

more than most people with their jobs, the amorality of their professional role will begin to infect their personal lives. The amorality will become its own impoverished morality by default: lawyers' sensitivities can atrophy or narrow to fit the constricted universe dictated by role.[14] Strict adherence to a strong role differentiation asks lawyers to engage in a form of moral schizophrenia. In such a role, their sense of moral judgment atrophies, they lose track of what is and is not important, and their clients are reduced to nothing more than fee-generating possibilities.

**PROBLEM 3: You specialize in tax. Knowing that Revenue Canada rarely question business expenses of up to 60 percent of revenues, should you tell your client this information when you are aware that her expenses are much less than that percentage?**

Legal ethics does not simply collapse into personal morality, but there has to be a recognition that role-differentiated behaviour has a legitimate claim on the attention of those who strive to be ethical lawyers. Although lawyers must assume personal responsibility for their professional activities, it does not mean that, as lawyers, they must do only what they would do as individuals. It simply asks them to answer to themselves about the extent of dissonance that a professional-differentiated role should allow. Mindful of the social and political realities in which they offer their professional services, lawyers must confront the consequences of their choices about who to represent, the methods of representation, and the broader consequences of their work. If lawyers permitted their own values and preferences to infiltrate all their work, it would mean that they were abusing their privileges by rationing a valuable public service only to those whose views happen to coincide with lawyers'. This broad scope does not mandate a wholescale abrogation of moral responsibility by lawyers. Instead, it suggests that lawyers should try to better integrate their professional and personal lives. Reworking the balance between role morality and personal conscience, a fresh account of legal ethics would place the individual at the centre of the process. It would encourage lawyers to develop a critical morality that encompasses such pressing issues as "What kind of lawyer do I want to be?" and "What interests am I going to spend my life serving as a lawyer?"[15]

---

14    R. Wasserstrom, "Lawyers as Professionals: Some Moral Issues" (1975) 5 Human Rights 1 at 5. See also G.J. Postema, "Moral Responsibility in Professional Ethics" (1980) 55 N.Y.U. Law Rev. 63.

15    A.A.J. Esau, "Teaching Professional Ethics and Responsibility at Law School: What, How and Why?" in R.J. Matas & D.J. McCauley, eds., *Legal Education in Canada* (Federation of Law Societies of Canada, 1987) at 308.

By asking lawyers to limit their moral judgment, such advice endangers the whole moral standing of the legal profession. In the traditional approach, there is little space for reflection or engagement; reference to the Rules is intended to provide definitive and authoritative answers. My approach suggests that legal ethics has more to do with a situated reasoning — with the interests, purposes, and consequences of the participants and their contexts. Reliance on codes atrophies the moral intelligence and leaves lawyers adrift without a moral compass when those professional rules run out or give conflicting advice. My approach encourages continual reflection and better prepares the lawyer for difficult situations. Indeed, the prospects for keeping lawyers in better moral shape and developing a more sensitive mentality should be enhanced if their regimen involves regular immersion in ethical dilemmas.

The other choice for the enlightened lawyer is to abandon the notion of a professionally differentiated role morality and to incorporate all their personal values into the professional arena. Such a solution seems unwise and undesirable, for lawyers would then be abandoning their public trust and abusing their monopolistic privileges. The challenge is to integrate the demands of a professional role with the dictates of a personal morality and be able to construct important bridges between the two, so they can each support and fructify each other. To provide sound professional judgment, it is necessary to resort to a well-honed and mature sense of moral acuity. Unless one subscribes to a formalistic account of law, a familiarity with and a sensitivity to moral issues is an essential quality for lawyers to have, if they are to advise clients about particular areas of law or what the courts are likely to do in particular cases. Without such resources, lawyers will be ill-equipped to fulfill the most basic skills of legal representation; they become only technicians, not advisers. To flinch this challenge or to settle it by default is to fail in both professional and personal responsibility. As Robert Megarry concluded, "clients, of course, come and go; but your conscience does not, and you will have to live with it for the rest of your life."[16]

The traditional approach fails to involve clients sufficiently in the provision of legal services, and so denies them satisfaction. They are seen to have fixed interests and to stand outside the moral domain of lawyers. The reality is that clients rely as much on lawyers to define their interests as they do to protect them. In my approach, clients are treated as conversational partners who can contribute to and be persuaded about particular courses of action and their likely consequences.

---

16   R.E. Megarry, "Convocation Address" (1983) 17 L.S.U.C. Gazette 41 at 44.

Indeed, client selection is one of the most important and most neglected issues for lawyers. Once a client is taken on, the lawyer has some responsibility to treat that person differently from other persons; they are engaged in a special relationship that lawyers cannot simply abandon as and when they choose. Notwithstanding rhetoric to the contrary, lawyers can choose whatever clients they wish. As such, lawyers must take responsibility for the clients they choose to represent.

# E.  DEVELOPING GOOD CHARACTER

The term *ethics* is derived from the Greek *ethike,* which was used to denote the science of character. This science was not considered to be solely or even mainly a matter of forming rules, but one that involved the development of good judgment — to respond to and be refined in particular situations. Rules and professional codes assume that lawyers have good character and can go about their lawyering lives with an ability to apply those rules wisely and appropriately. This is the idea of professionalism. Although it has become almost pejorative in popular usage and resonance, the idea of professional judgment is important; it involves more than the technical adept performance of a particular task, without any concern for its broader redeeming qualities or impact. As I use it, professionalism is an approach or attitude that embodies a justification for a particular course of conduct within a wider account of a morally defensible *modus vivendi*; it has a vital moral dimension that defines who lawyers are and what they aspire to be, individually and collectively. It is not simply a vague and general aspiration, but entails a definite response to such issues as the availability of legal services, the clients lawyers accept, and the causes they pursue.

A large part of that professional responsibility is to recognize that, except in the most egregious circumstances, there is no one clear role to fill and no obvious action to take; there is only the obligation to decide what that role should be and what action should be taken. Although this critical process will be heavily influenced by professional codes and the values of the informing collegial community, it is a personal responsibility that involves, but does not reduce to, professional norms; "lawyer morality is ordinary morality which takes into consideration the moral value of professional obligations."[17] In striving to cultivate such a practi-

---

17   J.L. Sammons Jr., *Lawyer Professionalism* (Durham, NC: Carolina Academic Press, 1988) at 47.

cal ethic of professional judgment, lawyers must not forget that it is not equivalent to an ethic of principle, in which ethical conduct is vouchsafed by the strong adherence to accepted and general codes. Character is reflected in all we do, and what we do affects our character; it is a lifelong process of development, readjustment, and determination. Character and judgment cannot be learned by requiring lawyers to prep for and take regular "integrity tests." While these tests are probably better than nothing, they tend to do as much to camouflage the problem as resolve it.

One critic who has lamented the demise of professional standards is Antony Kronman. For him, the rationalization and commercialization of legal practice has led to disenchantment within the profession of the "lawyer-statesman" ideal that used to dominate and inform good lawyering. This ideal put great emphasis on practical wisdom that both informed and transcended code following or rule adherence, and on the commitment to a shared set of communal ends.[18] For Kronman, the talent of good judgment is radically inegalitarian not only in the sense that it is unevenly distributed but also in that it is conducive to a political fraternity that recognizes that the legal community has a special responsibility and facility, as a trained élite, to do what is best for society at large. While Kronman is on to something when he urges greater attention to the development of practical wisdom and professional judgment, there is no reason at all why the cultivation of such attributes needs to be associated with such an élitist vision of the legal profession. Although it is true that judgment is a difficult quality to teach and acquire, it is not the God-given gift that Kronman and others imply. To adhere to such a position discourages people from seeking to enter the legal profession, and excuses those without good judgment from taking responsibility for what they do and from working to improve their judgment skill. Unlike Kronman, I believe that practical judgment is less a character trait that people either do or do not possess, and more a learned skill that people can be taught and can themselves refine with practice.

In teaching legal ethics and professional responsibility, considerable attention must be devoted to simulating situations in which lawyers can build moral character and good judgment. As Aristotle insisted, these attributes are developed by engaging in practical situations and reflecting critically on those experiences so as to enhance and refine their sense of judgment. Consequently, the achievement of moral character and good judgment cannot be grasped by feeding students the relevant

---

18  A.T. Kronman, *The Lost Lawyer: Failing Ideals of the Legal Profession* (Cambridge, Mass.: Belknap Press of Harvard University Press, 1993).

rules and a sense of the theoretical models; theory cannot substitute for practice, and logic cannot replace judgment. This does not mean that theory has no place, but it cannot dispense with the need for learning by immersion in practical situations and by the development of a context-sensitive sense of applied judgment.[19] It cannot be taught, but needs to be learnt in a trial-and-error way that has a built-in component of critical reflection and collegial dialogue. Instruction will need to contain a clinical element if it is to have any prospect of nurturing a sense of good judgment in law students and lawyers; it will not be sufficient to urge upon neophytes the necessity to develop good character, without some structured and supervised opportunities to cultivate a talent for making good decisions. The obvious virtue of ethical principles is often belied by the complexity of practical situations; obligation and duty are not on/off concepts, but vary in weight and force depending on the context. Moreover, "doing the right thing" will not always be apparent or persuasive to others.

The circumstances in which one is asked or expected to demonstrate good professional judgment are infinite. Nevertheless, there are a few general situations in which lawyers' character and judgment will frequently be put to the test — the selection of clients and the lengths to which lawyers are prepared to go on behalf of those clients (see chapters 4 and 6). In the two problems that follow, the issue arises whether you should use "moral" means to achieve "immoral" ends or "immoral means" to achieve "moral" ends. The solution is by no means obvious or uncontroversial; there are strong arguments to be made on both sides. The professional rules offer no genuine guidance, and professional consensus is divided:

PROBLEM 4: A well-dressed husband and wife come to your office to seek your services. They tell you that they made an arrangement a year ago for an elderly couple to take care of a property they own while they were out of the country. Now that they have returned, they no longer want to pay the couple the $3000 they had informally promised, even though the couple had done the work in exemplary fashion and need the money. Do you agree to help them get out of the deal? Would it make a difference to you if these people were already clients of yours in other matters, they were willing to pay you handsomely, they had discovered that the elderly couple were cheating Revenue Canada, or you were short of clients?

---

19   D. Luban & M. Milleman, "Good Judgment: Ethics Teaching in Dark Times" (1995) 9 Georgetown J. of Legal Ethics 31.

PROBLEM 5: You represent a large industrial firm that is being threatened with prosecution by a government regulatory body over broad-ranging environmental infringements. The chances of avoiding conviction on legal grounds do not look good. The CEO of the firm suggests to you that you should tell the government that, unless it drops the prosecution or makes a "sweet" plea bargain, the firm will legally lay off all its workers and relocate to the United States. Would you use this strategy? Would it make a difference if billings to the firm had accounted for over one-third of your legal practice in the last few years?

One of the ways in which lawyers will develop a sense of professional judgment is simply in being a lawyer and handling the different challenges that lawyering throws up, particularly in their early years as an articling student and associate. The influence of senior lawyers in this process will be crucial. Some provincial codes explicitly require lawyers who serve as principals to articling students to provide training that encompasses both the practical aspects of the law and an appreciation for the traditions and ethics of the law. However, the demands of practice mean that such ethics will be acquired more by default than design. A crucial ethical dilemma that is understated by most commentators is the real-world problem of what young lawyers are to do about ethical qualms they have about what they are asked to do by older, supervising lawyers. For instance, what do you do when you are instructed to take the client in Problem 3 and to follow the course mooted in Problem 4. Again, the Rules are not helpful. Apart from being generally unclear on what might and might not be unethical, they simply state that lawyers are to act "with integrity" and not to engage in "dishonourable conduct" (see I, c. 3). The only advice for young lawyers is to "talk" or find mentors in the firm. This avenue might be especially difficult for women and people of colour, who are already under considerable pressure to integrate and adapt to a different culture.

# F.  CONCLUSION

It is surely the case that, in answering Socrates' famous question about how should one live, lawyers cannot respond by simply mumbling that it is acceptable to do whatever is not expressly prohibited by law or disallowed by the professional codes. This is not so much an ethical stance as an abnegation of one. As Hazard observes, "when all has been said, however, the fact will remain that a lawyer's ethical deliberations are a process of personal thought and action."[20] In that process, students and

---

20   G.C. Hazard, "Personal Values and Professional Ethics" (1992) Clev. St. L. Rev. 133 at 140.

lawyers must be prepared to answer for the ethical choices they make and the legal practice in which they engage. Simply pointing to some rule is never enough on its own. There must be a greater acceptance of the fact that good professional judgment cannot be left to the untutored and catch-as-catch-can approach of the present legal community. An explicit and enduring focus on the cultivation of a strong sense of professional purpose and judgment must be pursued and institutionalized.

# CHAPTER 4

# LEGAL PRACTICE: THE ETHICAL DIMENSION

As part of their professional power and responsibility, law societies have shown considerable energy in regulating the circumstances and conditions under which persons can become lawyers and continue to engage in the practice of law. However, their eagerness to enact rules and regulation has not always been matched by their willingness to enforce them with any marked degree of enthusiasm. Indeed, like the common law itself, the regulatory process tends to be largely reactive, and lawyers as a group evince little genuine appetite for the exercise. Nevertheless, in this chapter, I will explain the basic structure that controls the attainment, monitoring, and performances of legal practice. In the first part, I introduce the terms for entry into the legal profession. Next, there is an inquiry into the "good character" test for admission into the legal ranks. The third section explores the standards imposed by the law generally and the Rules specifically for determining and sanctioning professional malpractice. In the last two sections, I round out the chapter by noting the control of unauthorized legal practice and the relevance of lawyers' private lives to their professional status and reputation. Throughout the chapter, I will concentrate on the impact of these structural arrangements for individual lawyers.

## A. ENTRY INTO THE PROFESSION

Lawyers in Canada are part of an integrated profession. Students are called to the bar as barristers and solicitors. This distinction (essentially between those who do and do not litigate as advocates in court) is traceable back to the English profession, which still remains split, with very different entry requirements and training for barristers and solicitors. Although there is a de facto split in the Canadian profession, with a small group of lawyers dominating the litigation process, there is still a much greater and healthier shifting between roles; many general practitioners do a small amount of court work. Indeed, there are many different kinds of lawyers and ways of lawyering — small firms, large firms, sole practitioners, urban practices, rural practices, generalist firms, specialist firms, female firms, ethnic firms, to name a few. Most important, the split organization of the English profession means that the relevance and applicability of its approach to professional responsibility and legal ethics is questionable; there is no obvious or easy equivalence between the English and the Canadian debates and initiatives. The American legal community, however, is structured in a more similar way to the Canadian as a joint profession, so American approaches have a greater salience and resonance. Nevertheless, there are significant organizational differences that caution against too easy a direct borrowing from the American profession.

A natural place for many lawyers to look for guidance on legal ethics and professional responsibility is the United Kingdom. However, apart from the tendency to be overly concerned with what the British do and the modern shift of the Canadian legal system away from its British heritage, there are certain dangers to be avoided. Unlike its Canadian counterpart, the English profession is formally divided into two sections — barristers and solicitors. Without going into the niceties and details of that split, suffice it to say that there are real organizational differences that make any simple borrowing from the United Kingdom a risky business. While the comparison with solicitors is the closest, barristers are in a special position as they do not have a direct contractual relationship with clients (only with the instructing solicitors) and see themselves more as officers of the court as anything else.

All Canadian provinces have a governing body that is controlled by lawyers and has a monopoly over the certification and discipline of lawyers. The requirements for call to the bar vary slightly from province to province. The basic pattern is that all students must possess a law degree from an accredited law school. After successfully completing a law degree, there follows a period of articling or apprenticeship with a lawyer and some combination of course work and examinations in subjects — such as business, corporate, family, tax, or criminal law — that are often taken by most students in law school. All provinces require a period of articles; it is only the length that varies. Articling is a largely unstructured affair in which students are supposed to learn more by osmosis than education and to prove their mettle under the pressure of deadlines rather than acquire the professional values and skills. While there is a vast variety of experience, articling remains too much a rite of passage and not enough a period of instruction. Of course, articling has a long and illustrious pedigree that harks back to the aristocratic aspirations and affectations of the legal profession. In the thirteenth century, the English Inns of Court were community colleges at which members studied, lived, worked, ate, and prayed. Modelled on old trade guilds and predating university legal education, students would be tutelaged in legal crafts and professional lore. As Sir John Fortescue described them in his fabled *De Laudibus Legum Angliae*, the Inns were not so much law colleges as schools for English gentlemen. For barristers in the United Kingdom, a more formalized version of this apprenticeship still applies today: solicitors follow less archaic rites of initiation into the secrets of the law. In Canada, while the aristocratic mien is gone, the lingering practice of training for hierarchy remains.

Many provincial law societies are in the throes of re-evaluating and reorganizing their post-LLB entrance requirements. It is likely that any changes will be modest and limited rather than radical and structural; possible alternatives being considered include the introduction of some kind of provisional or restrictive licence that might limit the kind of work that can be done without supervision. There is an increasing tendency to shift away from a once-and-for-all initiation into the legal profession to a continuing responsibility to maintain and relearn the lawyering craft. Law societies are beginning to recognize that new law school graduates are no more of a threat to the public than old practitioners who have not bothered to inform themselves about changes in the substantive law or lawyering techniques: inexperience is not the only or major source of lawyer malpractice. As a quid pro quo for abolishing articles, lawyers would be required to attend annual professional courses, devoted to substantive updates and fresh skills training. In some areas of practice, it might be appropriate to place limited restrictions on what lawyers can do; these constraints can be removed once a lawyer has practised for a period of years and taken appropriate professional courses. The main goal would be to ensure that lawyers understood that the call to the bar was a privilege that had to be constantly re-earned in order to maintain good professional standing.

# B.  TEST FOR MORAL CHARACTER

Apart from meeting the required educational and vocational standards, applicants for admission to the legal profession must be certified as being "of good character." The requirement for ethical behaviour and moral character flows from the idea that law is a profession, one in which its members are trustees for the public good in the administration of justice. Dating back to Rome's Theodesian Code and Anglo-Saxon England, lawyers have always been required to take an oath that they will fulfill their professional responsibilities in a good and virtuous manner. This is still the case today. New lawyers have to be certified as being of good character and to swear on oath on admission that they will uphold the highest standards of moral integrity. However, there is little consensus on what the requirement of moral character entails or demands. Apart from abstaining from criminal or illegal activities (or, at least, not getting caught), law societies seem to treat such inquiries in a pro forma way; there is only the most perfunctory inquiry into a person's moral character, one that is largely confined to the applicant's own admission and answers. Applicants are presumed to be of good character and, therefore, suitable for legal practice unless there is evidence to the contrary. If the requirement of moral character is to be maintained, law societies must begin to take more seriously its testing and certification. The acquisition of legal competence ought not to be treated as equivalent to the establishment of moral character: they are very different and mutually exclusive attainments.

The requirement of good character has an ancient heritage and is based on the obvious fact that, as lawyers hold considerable power and responsibility in society, they must give the public confidence in their capacity to act fairly and to maintain appropriate standards of conduct. However, although it suggests the maintenance of high moral standards, the test of good character has been used for improper purposes. Under the cover of lack of moral substance, women, people of colour, homosexuals, communists, and others. have been refused admission to the profession. While this exclusionary dimension has been more severely pursued and closely documented in the United States, it is undoubtedly a feature of Canadian legal history. Today, the requirement seems to be administered in a much less exclusionary and discriminatory basis. Nevertheless, the precise nature and scope of good character is far from clear or uncontested,[1] and efforts to provide more determinate guidance

---

1    For a broad-ranging discussion, see D.L. Rhode, "Moral Character as a Professional Credential" (1985) 94 Yale L.J. 491.

seem of little help. For example, the Law Society of Upper Canada has determined that "[c]haracter is that combination of qualities or features distinguishing one person from another. Good character connotes moral or ethical strength, distinguishable as an amalgam of virtuous attributes or traits which would include, among others, integrity, candour, empathy and honesty."[2]

The fact is that law societies have played fast and loose with what does and does not amount to good character. On some occasions criminal convictions for dishonesty have proved decisive, but on others they have not been used as a conclusive bar to admission. The first recorded Ontario case in which an applicant was denied admission for lack of good character did not occur until 1989. While at law school, the applicant had served a prison term for his conviction on serious sexual offences involving young girls; on completion of his law degree and successful psychiatric treatment, his application for admission was denied. In a case in which an applicant had been in prison for election fraud, however, his application for admission was accepted. These two cases not only testify to the muddiness of the character requirements but also demonstrate the rank inconsistency and arbitrariness that mark such assessments. It is reasonably clear that admission to the profession is unlikely to be refused for minor misdemeanours, such as traffic offences or drug possession. The law societies put great stock in the applicant's willingness to be entirely candid about the past, and failure to disclose some dubious earlier conduct can be as damaging as the conduct itself.

The standards of good character tend to be higher (in terms of the burden and standard of proof) for those seeking admission than for those already part of the profession. It is considered less punitive to deny admission to the profession to those who are not yet lawyers than to deprive those who have already been admitted and practised as lawyers. Indeed, in disciplinary proceedings, the focus is not on the lawyer's good character, but on "professional misconduct." Also, there is the anterior and hotly debated question of whether law schools should police the moral character of their students. In both the cases referred to, the criminal conduct occurred before or during law school. For some, the law school should at least bring these professional requirements to the attention of aspiring lawyers and might also perform a moral audit on the incoming students. For others, this censoring offends the life-changing possibilities of education and aligns the law

---

2   See G. MacKenzie, *Lawyers and Ethics: Professional Responsibility and Discipline* (Scarborough, Ont.: Carswell, 1993) at 23-6.

schools too closely with the profession. While universities need to ensure that members of its community are not exposed to immediate threat of harm, there is no compelling reason to impose added moral requirements on law students than on any other students.

A central problem is that, as one critic astutely observes, the inquiry into moral character is both too early and too late in the overall professional process.[3] Occurring on entry into the bar admission courses, it arises before applicants have experienced any genuine ethical dilemmas under real-world pressures; they have no practical context in which to put to the test their ethical intuitions and commitment (or lack of it). However, such institutional assessments occur only after a considerable investment of time and money in academic education by fledging lawyers. Like other skills and requirements, the testing and tutoring of a refined ethical sensibility should be part of a lifelong learning process. There needs to be substantial peer review and a regular auditing process that would both challenge and train lawyers about the worth and importance of ethical lawyering. Nevertheless, the question of whether law schools should police the moral character of their students is hotly debated and contested: Are law schools primarily academic institutions or gatekeepers for the profession?

Legal ethics is a lifelong challenge in which lawyers must be encouraged to go beyond simply learning the rules and how to apply them; they should constantly interrogate themselves and their colleagues about the moral status of their work and practices. Accordingly, lawyers must be helped to hone and question a sense of moral judgment about themselves and their work. While many lawyers lead ethical lives and carry much of that over into their professional lives, there is still a depressing indifference to issues of legal ethics and a lamentable ignorance about how to identify and deal with situations that raise ethical queries and challenges. The first task, therefore, is for people to enhance and interrogate their own sense of moral judgment and responsibility; these qualities are too often assumed to be in place. Mindful that ethical training is primarily concerned with learning about the self, students need to confront ethical dilemmas in concrete circumstances if they are to begin questioning and articulating their own moral views before they struggle with the complex demands of a professional ethic. There is an urgent need to stimulate all students' moral imagination and cultivate their sense of moral responsibility, so they are able to develop a moral

---

3   See R. Gerber, *Lawyers, Courts and Professionalism: The Agenda for Reform* (New York: Greenwood Press, 1989).

facility that is capable of recognizing ethical dilemmas, analyzing them, and responding to them in a responsible and realistic way. A pervasive difficulty in achieving this outcome is that legal ethics is more about responsibilities than rights and, therefore, does not sit easily or well with much of the legal education that lawyers receive.

Insofar as the practice of legal ethics is in disarray, the law societies and the law schools must shoulder a considerable share of the blame for failing to provide an institutional setting for establishing a sophisticated understanding of professional responsibility and its demands. Few law schools take very seriously the need to offer training, mandatory or optional, to its graduates. Certainly, the extent and sophistication of courses in legal ethics comes nowhere close to mirroring those of the substantive courses. Furthermore, the courses that do exist tend to treat the teaching of legal ethics as if it were simply one more course, often with less than the modest intellectual ambitions and innovative pedagogical techniques than in business associations or torts. In an important sense, although law schools have not taken the teaching of legal ethics seriously, they have still instilled within students and lawyers a certain sense of professional ethics. Indeed, law schools cannot avoid teaching legal ethics as "the very act of teaching . . . creates images of law and lawyering when we teach doctrine through cases and hypotheticals."[4] Unfortunately, reinforced by the general rule-centred attitude to the study of legal doctrine, law students settle neatly into thinking of legal ethics as involving a similar process of role-detachment and legalistic application.

To their credit, however, the law societies and law schools have begun to take responsibility in meeting this shortcoming more seriously. Stirred into action by some first-rate studies and reform proposals,[5] there is now a compulsory component in ethics in most provincial bar admission courses. Nevertheless, there is still a considerable way to go, as instruction remains closely tied to the rote-learning of the codes and the tendency to treat legal ethics the same as other subjects remains pronounced. Also, while continuing legal education programs are another step in the right direction, the law societies remain reactive in planning or pursuing the ethical practices of lawyers; they make little

4    C.J. Menkel, "Can a Law Teacher Avoid Teaching Legal Ethics?" (1991) 41 J. Legal Ed. 3.
5    See, for example, B. Cotter, *Professional Responsibility Instruction in Canada: A Coordinated Curriculum for Legal Education* (Montreal: Conceptcom, 1992), and D. Buckingham et al., *Legal Ethics in Canada: Theory and Practice* (Toronto: Harcourt Brace Canada, 1996).

effort to monitor the competence of lawyers on any regular or serious basis. All in all, the efforts to prepare young lawyers for the ethical rigours of legal practice are still very limited, more an afterthought than a core feature of the curriculum. It will take a sea-change in both the scope and substance of courses taught and the style and pedagogy through which they are presented (see chapter 11).

As well as altering their attitudes and their approach to the teaching of legal ethics, law societies must encourage their members to adopt a much more expansive understanding of their ethical responsibilities. They can do this in a number of ways. At an institutional level, lawyers can be constantly reminded that they must not neglect or overlook the opportunity to converse with other lawyers. This can be done by prolif-erating the forums — as in law schools, professional gatherings, law firms — within which dialogue and engagement can be nurtured and thrive. In this way, lawyers might explore their own moral intuitions in the different context of others' views without inviting public criticism or risk. Also, it can be made clear to lawyers that their moral obligations as professionals extend beyond concern with their own individual actions and encompass a responsibility to monitor the actions of other lawyers. In this way, professional responsibility is as much a collective as well as personal undertaking in which each lawyer should contribute to the moral health of the profession as a whole.

## C.  COMPETENCE AND MALPRACTICE

There are several ways in which lawyers are regulated to ensure that they acquire and maintain an appropriate level of professional quality and ser-vice. There are two main sources of obligation: professional discipline and legal regulation. Under the various codes of professional conduct, lawyers have a clear duty to be competent and to deliver services "in a conscien-tious, diligent and efficient manner" (see II, cc. 1, 2, 7, and 8). The stan-dard demanded of lawyers is that expected of "a competent lawyer in a like situation." Notwithstanding the circular nature of this standard, it is clear that it involves more than a basic understanding of legal principles, that lawyers must keep up to date, and that the required level of skill will vary depending on the subject matter and the experience of the lawyer (see II, cc. 3, 4, 5, and 6). However, the standard to be maintained is a reasonable one, and there is no expectation that particular lawyers will have to meet, even though they should aspire to, the perfection of the ideal lawyer.

Of particular importance is the requirement that lawyers should only take on specific cases in areas in which they have a sufficient knowledge or in which they could quickly become competent. Unfortunately, there is no evidence that anyone is disciplined for this failing, even though its incidence is likely far from negligible. At the very least, lawyers must be up front with their clients about their (lack of) knowledge and experience in certain matters. Accordingly, lawyers can take on cases in areas they do not usually practice, provided they explain this to their clients and are willing to refer the case to another, more expert lawyer at a later date if the circumstances so demand (see II, cc. 3, 5, and 6). Also, if lawyers undertake to offer non-legal advice or engage in other business, they must ensure that they make their clients aware of their limited knowledge or expertise in the matter, provide competent advice, and give precedence to their legal duties (see III, c. 10, and VII, c. 3). In both legal and non-legal business, lawyers must withdraw in situations where it becomes clear that they are not competent to continue acting (see VII, c. 4(d)).

**PROBLEM 6: After articling at a large corporate and commercial firm, you decide to set up your own suburban practice and offer a broad range of legal services. Business is slow at the beginning. A couple of local residents come to your office; they claim to be in ill-health as a result of emissions from a neighbouring textile plant. They also tell you that there are plenty of other local residents in a similar situation. You see the possibility for a large class action against the company. What do you tell the prospective clients?**

Like everyone else, lawyers are subject to the general rules of civil liability. Fortunately, Canadian courts have not been seduced by the dubious decisions of the Anglo-Australian courts that advocates in their court work are immune from negligence claims. However, the success of such actions is even more remote than in litigation generally; courts are sensitive to the difficulties that lawyers face in making judgments and assessing legal options. Although the most common action against lawyers involves negligence claims, these cases usually arise from a variety of contractual and fiduciary duties brought into play by the lawyer-client relationship. It must be emphasized that the general principles and fiduciary duties of agency law apply to dealings between lawyers and their clients: these are the basis of the obligations in regard to fidelity and full disclosure in accounting and profit making.[6] As professionals, lawyers assume power over others who are more vulnerable and they must, therefore, exercise that power in the best interests of their clients. For example, lawyers must not accept a referral fee from any

---

6    *Norberg v. Wynrib*, [1992] 2 S.C.R. 226.

person or organization, such as a mortgage broker or a real estate agent, to whom lawyers introduce one of their clients. Also, lawyers cannot accept any hidden fees and must disclose any collateral benefits they will receive from having someone as a client (see XI, c. 7).

Indeed, not only can clients proceed by way of contract or tort, whichever is most advantageous to them (i.e., limitation period or damages), but the responsibility of lawyers to act competently also can extend to others who have been foreseeably injured by their conduct (such as beneficiaries under a will).[7] It is not enough that a lawyer makes an error or a mistake. In addition, it must be shown that it was the kind of error or mistake that reasonably competent lawyers would not make. However, while the appeal to the common professional customs will often be determinative, the courts have held that those customary practices must be demonstrably reasonable if lawyers are to escape liability.[8] One primary responsibility of lawyers is to be knowledgeable about the law and to ensure that their skills are kept up to date, though the standard for such professional negligence is variable and will depend on a variety of factors, including the lawyer's skill and (in)experience, the nature of the work, and the level of remuneration. Lawyers should also remember that they can be found liable for giving negligent non-legal advice and might be held to a professional standard of care.[9]

Apart from the general law of civil obligations, lawyers are required by the Rules to be diligent in maintaining and exercising their legal skills. A failure to use an appropriate level of care can amount to professional misconduct, even if it falls short of establishing civil liability. In such circumstances, however, the finding of negligence does not lead to an award of damages, even though law societies are empowered to direct lawyers to compensate their clients. Although the general language of the Code suggests a high standard of care and competence, there is a clear comment to the effect that "a mistake, even though it might be actionable for damages in negligence, would not necessarily constitute a failure to maintain a standard set by the Rule" (see II, c. 9). It would seem that to warrant disciplinary action against lawyers, there must be "evidence of gross neglect." One might expect that the ethical standards of conduct imposed by the profession would be more strict and demanding than that imposed by the general law, but this does not seem to be the case. The profession takes the view that simply being

---

7    See *Central & Eastern Trust Co.* v. *Rafuse*, [1986] 2 S.C.R. 147, and *White* v. *Jones*, [1995] 2 A.C. 207 (H.L.(E.)).
8    See *Dorion* v. *Roberge*, [1991] 1 S.C.R. 374.
9    *Brumer* v. *Gunn*, [1983] 1 W.W.R. 424 at 443 (Q.B.).

found liable for tortious malpractice is not conclusive evidence of professional misconduct by a lawyer or, at least, a trigger for an inquiry to be made into the lawyer's general practice. That having been said, the professional rules do designate as unsatisfactory professional conduct such matters as failure to keep appointments and failure to answer communications within a reasonable time, matters that would likely fall short of tortious liability.

While a finding of incompetence under the Rules is not dependent on proof of prejudice or disadvantage to a client, the law societies have been less than vigilant in their efforts to monitor such matters. The initiation of disciplinary proceedings for professional incompetence, even in cases of gross delinquency, is rare, and the punishment of disbarment is almost unknown. It is more usual (but still infrequent) for lawyers to be brought to institutional task for disgraceful or dishonourable conduct (see chapter 1). Disciplinary actions following complaints of incompetency have been limited to extreme cases. Law societies are more concerned with eradicating behaviour that is "disgraceful and dishonourable," that affects their professional reputation. Moreover, although lesser penalties such as suspensions and reprimands are largely ineffective as general deterrents, it is extremely rare for lawyers to lose their right to practise because of incompetence. Indeed, there is a definite reluctance on the part of law societies to use their authority to discipline incompetent members; rather, the tendency is to apply the standard of the lowest common denominator (see chapter 1).

Finally, the courts possess a number of devices by which they can take direct and uninvited action against lawyers who act incompetently or improperly in the course of litigation. Occasionally, judges exercise their authority under their various contempt powers against lawyers who are found to be engaging in outrageous behaviour. They can also sanction lawyers by way of awarding costs directly against them, where their conduct is considered to have unnecessarily extended proceedings. Judges can also disallow costs between lawyer and client, or direct lawyers to reimburse their clients. It is also in the inherent power of judges to report the conduct of lawyers to their professional bodies so that disciplinary action might be contemplated.

# D.  UNAUTHORIZED PRACTICE

In all provinces, there is a statutory framework that prohibits unauthorized persons from engaging in the practice of law. Moreover, it is the duty of lawyers to "assist in preventing the unauthorized practice of law" (see XVII). This prohibition is intended to ensure that, in seeking legal advice, people can be confident that the person they consult has received appropriate training and is subject to institutional discipline. In contrast to those who are not authorized to practise law, lawyers can offer such exceptional benefits as confidentiality and evidential privilege. Also, because lawyers are members of a professional body, there are other safeguards that accrue to clients, such as liability insurance, the maintenance of compensation funds, and the direct supervision of lawyers by the courts (see XVII, c. 1).

Although this common-sense regulation is obviously intended to protect the public, it also permits the legal profession to maintain its monopoly over the provision of legal services and to exercise enforceable authority over competitive practices. For instance, there has been some litigation over the work that can and cannot be undertaken by paralegals (who are to be distinguished from law clerks, who work under the supervision of lawyers). In the case of *Lawrie and Pointts,* it was decided that a retired police officer with considerable experience in the conduct of traffic cases was not acting as a barrister or solicitor when he appeared as an agent for an accused person.[10] However, the court was adamant that this was the case only because of a statutory provision in regard to traffic offences: paralegals were still forbidden to perform many other legal tasks, even some that are trivial and generally unserviced by the legal profession. Paralegals remain more tolerated than encouraged. While the need to protect the public is paramount, it is difficult not to be concerned that the zeal with which the legal profession patrols its turf has as much to do with its own pecuniary and institutional interests as anything else.

PROBLEM 7: You have an LLB and an LLM in estate planning, but you are not a member of any law society. After some of your relatives and friends hear that you have done an excellent job in organizing your elderly parents' affairs upon death, they ask you to help them in planning their affairs and drafting their wills. While it is understood that you are not acting professionally, they insist on paying you a small sum for your time and effort. Is this unauthorized legal practice? Ought it to be?

Lawyers have very definite responsibilities in regard to the supervision and employment of non-lawyers. Indeed, lawyers are responsible not only for the competence of their own work but also for any work that is delegated or entrusted to others. As well as not employing any lawyer

---

10    See *R. v. Lawrie* (1987), 59 O.R. (2d) 161 (C.A.).

who has been disbarred or suspended, lawyers must be careful to ensure that they do not allow their staff or assistants to do work that should more properly be done by a lawyer personally (see XVII, c. 2 and c. 3). Most professional codes encourage the training and employment of legal assistants as being conducive to the more efficient and comprehensive provision of legal services. The adequacy of supervision will vary from situation to situation with subject matter and experience, but it is the responsibility of lawyers to draw a distinction between "the special knowledge of the legal assistant and the professional legal judgment of the lawyer" (see XVII, cc. 4, 5, and 6). Although there is considerable economic pressure on lawyers to rely heavily on legal assistants, such pressure must be resisted if it results in an overreliance on them. Asking legal assistants to undertake too much responsibility can lead to a breach of the ethical rules, and might also result in clients being charged for work done and at a rate that is not matched to the actual status of the person doing the work.

## E.  LAWYERS AS CITIZENS

It is generally understood that law societies are "not concerned with the purely private or extra-professional responsibilities of a lawyer" (see I, c. 4). However, it will become a matter of institutional concern where such activities "bring into question the integrity of the legal profession or the lawyer's personal integrity or competence." Indeed, disciplinary action is considered justified where lawyers engage in "dishonourable or questionable conduct in . . . private life" (see I, c. 3). With regard to lawyers' competence and quality of service, the Rules explicitly note that "self-induced disability, for example from the use of intoxicants or drugs," will be considered prima facie to interfere with lawyers' ability to act in a required professional manner (see II, c. 7(m)).

The breadth of these provisions is typically open ended and gives law societies wide powers not only to regulate lawyers professionally in their private lives but also offers them little guidance about what they can and cannot do in their private lives. Nevertheless, there are many illustrations of conduct that has been or would be considered disgraceful or questionable — such as fraud or dishonesty (e.g., knowingly filing a false tax return), conviction of a serious criminal offence (e.g., homicide), embezzlement, or taking advantage of a client. In *Cwinn*, a lawyer was disbarred following his criminal conviction in the United States for "transporting a woman across state lines for immoral purposes." The fact that he was not acting as a lawyer did not detract from the fact that his conduct was so lacking in integrity that it would undermine public confidence in his continued ability to provide legal services.[11] However, the nature and scope of good character is by no means universally agreed within the legal profession and is changing, albeit slowly, in response to changing social mores (see chapter 3).

When lawyers engage in non-legal business or in outside work, they must take care that such activities do not "jeopardize [their] professional integrity, independence or competence." Where lawyers' clients are involved, the usual duties and expectations will remain in play. However, if the activity is in no way connected with the provision of legal services to clients (e.g., politics or acting), lawyers are constrained only by the general obligation not to bring themselves or the profession into disrepute (see VII, c. 2 and c. 3). When involved in outside activity, it is incumbent on lawyers not to leave any impression that they are acting in a legal capacity and not to act in a dishonourable way (see VII, c. 5 and c. 6). In dealing with the media, the professional rules advise caution and circumspection. If the interests of clients are implicated, lawyers must observe all the usual proprieties. In other situations, while lawyers are not actively discouraged from such involvement, it is clear that there is a strong desire on the part of the profession for public appearances to be limited and constructive rather than critical and opinionated. In short, lawyers are expected to "encourage public respect for and try to improve the administration of justice" (see XVIII, cc. 4, 6, 9, 11, and 13). In no circumstances are such media appearances to be used as a way to solicit business (see XIV, c. 7).

To what extent should the conduct of lawyers in their private capacities be cause for concern or censure in their professional capacities? What some lawyers might consider acceptable and even laudable might well be viewed by others as inappropriate and deplorable. One particularly difficult area is the involvement of lawyers as citizens in political protest and disobedience — for example, around Native issues or anti-war activities. Leaving aside engagement in criminal activities, lawyers should be at liberty to do what any other citizen can do, provided they do so in good faith and with a sense of ethical proportion. It is only when they use their status as lawyers or participate in law-related activities that the collective morality of the profession ought to stand in judgment on them. Consequently, it is recommended that law societies shift their attention from what is being done to whether lawyers are taking moral responsibility for what they are doing: there needs to be a balance in the pull of professional expectation and the push of personal conscience.

---

11    *Cwinn v. Law Society of Upper Canada* (1980), 28 O.R. (2d) 61 (Div. Ct.).

# F. CONCLUSION

In this chapter, I have sought to introduce critically the organization of the legal profession and its implications for the ethical practice of law. Although law societies are vocal in demanding very high standards of lawyers in order to gain and keep membership, there is less action than might be expected. The moral standards for entry are more notional than real, and the profession too easily hides behind the professional rules rather than vigorously using them in maintaining high standards of professional conduct. Nevertheless, this collective hesitancy ought not to signal to the public or to individual lawyers that the development of an ethical legal practice is something that is secondary to lawyers' involvement in the business of law. It is for each lawyer, encouraged by responsibility to both clients and the public, to ensure that law societies exercise their considerable power and authority in a way that reinforces the actual, not merely rhetorical, importance of legal ethics in the contemporary practice of law.

# CHAPTER 5

# DEALING
# WITH CLIENTS:
# FROM START TO FINISH

Lawyers' relationship with their clients stands at the heart of any discussion about legal ethics and professional responsibility. Whatever the appropriate dynamics and limits of the duties owed to clients and non-clients are considered to be, it is essential to have an informed understanding of the nature and extent of the lawyer-client relationship. Accordingly, before proceeding to tackle some of the more traditional and obvious ethical tensions in the dealings between lawyers and clients, it is important to grasp the ethical opportunities and restrictions that make up and define this area. Although often neglected in debates on legal ethics and professional responsibility, these issues raise important moral dilemmas and professional challenges. Indeed, it can be argued that there is no more important issue for lawyers than how they are going to select the persons to whom they agree to provide their services. In many circumstances, it is the most important, yet least considered, decision that lawyers make.

This chapter examines the relationship with clients from start to finish. In the first section, I consider the crucial issue of client selection and whether there are any compelling ethical responsibilities to reject or adopt certain potential clients or causes. The second section deals with the broad topic of compensation and, after providing a realistic context for discussion, highlights the professional regulation of what amounts to fair and reasonable fees. In the third section, I look at the circumstances in which lawyers must or can withdraw their services from their clients. The fourth section is devoted to inquiring into whether lawyers have an obligation, through legal aid and pro bono work, to meet the needs of those people who cannot afford legal services. Finally, the fifth section examines the possibilities and prohibitions around solicitation and advertising by lawyers. Throughout the chapter, emphasis will be placed on the profession's and individual lawyers' ethical responsibility to give persons reasonable access to justice.

## A. THE CHOICE OF CLIENTS

Client selection is one of the most important and most neglected issues for lawyers. There is little discussion of the ethical issues that such a decision entails. Indeed, it is arguably the most important decision that any lawyer makes because, once a client is taken on, the lawyer has become committed to a whole host of ethical and moral obligations (see chapter 6). They are engaged in a special relationship that lawyers cannot simply abandon as and when they choose. Moreover, all clients are entitled to the same level of competence and commitment from their lawyers. Once the lawyer-client relationship is established, a large part of the ethical die is cast; the lawyers' options about what they are and are not prepared to do are severely curtailed and their obligation is closely circumscribed. This is entirely reasonable because, under any realistic vision of professional responsibility, it would be unconscionable to take on clients and represent them in an incompetent or half-hearted way; that would be a travesty of any kind of ethical expectation.

In Canada, lawyers can choose to represent whichever clients they wish. While the oath taken on call to the bar often contains a commitment to "refuse no man's just cause," this is more of a token gesture of ceremonial window-dressing. The professional rules are imbued with a general sense that legal services are important and should be made available to everyone, but there are no prohibitions on lawyers refusing to represent particular clients or causes. Some provinces have recently declared that lawyers must not make their choice of clients in a way that discriminates on the basis of race, gender, or other similar distinctions, though it is arguable that that was already the case under most general provincial laws. Other than this, lawyers are not formally constrained in their decision of how to allocate their services and expertise. Nevertheless, there are two major and interrelated ethical issues that pervade this important decision: Is there an obligation to take unpopular cases, and is it ever professionally responsible to refuse certain cases?

Although there is much rhetoric to the contrary, the traditional practice on client selection is that lawyers are not under any obligation to take unpopular cases, nor are they ethically compromised by the moral (un)worthiness of their clients' causes. Although lawyers are conferred with special privileges in pursuing their profession, they still retain considerable autonomy in how they use those privileges: the importance of the public's need for legal services does not entirely submerge lawyers' own sense of choice over how they work. However, once lawyers do make a decision to enter into a lawyer-client relation, their unswerving commitment to the cause of their clients is not to be interpreted as in any way supporting or condoning that cause. Unless they participate directly in unethical or illegal behaviour themselves, lawyers are to be treated as independent and moral agents; the sins of clients are not to be inflicted upon their lawyers. As Charles Fried argues, "as a professional person, one has a special care for the interests of those accepted as clients, just as his friends, his family, and he himself have a very general claim to his special concern."[1]

For some commentators, lawyers not only can but should accept all requests for legal assistance, no matter how unpopular or unjust, because any other course would deprive people of their rights and usurp the function of the jury. While this argument might have some bite in the criminal area, it has little to recommend it in civil matters. Moreover, even in the criminal area, it offers no compelling reason for why that lawyer has to be *you*. Although it is true that everyone has the right to be legally represented, this is not an argument as to why a particular lawyer should have a duty to be anyone's lawyer. Of course, there might be circumstances where lawyers believe that undeserving clients are entitled to their services because they think that such clients should have a lawyer, even though they cannot afford one, or because they will be treated unfairly by the system.

According to Duncan Kennedy, the right not to take clients has a much wider moral ambit than simply refusing to represent people or organizations that you think have evil intentions or of whose activities you disapprove. He maintains that lawyers should take full responsibility for the clients they take and the causes they advance: it is ethically wrong to argue a case or a cause that will do more harm than good if you think that your client should not be in court in the first place or that your client should lose. In particular, you should not represent clients who are using technical defences to avoid justified liability or who are enforcing their valid legal rights in a bad cause. For Kennedy, "you are

---

1    C. Fried, "The Lawyer as Friend: The Moral Foundations of the Lawyer-Client Relation" (1976) 85 Yale L.J. 1060.

tarred with bad actions of clients that you facilitate in your work as a lawyer."[2] Working against/for unionization if you are pro/anti-union, or advising for the postponement/implementation of environmental controls if you are pro/anti-environmental rights is something that lawyers should not do, and they should not do it as a matter of professional ethical responsibility. This does not mean that lawyers should choose to represent only those clients whom they or anyone else would approve of. It simply means that lawyers should represent only those clients or causes they are prepared to defend as being more, rather than less, beneficial for society.

The argument that lawyers should have an obligation to take any and all clients founders on a number of critical reefs. First, most lawyers draw the line at representing clients free of charge. This restriction is not unreasonable; lawyers are not charities. There is no particular reason why some lawyers should shoulder singly a problem of non-accessibility that has public and collective causes and that could be dealt with by a more compelling pro bono obligation. Second, there is an obligation on the legal profession to ensure that people have access to lawyers; only a hypocritical profession and process would trumpet people's rights, but fail to provide a means to exercise them fully. However, while the profession has this collective responsibility, it does not provide an obvious answer as to why any particular lawyer should be obliged to take on any particular client. This argument has bite only where the lawyer is the "last lawyer in town" and the client has no other means of legal representation to which to turn. While some unpopular clients or causes are going without legal representation, it is likely that more potential clients fail to get a lawyer because of their inability to pay than the unpopularity of their case. Nevertheless, there are clearly cases where people have been refused representation by lawyers as a result of considerations that are unrelated to their legal cause. To deal with this problem, a rule has recently been added that states that lawyers must not "deny services or provide inferior services on the basis of [discriminatory] grounds" (see XX, c. 1(a)).

PROBLEM 8: Times are tight: you are a single parent and the bills are mounting up. With a mixed law school record and after being unemployed for six months, you are offered a reasonably well-paying job with a small firm whose main business is debt enforcement for large corporations and banks. As well as drafting air-tight loan agreements for the lenders, you are expected to be a vigorous and unyielding litigator. Would you take the job, and why?

---

2    D. Kennedy, "The Responsibility of Lawyers for the Justice of Their Causes" (1987) Texas Tech L. Rev. 1157 at 1159.

**PROBLEM 9: At a meeting of your law firm, it is suggested that members of the firm should represent only women in spousal abuse cases. Do you agree with such a policy? Does it make any difference if this policy is adopted by a publicly funded legal-aid clinic?**

It is no excuse or justification to argue that, if you do not take the case, somebody else will or that it is a wealthy client — these are weak efforts at rationalization. While it is important that your client has a legal basis for action, it is only a necessary but not a sufficient condition for your involvement. Also, because lawyers influence the law's content through their advocacy, they must take some responsibility for the way in which the law develops and unfolds. For instance, tax lawyers earn their keep by advising rich clients on how to get around tax laws and, in the process, affect the interpretation of the law itself, often bringing about legislative changes and revisions. Often, tax lawyers are consulted by the government on the wisdom or merit of particular changes to the tax system. It ill behoves such lawyers to pretend that they merely respond to a system that functions independently of them. Because tax lawyers largely represent the business and investment sector, they do little to help the rest of the population — and might, indeed, have some responsibility for shifting the tax burden onto the poorer parts of the population.[3]

Before taking on any clients, it seems ethically incumbent on lawyers to talk to them. This need not be a one-way lecture to the potential client about the lawyer's ethical values, but it might be a conversation in which lawyer and client outline their basic expectations of each other. Questions lawyers might ask before taking on a client include whether the objective of the case is worthy and whether the means that might be required will be allowed to be used. It is important that lawyers inform potential clients of the ethical limits they place on their provision of legal services — negotiation tactics or cross-examination style. In general, lawyers should treat their potential clients as moral persons who are capable of engaging in debate and changing. It is unrealistic to imagine or expect that every lawyer will, like Socrates, be guided only by the need to do right rather than wrong: most lawyers are reasonably concerned about their jobs, paying their mortgages, providing for their children. Also, it is impractical to believe that lawyers and clients will have to share a whole ethical outlook on life to be able to establish a workable and moral professional relationship. It might be that lawyers will need to make an important distinction between "values" and "convictions." For

3    See L. McQuaig, *Behind Closed Doors: How the Rich Won Control of Canada's Tax System* (Markham, Ont.: Penguin Books Canada, 1987) at 95–102.

example, while lawyers might refuse to represent people associated with a particular side in the abortion struggle, they might not have any difficulty in representing such persons in unrelated property transactions.

## B. COMPENSATION

There are many jeremiads about the decline of the legal profession from an honourable and public-spirited calling to a highly commercial business. Notwithstanding the naively nostalgic tone, the fact is that lawyers are entitled to make arrangements with their clients that allow for handsome remuneration, and no general justification is required. Like any contractual arrangement, such agreements must comply with the usual legal requirements, including the fact that they are made without duress or unconscionability. Also, clients are provided with other special devices, such as taxing, for challenging the fees charged. Nonetheless, the way in which lawyers arrange for themselves to be compensated raises important questions of ethical principle as well as legal doctrine and business practice. Although the billing of clients is treated as a matter of economic bargaining, it is also very much a moral matter. Because lawyers exercise a monopoly over the important services rendered and such services are not optional in social life, there is a special need to ensure that the terms and amount of compensation are fair and reasonable.

Actual rates of compensation, and whether they are fair or reasonable, are notoriously difficult to assess; there has been a thick fog around the whole issue of legal fees and lawyers' earnings. Nevertheless, indications are that there is an unexpected consistency in the price of legal services across Canada and across the different forms of legal practice.[4] The average hourly rate is about $110 for a lawyer with one year of experience, $140 for a lawyer with six years, and $170 for a lawyer with ten or more years. While these are only ballpark figures and should be viewed with the usual caution given to "average" figures, they do imply that lawyers are reasonably well rewarded for their exertions. For instance, lawyers who charge an hourly rate of $140 will, on the assumption that they bill about (a conservative) 1600 hours a year, earn $224,000. If even as much as 50 percent of that sum is set aside for costs and expenses, this amounts to an annual salary of $112,000 for the average lawyer.

---

4   M.G. Crawford, "The Going Rate: The Canadian Lawyer 1997 National Legal Fee Survey" (1997) 21 Canadian Lawyer (Sept. 1997) 18.

**TABLE 5.1**    National Fee Range

| | High | Average Range ($)<br>(Average) | Low |
|---|---|---|---|
| **Family** | | | |
| Uncontested divorce | 15,000 | 525 – 1,250<br>(775) | 100 |
| Contested divorce | 90,000 | 2,535 – 14,725<br>(6,715) | 500 |
| Separation agreement | 6,000 | 575 – 1,800<br>(985) | 100 |
| Child custody<br>and support | 50,000 | 2,650 – 10,650<br>(5,140) | 250 |
| **Criminal** | | | |
| Summary offence<br>(guilty plea) | 5,000 | 400 – 1,100<br>(750) | 100 |
| Criminal offence<br>(1-day trial) | 15,000 | 1,575 – 2,150<br>(1,725) | 300 |
| **Estates** | | | |
| Simple will | 800 | 115 – 180<br>(135) | 35 |
| Complex will | 2,500 | 190 – 495<br>(315) | 30 |
| Power of attorney | 1,500 | 105 – 430<br>(200) | 10 |
| Probate | 20,000 | 795 – 6,460<br>(2,790) | 200 |
| **Civil litigation** | | | |
| Civil action<br>(inc. 2-day trial) | 35,000 | 4,910 – 13,470<br>(8,325) | 500 |
| Civil action<br>(appeal only) | 15,000 | 3,825 – 12,660<br>(7,015) | 200 |

| | High | Average Range ($) (Average) | Low |
|---|---|---|---|
| **Real Estate** | | | |
| Residential purchase | 10,000 | 390 – 865 (615) | 100 |
| Residential sale & purchase | 20,000 | 645 – 1,520 (930) | 100 |
| Commercial property purchase | 10,000 | 700 – 3,000 (1,540) | 100 |
| Commercial lease agreement | 15,000 | 430 – 1,985 (965) | 150 |
| **Corporate/commercial** | | | |
| Simple incorporation | 1,500 | 475 – 720 (555) | 150 |
| Shareholders agreement | 73,000 | 515 – 3,965 (1,520) | 150 |
| Secured financing agreement | 10,000 | 835 – 2,280 (1,185) | 80 |
| Simple prospectus | 40,000 | 2,000 – 22,500 (10,085) | 1,000 |
| Merger/acquisition | 35,000 | 1,805 – 10,055 (5,000) | 500 |

Hourly rates appear to be on the way out, with clients pressing for capped fees, flat fees, and other billing alternatives. One of the reasons is that such billing can too easily reward inefficiency, incompetence, and even encourages duplicity. Moreover, for all the emphasis placed on the traditional practice of hourly billing, there is evidence to suggest that the cost of legal work is not closely tied to the actual time expended in performing that work. As Table 5.1 seems to confirm, in some cases the actual hourly rate is much lower; in other cases, the rate is much higher. As the professional rules highlight, the reasonable price to be charged for a similar service can be influenced by a wide variety of factors (see XI, c. 1), including the time and effort involved, special skills required, customary charges of other lawyers in like matters, the amount involved, the results obtained, special circumstances, and the relevant agreement between the lawyer and the client. In any market there will be a range of charges for similar products and, provided the client/consumer is not misled or taken advantage of, this is a matter for consumer choice, albeit on typically imperfect information. From an ethical standpoint, a more relevant question is whether legal services should be treated as any other traded commodity and whether, in light of the profession's monopoly on the provision of legal services, there should not be a more vigorous monitoring and regulation of fees charged. For instance, exactly why "the amount involved" is relevant or determinative is unclear, if the same time is spent on files that are only distinguished by the amounts involved.

**PROBLEM 10:** A client wants you to advise her about her overall tax liability. You tell her that your rate is $200 an hour. You are able to devise a simple solution after a couple of hours work that will save her almost $30,000 annually in tax. Rather than bill her for $600 (which represents the time you spent on her file), you send her a bill for $2000, on the basis that this amount is reasonable in light of the money you have saved her. Should you do this? What might you have done differently?

The professional rules have little to say about the actual prices charged, other than that they be "fair and reasonable," and are more concerned with ensuring that lawyers do not engage in dubious practices, such as charging for hidden fees, splitting fees with non-lawyers, or not giving full disclosure to clients of the basis for fees charged (see XI). The relationship between lawyers and their clients is a fiduciary one and requires more than a standard commercial arrangement. Lawyers must disclose all possible conflicts of financial interests and whether they have a financial connection with persons to whom disbursements are made. Further, it is the right of all clients to invoke a formal procedure for determining whether lawyers' charges are fair and reasonable in the particular circumstances; this process is known as "taxing the bill." However, the commentary to the Rules exhorts lawyers to remember that "it is in the best traditions of the legal profession to reduce or waive a fee in case of hardship or poverty." While this sentiment is to be applauded, it is typical of the Code generally that such matters are to be left to the discretion of individual lawyers. While some lawyers follow such a practice, some clients could be forgiven for thinking that it was unjustified self-congratulation on the part of the profession as a whole. The incidence of discipline for charging unfair or excessive fees is extremely rare; action is taken only where there is evidence that the lawyer has actually cheated or duped the client.

PROBLEM 11: You have agreed to go out of town for a client. While travelling, you take the chance to work on another client's file. Can you simultaneously bill one client for your time spent travelling and the other client for the work done?

PROBLEM 12: You spend a considerable amount of time researching and preparing a memorandum of law for a client. You charge the client on the basis of the hours worked. A couple of months later, another client seeks your advice on almost exactly the same point. On what basis should you charge the client? Does the fee arrangement with the later client affect the interests of the earlier client?

One compensatory arrangement that has come in for considerable scrutiny is the contingency fee. This is where the lawyer agrees that payment will be received only if the outcome of litigation (or the agreed services) is favourable to the client; the fee is usually calculated as a percentage of the actual amount recovered or obtained. All provinces, except Ontario, allow lawyers to work under these arrangements, and have introduced a framework of rules that covers issues such as type of cases permitted and the maximum percentage chargeable. The basic argument in favour of contingency fees is that they allow persons who would otherwise be unable to afford litigation to exercise their legal rights. The scope for abuse in such arrangements is great: lawyers might easily be tempted to exaggerate the difficulty of the case to boost their fee, or they might engage in unsuitable tactics to inflate the amount that a case is worth. The response of the profession has been that "it is not improper" for lawyers to enter into such arrangements (see XI, c. 10). This odd turn of phrase indicates that the profession has some reservations about such matters, but is prepared to accede, mainly because there is a battery of statutory rules that limit the scope for abuse. However, the fact that Ontario is not yet fully prepared to allow its lawyers to enter into contingency fee arrangements is indicative of some of the ethical dangers in such matters (an exception has been made in class action proceedings).

Ironically, lawyers themselves have become exercised about fees and the cost of legal services. While much public debate is about whether fees are too high and whether clients receive value for their money, some lawyers (and law societies) are concerned that a few lawyers are not charging enough. The claim is that a small number of lawyers are engaging in unfair competition by offering cut-price services and, because they cannot be putting in the time to do the job properly, they are not serving the public interest. While there are some definite dangers in low-priced services (as with any other cheap product), it is not immediately obvious why the interests of those who want or are obliged to charge such rates, and those who can afford only such fees, should be ignored. The better course is to look at the particular arrangements made and the work done rather than prohibit the charging of such fees.

With the expected emphasis on the size and nature of billing practices, there is a grave danger that one of the most pressing ethical issues in this area will be overlooked. Perhaps the most pervasive and unstated ethical dilemma is whether lawyers are really in a position to devote as much time to cases and clients as they deserve. It is often not sophisticated legal arguments that are most needed, but the simple expenditure of time to do the necessary work in a detailed and attentive way. It might well be the case that, while lawyers bill only for time spent on files, they know they are not giving clients and their problems as much attention as they deserve. It is less a matter of the clients' ability to pay and more an issue of lawyers' taking on too many clients and files. This dilemma is well put by Robert Megarry: "Obviously, you would never 'sell out' a client in any way, and obviously you would never let him down in order to obtain some personal benefit. But the law demands more than this. You will often have to ask yourself whether you are satisfied with what you have done. Have you really done everything that is humanly possible to solve your client's problems? Did you abandon research on his behalf a little too readily? Did you rely on your client never discovering that you had not spent enough time in preparing his case?"[5]

# C. WITHDRAWAL

As well as the general right to decline employment, lawyers are entitled to withdraw their services once they have entered into a professional relationship with clients. However, as might be expected, there are restrictions on the situations and the ways in which lawyers can withdraw. There are a few circumstances in which lawyers are obliged to withdraw from the case. In litigation, this occurs where clients want the lawyers to engage in prohibited conduct, such as knowingly deceiving the court or tribunal, taking malicious action, attempting to influence decisions or officials improperly, and harassing witnesses (see IX, c. 2 and c. 4). In such circumstances, after efforts to persuade clients of the impropriety of such conduct, lawyers must withdraw or seek the leave of the court to do so. In non-litigious matters, lawyers have a similar obli-

---

5    R.E. Megarry, "Convocation Address" (1983) 17 L.S.U.C. Gazette 41 at 44.

gation to withdraw where clients instruct them to act improperly, where they learn that a conflict of interest has occurred, or where they realize that they are no longer competent to handle the matter (see XII, c. 4).

However, as a general matter, lawyers can withdraw only where there are compelling and justifiable reasons to do so. While clients have a clear right to dismiss their lawyers as and when they wish (provided they settle their outstanding account), lawyers do not have an equivalent right to withdraw their services arbitrarily from their clients. For lawyers to choose to withdraw, there must have been "a serious loss of confidence between lawyer and client" such as the clients' persistent failure to follow the lawyers' advice, to provide necessary instructions, and, most important, to pay their bill after a reasonable time (see XII, c. 5). In effecting withdrawal, lawyers must take all reasonable steps to protect the clients' interests, especially if the case is at a particularly crucial phase in the action or dealing, and to deliver all documents, papers, and property to their clients or the successor lawyer. Nevertheless, lawyers do have a lien over such papers and property until their fees are paid (see XII, c. 8 and c. 11).

PROBLEM 13: The day before a manslaughter trial for which you are thoroughly prepared, you have exhausted the retainer and your client says she is unwilling or unable to pay anymore. Can you withdraw? Can you threaten withdrawal if she does not pay?

## D. LEGAL AID AND PRO BONO

In matters of regulation, the legal profession engages in much talk about its public responsibility to ensure that the Rule of Law is upheld and that there is genuine access for all citizens to the legal process. However, lawyers have tended to be more concerned with the total amount and general quality of legal services available than with their distribution or general availability. Not only is the allocation of legal assistance unequally distributed but its maldistribution further increases the advantages of the "haves" over the "have-nots." Without access to reasonably priced lawyers, many people will neither know their legal rights nor be able to protect or enforce them. Indeed, a clear part of the compact between the state and the legal profession is that it can have a monopoly only if it assumes some moral obligation for ensuring that legal representation is reasonably available to all. Without such a responsibility, the profession would be a crude cartel that existed simply to limit the supply of legal services, inflate prices, and create market dislocations. Accordingly, it would seem important that those who are already "have-nots" are not made worse off by their inability to afford proper legal representation.

There are three possible ways to approach inequalities in the allocation and distribution of legal services: to reduce all barriers to competition among lawyers, including admission, articling, and compulsory fees; to subsidize assistance (e.g., legal aid, pro bono, insurance, and tax relief) to those who presently cannot afford legal services; and to change the substantive law so that the "have-nots" are better protected and favoured (e.g., rent control or a minimum wage). Canadian society has attempted to take initiatives in all three areas, but the overall practical effect manages to be far smaller than the sum of the theoretical parts. Notwithstanding recent efforts at reform, the delivery of legal services is characterized by a strange mix of market discipline and social regulation. The discourse surrounding this contentious topic is also marked by a similar mix of private and public rhetoric. However, the pattern and logic of the mix is far from consistent or convincing; lawyers tend to favour market discipline for their clients and communal regulation for their own interests. The bottom line is that the cost of legal services continues to be beyond the purse of an increasing number of Canadians. At the same time, the resources of legal aid plans, financed by both government and the legal profession, are being steadily depleted rather than replenished.

Apart from the exhortation "to reduce or waive a fee in cases of hardship or poverty," the Code is almost silent about lawyers' duty or willingness to provide services to those who cannot afford legal services (see XI, c. 2). While there is much talk about the fair administration of justice and the basic commitment to equal justice for all, lawyers are on their own when it comes to dealing with the less fortunate in society. There is no sense that lawyers as a professional community have any enforceable obligation to serve all sectors of society, rich and poor alike. Rather, there is a grudging concession that lawyers "*may* assist in making legal services available by participating in legal aid plans and referral services" (see XIV, c. 5). In a code that is partial to the use of "should," this variation in this circumstance is troubling. Moreover, professional rules make it clear that, in the name of free choice, lawyers have a strong right to decline particular employment that is conditional only on the weak duty not to exercise such a right too quickly, not to be too influenced by the unpopularity of the person's cause, and to help rejected clients to find another lawyer (see XIV, c. 6).

When private and lay-initiated steps have been taken to deal with the high costs of legal services by making access to lawyers more cheaply available, the profession has almost always taken an adversarial stance. For instance, initiatives to establish legal benefits plans, similar to medical and dental plans, have initially been resisted by law societies, especially when the plan has sought to restrict the number of lawyers involved and to cap the amount that lawyers can charge under the plan. The main thrust of the law societies' position is that attaching such terms and conditions on lawyer availability infringes on the societies' regulatory role and is an unfair limitation on individual lawyers' freedom to deploy their services as and how they see fit. This instinctive resistance to innovative initiatives to improve access speaks volumes about the profession's collective concerns: it gives the distinct impression that lawyers are concerned less about the purses of clients and more about the coffers of lawyers. Functioning more as trade associations than public regulators, law societies and, therefore, lawyers have not done enough to respond to the needs of low-income Canadians.

If the profession is to have any real chance of matching its rhetoric of service to the reality of social need, lawyers must begin to take seriously the obligation to provide their services at reduced rates, to take legal aid clients, and to engage in pro bono work. It is not enough to heap praise on those lawyers who undertake such work. This obligation must be built into the basic ethical fabric of professional responsibility. "Access to justice" is a hollow slogan unless there is genuine access to legal services. The legal profession is too quick to trumpet the moral obligation to perform pro bono work, but very slow at fulfilling it. Even when it is done, it is seen as a virtuous act of *noblesse oblige* rather than a basic responsibility that comes with being a lawyer. The argument is made that, if there is a shortage of affordable lawyers, "it is grossly unfair to conscript the legal profession to fill those needs: if the obligation is one of justice, it is an obligation of society as a whole."[6] However, in light of lawyers' monopoly on a vital social resource, it seems that it is such hyperbole that is "grossly unfair."

Of course, any proposal to require lawyers to do compulsory pro bono work is not without problems. Apart from the ideological argument about infringing lawyers' autonomy, it is seen to devalue the altruistic nature of the work. It is also likely to operate in an inequitable way in that its burden will be greater for the already economically marginalized practitioner than for the partners in large firms. Moreover, it might lead to the wrong kind of work being done, and lawyers doing work that they are not trained to do (such as corporate lawyers representing poor clients for welfare claims). While these objections cannot be ignored,

---

6    Fried, above note 1 at 1066.

they are insufficient to invalidate the worth of such a proposal: the trans-formative value of having establishment lawyers appear in provincial courts ought not to be underestimated. Nevertheless, in response to the traditional concerns, it might be possible, for example, to introduce a coupon scheme whereby clients are directed to appropriate lawyers, and those lawyers who do not receive enough pro bono coupons will be required to pay into a pro bono fund an equivalent amount to the hours not done.[7]

# E.  SOLICITATION AND ADVERTISING

An interesting aspect of the more general debate over the provision of legal services is the particular topic of solicitation and advertising. The traditional attitude has been that professionals should wait for business to come to them because, to do otherwise, would be to become crass merchants; it might confirm the popular suspicion that an organized legal profession is little different from "a retail grocers' association."[8] The assumption behind the restrictive rules was that lawyers worked in small communities in which there were few lawyers, each generally competent in most matters and with a reasonable share of the market. However, the realities of late twentieth-century law practice render this assumption problematic. Indeed, there has always been the suspicion that, behind much of the high-flying rhetoric, lurked other crass concerns. Often restrictive rules were driven by barely latent ethnic hostility and the desire to neutralize competitive practices. Of course, there were and still are some genuine issues about which to be concerned — "ambulance chasing," intrusiveness, misrepresentation, but it has never been entirely obvious why these abuses could not be dealt with by less blanket and more nuanced regulation.

Consequently, although frequently expressed and justified in the name of the public interest, the Rules were much more concerned with established lawyers' interests than with potential clients who would most likely have benefited from the increase in broader and cheaper legal services. For both lawyers and clients, advertising has advantages, such as increased market and revenue for lawyers, and greater choice

---

7    See D. Luban, *Lawyers and Justice: An Ethical Study* (Princeton, NJ: Princeton University Press, 1989). See also S. Lubet & C. Stewart, "A 'Public Assets' Theory of Lawyers' Pro Bono Obligations" (1997) 145 U. Pa. L. Rev. 1245.

8    R. Pound, *The Lawyer from Antiquity to Modern Times: With Particular Reference to the Development of Bar Associations in the United States* (St. Paul, Minn.: West Pub. Co., 1953) at 89.

and (possible) reduction of costs through economies in scale for clients. There are also disadvantages, such as increased costs of service and overreaching by some lawyers. Some traditionalists continue to complain that it will irreparably impair the image of the profession and the ethic of service on which it is built.

As part of their general responsibility to ensure that legal services are made available to the public in an efficient and convenient manner, lawyers have acknowledged recently that a limited amount of informational advertising might be necessary if members of the public are to make an informed choice about the lawyer they want. This concession has been driven as much by *Charter* decisions on other professionals' freedom of communication as any concern with enhancing access to legal services. Accordingly, in addition to using telephone directories, legal directories, and referral services, lawyers are entitled to advertise. As well as being truthful and low key, the extent and content of that advertising is to be determined both by local conditions and what is consistent with a dignified and serious profession. Such advertising must not be "in bad taste or otherwise offensive as to be prejudicial to the interests of the public or the legal profession" (see XIV, c. 1 and c. 3). Many different regulations have been enacted by provincial law societies, but their main gist is that the advertising is to be largely informational and non-competitive. Crass commercialism is less likely to be good business in Canada than in the United States. In fact, there is still very little advertising of a substantial or serious kind.

The most high-profile issue in this area is the vexed practice of "ambulance chasing." This term was originally intended to refer to seedy practices in which lawyers tout for business at the scenes of accidents or other potential sources of legal work, but it has come to be used unfairly to stigmatize a variety of efforts to generate legal work where there is an unmet social need. Although it is accepted that activities designed to stimulate legal work where none exists, to harass or mislead potential clients, or to offer referral incentives are of ethically dubious provenance, it is clear that lawyers solicit work by more dignified and less intrusive methods — club memberships and schmoozing, to name but two. Nevertheless, the problem remains how lawyers who are driven as much by public spiritedness as commercial gain can take effective steps to ensure that the least advantaged in society are made aware of their legal rights and the means to enforce them.[9] As with

---

9   M.H. Freedman, *Understanding Lawyers' Ethics* (New York: M. Bender, 1990) at 252–53.

advertising, it seems that the best course would not be to prohibit solicitation generally, but to regulate its abuse.

PROBLEM 14: A nurse friend tells you that he visited an old persons' home
in which people were living in intolerable conditions. You are appalled by
this and ask your friend to return to the home, tell them about the possibility
of commencing a possible legal (class) action. You suggest that your friend
might tell them, without pressuring them in any way, about your personal
concern and professional interest. Is this appropriate conduct?

## F. CONCLUSION

The legal profession's approach to the formation and continuance of the
lawyer-client relationship seems to be driven as much by concern with
the economic interests of lawyers as by a desire to enable persons to
obtain necessary legal services. The institutional force of moral imperative is reserved for those circumstances in which the commercial freedom of lawyers might be infringed rather than when the unmet needs
of citizens are at issue. While there are few actual restrictions on lawyers
making their services known and available to those who are least able to
afford them and most likely to need them, there is no ethical obligation
to ensure that such people's needs are met. Again, insofar as lawyers
hold a state-backed monopoly over an indispensable social resource,
and insofar as many make a handsome living from that privilege, there
ought to be more of a collective and personal commitment to sharing
access in a more egalitarian and less restrictive way.

# CHAPTER 6

# THE DUTY TO CLIENTS: CHECKING ZEALOUS PARTISANSHIP

The core of legal ethics and professional responsibility is the general duty that lawyers are required to fulfill in dealing with their clients. Lawyers are under a strong obligation to put their clients' interests ahead of all others and to act as zealous partisans on their behalf. While there is little disagreement about the existence of this duty to act zealously for clients, there is considerable debate around the limits to which such zeal ought to go in light of the interests of other parties and the legal process itself. As Macaulay put it caustically in complaining about lawyers: "Is it right that a man . . . will do for money what . . . he would think it wicked and infamous to do for an empire."[1] The challenge is not only to understand the force and requirements of lawyers' duties to their clients but to work towards an appreciation of what the limits might be on such a single-focused duty. While loyalty and trust are important qualities, it is important to question to whom or what the lawyer is being loyal and trustworthy. Indeed, it is in the efforts to chart the limits upon lawyers' duties to their clients that the study of legal ethics and professional responsibility is at its most challenging and controversial.

I begin this chapter with a broad statement of the nature and rationale of lawyers' general duty to act as zealous partisans on behalf of their clients. In the second section, I will unpack the general duty and explain its various and discrete components. Next, I will examine the limits that

---

1    G. Macaulay, *The Works of Lord Macaulay*, ed. Lady Trevelyan (Boston 1900) at 163.

are placed on lawyers' zeal on behalf of their clients by their duties to the courts and the profession generally. And, in the fourth and final section, I tackle the difficult and revealing issue of whether and to what extent lawyers can or should take into account the interests of opposing parties or other persons. Throughout the chapter, the emphasis will be on the need to balance zealous partisanship against competing responsibilities.

# A.  GENERAL DUTY OF PARTISANSHIP

The duty of lawyers to work loyally and zealously for their clients is the corollary of the freedom to choose their clients. Having done so, lawyers are taken to have curtailed their freedom of action and to have thrown their professional weight in with that person or institution. Henceforth, lawyers must strive to represent clients to the best of their ability. The basis of the relationship between lawyers and their clients is a combination of legal requirements and ethical responsibility. In legal terms, the lawyer holds a fiduciary capacity in relation to clients' interests.[2] This means that, because there is an asymmetry of power between lawyers and clients, lawyers must exercise their skill and expertise only for the clients' benefit. The power imbalance between lawyers and clients imposes special and exclusive duties on lawyers to act only with good faith and loyalty to the client; the fiduciary obligation entitles clients to receive a higher standard of attention than a purely commercial contract for services would entail. In short, lawyers are supposed to serve their clients, not themselves.

While these legal requirements are considerable, lawyers also assume a wide variety of obligations to persons for whom they agree to act. These different obligations place lawyers under a heavy burden of commitment to clients — competence, loyalty, candour, confidentiality, and pro-action. The rationale behind this exacting duty is directly traceable to the law's reliance on the adversary system and its accompanying model of professional responsibility. If persons are to be able to know and exercise their rights or defend themselves against prosecution, it is imperative that they are able to rely on the professional expertise of those who are learned and experienced in such matters. Moreover, such reliance must be uncompromised and uncompromising. Without such confidence, people might be inhibited in seeking legal advice and, therefore, unable to function as full and active members of the community.

---

2   *Norberg v. Wynrib*, [1992] 2 S.C.R. 226.

Although this justification receives its most compelling expression in the criminal law area, it works to powerful effect in civil matters of both a litigious and a non-litigious nature.

A famous example of the force and rationale of this duty of zealous partisanship is offered by the reasoning of Lord Brougham, who was retained by Queen Caroline, the king's wife, to defend her against charges of treason. In pursuing the case, he took the daring step of alluding to evidence that might harm the king:

> An advocate, by the sacred duty which he owes his client, knows in the discharge of that office but one person in the world, that client and none other. To save that client by all expedient means, to protect that client at all hazards and costs, to all others, and among others to himself, is the highest and most unquestioned of his duties; and he must not regard the alarm, the suffering, the torment, the destruction which he may bring upon any other. Nay, separating even the duties of a patriot from those of an advocate, and casting them, if need be, to the wind, he must go on reckless of the consequences, if his fate it should unhappily be to involve his country in confusion for his client's protection.[3]

Again, the tension around the duty of zealous partisanship is over the extent of this duty and, in particular, when it should give way to the public interest. For some (American) commentators, this exception is very rare; they believe that lawyers have an almost undiluted obligation to put their client's interests above and beyond those of everyone else and at almost any cost to anyone else. Some go as far as to argue that it is not only permissible but necessary for lawyers to lie and be disingenuous on behalf of their clients. According to Charles Curtis, the duty to clients is so strong that lawyers must "treat outsiders as if they were barbarians and enemies." Indeed, he argues that lawyers should see themselves as actors who take pride in how well they play their part, but not take responsibility for the part they are asked to play. Curtis's blunt view is not widely shared by professional opinion in Canada, and it is directly rejected by the Rules. Although some lawyers might wish to act in this way, they prefer to justify their approach and actions by a more sophisticated and less cavalier justification. Charles Fried, for example, offers a less jarring justification for the traditional account: "[A]s a professional person," he argues, "one has a special care for the interests of those

---

3    See W. Forsyth, *The History of Lawyers: Ancient and Modern* (Union, NJ: The Lawbook Exchange, 1996) at 380.

accepted as clients, just as his friends, his family, and he himself have a very general claim to his special concern."[4] Although this general friendship analogy is sound, it is Fried's understanding of what it means to be a friend that is disturbing (see chapter 2).

One particular instance in which the legal and ethical responsibilities combine to telling effect is in the case of mentally incapable clients. Lawyers have a special duty, over and above the already onerous general obligation and fiduciary duty, to clients who are considered not fully able to make decisions for themselves as a result of age, infirmity, incapacity, or other reasons. In such circumstances, lawyers must be especially careful to ensure that their decisions are in their clients' best interests. Unlike other clients, lawyers will not always be able to refer to such clients' instructions to justify or defend their actions. When lawyers form the opinion that their clients are unable to appreciate the options for action or their consequences, it ought to be incumbent on them to seek a substitute decision maker under relevant legislation. For instance, in child protection proceedings, children are considered incompetent clients, so litigation guardians may be appointed. Where no litigation guardian has been appointed, lawyers' duties will depend on the age and ability of the child to give instructions. Younger children should be advised on the basis of what decision they would likely make if they were capable, as viewed by their lawyers, and older children should be allowed to make their own decisions. Ultimately, however, the court will decide what is in the child's best interests.[5]

PROBLEM 15: A lawyer represents a young person who is claiming social welfare. After dealing with the client and inspecting the records she has provided, the lawyer realizes that she is "mentally challenged" to a considerable degree. While this information will be important in establishing her case, the client insists that she has no disability and that this matter is not to be discussed further. At the tribunal hearing, the lawyer arranges to have the client leave the room under some pretext and proceeds to bring evidence of her disability into evidence. The tribunal decides to award the client benefits and to declare that the evidence of disability was crucial to the decision. Would or should you have taken this approach?[6]

---

4   See C.P. Curtis, "The Ethics of Advocacy" (1951) 4 Stanford L. Rev. 3, and C. Fried, "The Lawyer as Friend: The Moral Foundations of the Lawyer-Client Relation" (1976) 85 Yale L.J. 1060.
5   See *Strobridge* v. *Strobridge* (1992), 10 O.R. (3d) 540 (Gen. Div.).
6   See S.G. Kupfer, "Authentic Legal Practices" (1996) 10 Georgetown J. of Legal Ethics 33 at 48.

In deciding on the scope of their general duty to clients, lawyers ought to recognize that there is a significant difference between acting legally and acting ethically. Of course, it is clear that lawyers must not "knowingly assist in or encourage any dishonesty, fraud, crime or illegal conduct" (see III, c. 7). However, such involvement must be active. While lawyers are probably not in breach of the rule if they advise clients about the degree of criminal risk attendant on a proposed course of conduct, they may still face criminal prosecution for helping clients commit any offence, even though they initially advised against committing illegal action.[7] There is a strand in traditional thinking, particularly in criminal law, that lawyers not only can but should do everything for their clients which is not legally prohibited (see chapter 9). But this approach is now rejected by most commentators and professional codes. It is generally accepted that, in order to act ethically as a lawyer, there is an obligation to refrain from certain conduct that is entirely permissible as a matter of legal liability: to act legally is not the same as acting ethically. Just where the ethical line is to be drawn in relation to the legal line is at the heart of the professional and personal approach to professional responsibility.

# B. COMPONENT OBLIGATIONS

The general duty to be a zealous partisan on behalf of the client can be broken down into several separate components, each of which places an obligation on lawyers. Consequently, in the context of the overall responsibility to act zealously on their clients' behalf, lawyers must ensure that they are loyal to the client, that they are candid with the client, that they take pro-active steps on behalf of the client, and that they maintain confidentiality in all their dealings with the client. In each situation, the key issue is the limits to which lawyers can or should go in fulfilling these duties.

## 1) Loyalty

It is the primary obligation of lawyers to be loyal to the interests of their clients. They must ensure that, once they enter into a lawyer and client relationship, they give priority to the concerns and affairs of the client.

---

7   See M.H. Freedman, *Lawyers' Ethics in an Adversary System* (Indianapolis: Bobbs-Merrill, 1975) at 59, and G. MacKenzie, *Lawyers and Ethics: Professional Responsibility and Discipline* (Scarborough, Ont.: Carswell, 1993) at 14-4.

In particular, lawyers must act impartially and avoid any conflicts that might prejudice the clients' interests or compromise their own integrity. For instance, lawyers who have acted for clients in a previous matter should not act against those clients in a related matter, and lawyers should not act for more than one client in a transaction (e.g., vendor-purchaser), unless they have first advised the clients about the benefits and safeguards of being separately represented (see V, c. 8 and c. 10). Lawyers must also be very careful to prevent outside social, political, and economic considerations from influencing their judgment (see VII, c. 2 and c. 4). Many issues can give rise to conflicts of interest (see chapter 8).

There are limits to the extent to which lawyers can go in meeting the obligation to be loyal to their clients:

- Lawyers have a duty to refuse to follow clients' instructions that would place them in breach of the professional rules. Examples might include abusing process by launching legal proceedings motivated by malice, assisting clients in dishonest behaviour, deceiving a court or tribunal, misstating the contents of a document, and suborning a witness (see IX, c. 2 and c. 4). If clients do not desist, lawyers should withdraw from the case (see chapter 5).
- Lawyers can override their clients' instructions in matters of general strategic approach. They must remember that they are under a tortious duty to act with appropriate professional care, and this obligation ought to influence their decisions and tactical considerations. It might be negligent to follow certain tactics in certain situations, whatever the clients' wishes. However, some decisions are so important (such as the commencement of civil proceedings or the plea to a criminal charge) that clients' instructions must be treated as paramount. Nevertheless, even in such circumstances, lawyers would be wise to advise their client about all the probable and likely consequences that might flow from particular decisions.
- Even though there is no express prohibition against lawyers engaging in sexual relations with clients, lawyers are well advised to consider the propriety of such conduct. It might be preferable to wait until the professional relationship ends or to transfer the client to another lawyer. Of course, any sexual relation that involves harassment or other forms of intimidation will make lawyers liable to both legal prosecution and professional misconduct charges.

## 2) Candour

It is incumbent on lawyers to deal with their clients in an entirely "open and undisguised" manner. They must ensure that they provide candid advice and guidance to clients on all legal and professional matters. Such advice should comprise a competent legal opinion, based on an informed knowledge of facts and the law, which states the merits of the case and the probable outcomes. If lawyers realize that clients have misunderstood the advice, they must inform them of (and make certain that clients understand) the "true position" (see III, cc. 1, 2, and 3). However, although lawyers must take all reasonable efforts to be candid and avoid too many caveats and conditions in the giving of advice, they must be "wary of bold and confident assurances" that might also mislead clients or lead to them taking inadvisable action (see III, c. 4). Some particular matters that require complete candour are as follows:

- Lawyers must disclose all costs and may not accept hidden fees. As well as making full disclosure, express consent must be obtained from clients in order to accept compensation from anyone other than the client. Moreover, if someone other than the client (e.g., legal aid or a spouse) is paying the lawyer's fees, that institution's or person's consent is also required. Also, where disbursements are to be paid (e.g., brokerage or copying agency), disclosure must be made to the clients (XI, c. 7).
- If lawyers "unknowingly" do or fail to do something that, if done or omitted knowingly, was prohibited conduct under the professional rules, they have a duty to disclose and rectify their errors or omission on discovery (see IX, c. 2 and c. 3). However, if the error or omission is one that "cannot readily be rectified," lawyers must so inform their clients and advise them to seek out independent legal advice concerning their rights. Furthermore, lawyers should give prompt notice to their own insurer so that any claim can be dealt with fairly and expeditiously (see III, c. 11).

## 3) Pro-activity

It is the lawyers' duty to ensure that their clients' interests are pursued in an active and vigorous manner. They must not take a half-hearted or reactive attitude to following those legal tactics or procedures that would benefit their clients. However, lawyers must not let their zeal get the better of them and engage in disreputable practices. For instance, lawyers representing one party should not negotiate personally or approach directly any other party who is represented. They must negotiate through their lawyers.[8]

---

8    See *Bank of Montreal v. Wilson* (1867), 2 Ch. 117.

In particular, in regard to their work as advocates, lawyers must advance all arguments and seek all remedies. They must be vigourous and thorough in pursuing their clients' case, even if it involves asking certain "distasteful" (but necessary) questions (see IX, c. 1). However, this duty must be tempered by two particular restrictions:

- Lawyers must represent their clients by "fair and honourable means," as lawyers also have a duty to treat the court with respect and courtesy; it is not appropriate to engage in tactics or initiatives that will taint the overall process of the court (see IX, c. 1).
- Lawyers are not expected to engage in "frivolous or vexatious" behaviour that will "delay or harass the other side" (see IX, c. 7).

## 4) Confidentiality

A duty of secrecy is owed to all clients, both continuous and casual. This duty can arise even before a person or an institution becomes a client, and it can outlive even the professional relationship. For instance, not only are lawyers not to divulge information to any third party but they cannot use such information for their own benefit, even where it will have no detrimental effect on the clients' interests and affairs. Of course, a lawyer's duty to retain the confidentiality of his clients' communications can be abridged by rules of law. (The nature and scope of the duty of confidentiality is discussed at length in chapter 7.)

In performing these duties, lawyers will need to decide for themselves the vigour and style they will use on behalf of their clients. As is so often the case, while the professional rules provide general instruction, it will be left to individual lawyers to decide what to do and how to do it in particular circumstances. There are no easy answers in these situations. All lawyers should reflect upon what they do and include a self-critical reflection in their overall development of a professional *modus vivendi* that suits them and of which they can be ethically proud. As suggested earlier, lawyers might want to engage in a conversation with their clients both generally at the beginning of the professional relationship and as and when tricky situations arise (see chapter 5). In this way, lawyers might begin to contribute to a different ethic of professional responsibility that incorporates their clients' and their own values and ideas on what is appropriate and desirable. Again, this injunction does not insist on any particular response to the inevitable dilemmas that will occur, but it does demand that lawyers take personal responsibility for what they do rather than rely on the weak and ultimately convincing ruse of "group absolution."

This difficulty is particularly acute when lawyers have to determine how far they can or should go in cross-examining a witness who is thought to be testifying accurately and truthfully in order to make the witness appear mistaken, unreliable, or dishonest. In such circumstances, lawyers should carry out such a cross-examination only if they have reasonable grounds for believing that the imputation is well founded or true, and that the examined party's answers might reasonably affect credibility. As with most ethical matters, lawyers have no obligation to become the dupe of an unscrupulous client, and they should exercise their own judgment about the best course to follow.

**PROBLEM 16: You defend a client in a defamation action. Your client has alleged information about the plaintiff's odd sexual proclivities. The client maintains that the plaintiff is likely to deny this allegation initially, and then you can expose his failure to be truthful. You are convinced that the plaintiff is probably telling the truth in his evidence, but agree that these revelations, although unrelated to the dispute in hand, will severely damage the plaintiff's credibility at trial and his general public reputation. What do you do?**

Although it is not a problem in most cases, there are examples where it is not clear who counts as the lawyer's client. Family law can throw up several difficulties in this regard. Lawyers should represent both spouses in an uncontested divorce only when all matters concerning custody, access, maintenance, and the division of the parties' property were previously settled in negotiation/litigation where the parties had separate representation. Also, lawyers who have been retained by families are often asked to draft wills for spouses. While there might appear to be a common interest, conflicts can easily arise. Consequently, in preparing wills for couples or other parties who seem to have common interests, lawyers should inform both clients that information collected from one client will not be held confidential from the other client. Similar concerns arise when lawyers act for executors to an estate, since lawyers also have duties towards the beneficiaries (usually family members).[9]

As the character of litigation becomes less private and more public, the question of who it is that counts as the lawyer's client is potentially problematic when lawyers act for public organizations or groups. From whom does the lawyer take instructions? To whom is a duty of confidentiality owed? What is to be done if the group members disagree? These questions receive short shrift in the professional rules. The most that is stated is that lawyers represent "that organization acting through

---

9    See MacKenzie, above note 7 at 5-3 and 18-3.

its duly authorized constituents"; they must make it clear to all such constituents that the interests of the organization are paramount to those of any constituents who become "adverse" in interest (see V, c. 12). This rule is based on the notion that lawyers do not represent the interests of the people involved, but the artificial entity of the organization they form, whether it is a corporation or a loose association. The problems with this assumption are many,[10] and two important implications warrant comment. First, this brief reference reflects both the law and lawyers' concentration of individual autonomy; even when there are group interests at stake, they are treated either as reducible to one individual-like conglomerate interest or as separate interests whose combination does not change the nature of the interests represented. Second, there is an assumption that the client group will remain constant; it might begin to change as a result of what the lawyer does or suggests.

PROBLEM 17: A number of tenant families consult you. Along with other tenant families, they have argued for years with the landlord over the building's condition and safety. Some tenants have left, others have withheld rent. Although they now want to take action as a group to confront the landlord, you realize that some families would continue living there whatever, some might leave, and still others might accept a cash settlement. Also, the appetite of the families for aggressive tactics is varied. Who is your client? And how do you deal with future difficulties over strategy and settlement?

## C. DUTY TO COURT AND PROFESSION

Although the professional rules are permeated with reminders that lawyers should be zealous partisans of their clients' cause and that they should place their clients' interests ahead of all others, there are also limits to such obligations. The two primary ones are based on lawyers' duties to the courts and to the profession generally. While these requirements are accepted and established, their precise reach and force are predictably uncertain. Indeed, the Rules give little guidance as to how lawyers should resolve any competing demands and duties. This difficulty is shared with constitutions, statutes, and other regulatory schemes (see chapter 3). However, it seems reasonable and fair to suggest that the wording and structure of the professional rules, as well as

---

10    See S. Ellmann, "Client Centeredness Multiplied: Individual Autonomy and Collective Mobilization in Public Interest Lawyers' Representation of Groups" (1992) 78 Virginia L. Rev. 1103.

the ethical pull of a less traditional and more subtle account of professional responsibility, would recommend that the duties to court and profession trump those to clients. Accordingly, it is crucial that lawyers have a firm grasp of the overarching responsibilities they owe to institutions and persons other than their clients.

Loyalty to the client is tempered by lawyers' duty to be honest. If the adversary system is to have any chance of working, the court must be able to rely on the fact that it is not being fed out-and-out lies. As advocates, lawyers are under a duty to use tactics that are legal, honest, and respectful of courts and other tribunals. They must be courteous to the court and the opposing party. In particular, they ought not to employ strategies that are intended to mislead the court or to influence decisions by anything other than open persuasion. Lawyers should not mislead courts about clients' agreements with one or more parties (see IX, cc. 1, 2, 14, 17, and 18), though difficulties arise when it comes to "omissions" — in the sense of failing to bring relevant evidence before the court. Speaking generally about the barrister's duty, Lord Denning framed the issue in characteristic grandiloquent style:

> [The advocate] has a duty to the court which is paramount. It is a mistake to suppose that he is the mouthpiece of his client to say what he wants: or his tool to do what he directs. He is none of these things. He owes allegiance to a higher cause. It is the cause of truth and justice. He must not consciously mis-state the facts. He must not knowingly conceal the truth. . . . He must produce all the relevant authorities, even those that are against him. He must see that his client discloses, if ordered, the relevant documents, even those that are fatal to his case. He must disregard the most specific instructions of his client, if they conflict with his duty to the court. The code which requires a barrister to do all this is not a code of law. It is a code of honour. If he breaks it, he is offending against the rules of the profession and is subject to its discipline.[11]

What it means to lie is something that has been the occasion for much debate and, alas, legal sophistry. For instance, in the leading case of *Meek*,[12] a police inspector was being sued for assault and wrongful imprisonment. Between the alleged tortious incident and the trial, the defendant had been demoted to the rank of station sergeant as a result of an unrelated incident. Nevertheless, the defendant's counsel made a

11  *Rondel v. Worsley*, [1966] 3 W.L.R. 950 at 962–63 (C.A.), and *Rondel v. Worsley*, [1969] 1 A.C. 191 at 227 (H.L.(E.)), Reid L.J.
12  *Meek v. Fleming*, [1961] 2 Q.B. 366 (C.A.).

positive decision not to reveal these facts at trial on the basis that the demotion went to credibility, not "facts," and that it was for the plaintiff's counsel to draw out these events and their relevance: this decision was made only after serious reflection by the defendant's counsel about his ethical responsibilities. Moreover, at the trial, the defendant attended in plain clothes (a privilege not normally extended to station sergeants) and was not asked his rank in the usual manner. Also, throughout the trial, plaintiff's counsel and the judge referred to him as "inspector" without being corrected. The plaintiff lost the action. On appeal, the plaintiff's lawyer moved for a new trial because of the misconduct by the defendant's counsel.

The English Court of Appeal held that the appeal should be allowed and a new trial ordered. With regard to the lawyers' obligations, the judges drew a distinction between having to reveal something to a party's discredit and actively continuing a false pretence, where counsel knows that the court is so deluded. While the former is acceptable, the latter is not. Accordingly, the court took the view that each party has the primary responsibility to prove its own case and that the other side had no affirmative duty of disclosure. While it is acceptable for lawyers to remain silent about relevant matters, they must not take active steps to mislead the court. Nevertheless, the line between ethical and unethical conduct is very thin and blurry. In *Meek*, the defendant's lawyer was a very experienced and respected QC who had taken this course of action only after considerable reflection and on the basis that it was ethical to so proceed.

**PROBLEM 18:** What would have been acceptable for the defendant's lawyer to do in *Meek*? At what point would the lawyer cross the line between acceptable and unacceptable conduct? Would such a strategy be more acceptable in negotiations and, if so, why? (See chapter 10.)

**PROBLEM 19:** You represent the plaintiff in a civil action for the recovery of a car. At trial, an important part of your client's case is that an alleged receipt for goods received was a forgery. Although you did see an alleged original receipt in the hands of the police, you have since been unable to obtain a copy of the original receipt. You fake a copy of the original, being extremely careful to use the exact words that you remember were on the original. While cross-examining the defendant, you introduce the copy as evidence and ask the defendant, "Have you ever seen anything like this before?" Have you acted improperly?[13]

---

13   See R. v. *Visitors to Inns of Court, Ex. P. Calder*, [1994] Q.B. 1 (D.C.).

The fact that lawyers' duties to their clients can be overridden by their higher obligation to the court and the profession sometimes means that the overall outcome is not what everyone will consider just or fair. Some might reasonably contend that, unless lawyers place the interests of their clients above such institutional values, their clients' quest for justice might be sacrificed to or compromised by a dubious commitment to professional solidarity or established interests. Without single-minded attention to the clients' interests, lawyers might find themselves co-opted into the very system that the best traditions of the legal profession are devoted to challenging. This argument has some appeal if (and only if) lawyers are willing to take responsibility for the clients they represent and the tactics they employ. Otherwise, such a justification is hollow and will only serve to clothe the mundane defence of the status quo with the vestments of undeserved legitimacy. Like so much else in matters of legal ethics, the profession cannot have it both ways.

# D.  DUTIES TO OTHERS

While it is clear that lawyers must and should put their clients' interests first, this obligation does not mean that they should not or need not take into account the interests of others. Even if the other party has little or no legal representation, lawyers are legally obliged and morally required to be more concerned with the interests of their clients. This duty does not mean, however, that they should be oblivious to the interests of others. Indeed, on a more sophisticated account of what friendship involves, the traditional Friedian justification of the demanding duty owed to one's client in terms of lawyers being their clients' friends need not be considered to oblige lawyers to ignore the interests or concerns of any-one and everyone else. The duty to be a zealous partisan in the pursuit of clients' interests involves the prioritizing of clients' interests, not the obliteration of everyone else's: it simply means that lawyers can give their clients' interests more weight on the scales than those of others. Other interests still count, but for less.

Accordingly, the question of whether lawyers can owe some obligation, admittedly of a lower order than that owed to their clients, to other persons seems to be answerable in the affirmative: they can. For instance, there seems to be little or no reason for lawyers to facilitate their clients' efforts to harm another's interests deliberately, especially if such actions would not improve the situation of their clients. The more difficult and controversial question is what the nature of those obligations might be, when might they arise, and what is their extent. For some, it might be misleading to talk of such matters in terms of "obligations"; it might be thought better to treat them as considerations that might permissively, but not necessarily, be taken into account by lawyers in determining the most ethical position to take or course of conduct to follow. Either way, the question remains of how tensions might be resolved in practical contexts. This issue is particularly pressing in regard to the interests of other parties and their witnesses. For instance, is it ever acceptable to take advantage of another lawyer's error or inexperience? It will likely be difficult in most situations to distinguish between a genuine mistake and bad judgment (e.g., a poorly drafted separation agreement by a young lawyer). This example is a tough ethical call, as it goes to the heart of the competing stresses and strains on lawyers. Of course, there is no simple, straightforward, or single answer. It will not only depend on the personal views of the individual lawyer but will be influenced by the precise context (e.g., if the other lawyer or his client have themselves been acting badly throughout the dispute).

One area where the professional rules place some ethical responsibility on lawyers to consider the interests of other parties is in slips or errors by other lawyers. In encouraging lawyers to avoid "sharp practices," lawyers are urged not to take advantage of any "irregularities" on the part of other lawyers. However, this admonition is restricted to those mistakes that do not "go to the merits" or involve "any sacrifice of the clients' rights." Moreover, even then lawyers can take advantage of errors or slips provided that "fair warning is given." In a similar vein, lawyers should not impose unreasonable conditions or time restraints on other lawyers (see XVI, c. 4).

**PROBLEM 20: You have a few years' experience under your belt in a family law practice. You negotiate for your client in a divorce where the other spouse is represented by a brash, know-it-all young lawyer with little family law experience. In the final negotiations, you agree on a deal that is, because of tax consideration, very beneficial to your client and very onerous to the other spouse. You are almost certain that the other lawyer is not aware of the disadvantageous tax consequences of the deal. What can or should you do?**

The Rules leave no doubt that a lawyer's function is to be "openly and necessarily partisan." In particular, the Rules make it explicit that lawyers are not obliged "to assist an adversary or advance matters derogatory to [their] clients' case" (see IX, c. 15). Apart from those situations expressly required by law, there are three exceptions to this general situation:

• When the opposing party is not represented by a lawyer, lawyers must take "particular care to be accurate, candid, and comprehensive" in going about their work (see IX, c. 15).

- Lawyers should not take advantage of "slips or oversights not going to the real merits" (see IX, c. 7).
- Lawyers are responsible for ensuring that all legal authority that is "directly on point" is brought to the attention of the court. This requirement extends to mentioning binding authorities that are damaging to their own case and which have not been mentioned by their opponents (see IX, c. 2(h)).

Nevertheless, while the Rules do not demand that lawyers take into account the interests of others and do not condemn lawyers for not doing so, neither do they instruct lawyers to ignore those interests or prohibit lawyers from considering them. This distinction is vital. While there is some justification for adhering to a strong adversarial ethic in criminal matters where the individual is pitted against the state, with all its resources and power at its disposal, there is much less reason for doing so in civil cases (see chapter 9). Obviously, in paying any attention to the interests of others, lawyers must be careful not to jeopardize or undermine the interests of their own clients. In circumstances where such possibilities arise, it will be essential to include the client in any discussion about the appropriate or ethical course to be followed. It is simply a mistake to assume that all clients have no concern for the interests of the other side. For instance, although matrimonial disputes can become very bitter, there is no reason why lawyers should not try to reduce rather than exacerbate the problems by suggesting to their clients that it might be in the clients' long-term interests to act in a more reasonable and less hostile manner. Also, even if clients do want to take a scorched-earth approach to such matters, lawyers are well within their ethical rights to inform their clients that they are not prepared to engage in or condone such an approach.

PROBLEM 21: What should lawyers who represent a wealthy corporation do in an action against an unemployed and illiterate individual (with or without a lawyer)? Should lawyers' approaches to negotiation or advocacy depend on the identity of the plaintiff and the defendant? Should lawyers take advantage of the other side's lack of experience or expertise?

As mentioned, lawyers are under an obligation to represent their clients by "fair and honourable means" and not to engage in tactics or initiatives that will taint the overall process of the court (see IX, c. 1). Such tactics might include abusing, hectoring, harassing, or needlessly inconveniencing a witness (see IX, c. 2(k) and (l)). Nevertheless, notwithstanding these established and reasonable guidelines, some lawyers still resort to an aggressive strategy whose dominant purpose is to inconvenience and intimidate the opposing party. The difficulty is that, while these tactics are not always beneficial for clients (and may occasionally be to their detriment), many lawyers are reluctantly drawn to adopting such tactics on the basis that they will not be competitive enough and will not be able to defend their client successfully against those who still persist in using such tactics. Such a vicious cycle of justification is to be resisted: each lawyer has to take personal responsibility for the tactics he or she employs, and it is far from persuasive simply to point to the fact that other lawyers do it. For instance, in cross-examining witnesses, lawyers are in a position to wreak considerable havoc on the public reputation and private lives of witnesses. Yet, in most circumstances, there is no need to embarrass or humiliate witnesses in order to make the necessary and relevant points. In some situations, it might be counter-productive, as the judge or jury might take a definite dislike to the lawyer's tactics and, as a result, lean against the client's case. Also, there is a huge difference between performing a vigorous and uncompromising cross-examination and terrorizing the witness. In particular, it seems unconscionable to make a concerted and deliberate attack on witnesses' characters when there is no reasonable basis for such an attack and especially when credibility is not an issue.

As part of their overall responsibility to maintain the integrity of the profession, all lawyers have a duty to report breaches of the professional rules by lawyers where it is reasonable to believe that, as a result of such a breach, someone will suffer serious damage. The only exceptions exist where information is privileged or such reporting would be unlawful (see XV, c. 1). Of course, because such reports could lead to severe damage to a lawyer's reputation, they must be made without malice or ulterior motives. Finally, to enhance the public standing and performance of the profession and the legal process generally, lawyers are urged to engage in all activities (continuing education, legal aid programs) that would assist the proper and effective functioning of the profession.

# E. CONCLUSION

In this chapter, I have sought to explore the main dynamic of "zealous partisanship" that is at the heart of legal ethics and professional responsibility. However, while it is the fulcrum around which other obligations swing, it is the central but not the most important duty that lawyers have. Indeed, contrary to common understanding, lawyers' duty to their clients is only a secondary one; the duty to the court and the profession is primary. Further, lawyers' primary duty to their clients does not automatically justify acting with complete disregard for the interests of opposing parties. Winning on behalf of your client does not mean destroying or humiliating the losing party. Also, I have emphasized that the traditional approach fails to involve clients sufficiently in matters of tactics and strategies; they are too much seen to have fixed interests and to stand outside the moral domain of the lawyer. In the pragmatic approach that I encourage, lawyers should treat their clients as conversational partners who can contribute to and be persuaded about particular courses of action and their likely consequences.

# BEING CONFIDENTIAL:
# SECRETS AND LIES

Confidentiality is one of the most important, yet misunderstood, obligations to their clients that lawyers undertake. Notwithstanding Bentham's earlier opposition to the privilege on the basis that it protects only the guilty, the basis and need for some duty of confidentiality is now undisputed. There still remain considerable confusion and controversy about when the duty arises, to whom the duty is owed, what it covers, what its limits are, and what the consequences are of any breach. All these matters go to the heart of lawyers' duties to their clients in light of the competing demands that are placed on lawyers by both the system and their own consciences. While the duty is fundamental, it is not absolute: it cannot be allowed to work as a cover or a pretext for abuse. There is a public interest defence to any claims by clients that lawyers have breached the duty. Indeed, there are some instances in which lawyers are under an obligation to breach the duty. All in all, therefore, the duty of confidentiality is as confusing as it is central.

Accordingly, in this chapter I will try to make sense of the duty of confidentiality and its limits. There are two main sources that place obligations of confidentiality on lawyers: the law of evidence and the professional rules. Under evidentiary rules, lawyers are entitled and required to keep confidential all communications between clients and themselves that pertain to the giving of legal advice and assistance; this is a privilege to the client, and it applies regardless of whether litigation is involved or is imminent. Also, there is the litigation privilege that requires and entitles lawyers to keep confidential any information they get in contemplation of and in preparation for litigation. Further, lawyers may, in special circumstances, come under a legal obligation to keep confidential certain dealings with non-clients, though this is a narrow and infrequent situation. As well as such evidentiary privileges, lawyers are under a strong professional duty to keep all their communications with their clients confidential, whether they relate to legal or to non-legal matters. This professional duty is broader than the evidentiary privilege, but lawyers can be relieved of such an obligation at the direction of a court. Whereas the first two sections of this chapter will deal with the evidential privileges attaching to lawyer-client communications and general litigation preparation, the third section explores the ethical duty of confidentiality. The fourth section covers the limits that are imposed on the duty of confidentiality, and the fifth section canvasses the circumstances in which clients can authorize disclosure.

## A. THE LAWYER-CLIENT PRIVILEGE

Under the law of evidence, communications between lawyers and their clients are privileged and impose on lawyers a duty not to reveal them or use them in any way to the clients' disadvantage. From the outset, it is important to establish that, although this privilege to withhold information and documents can and does benefit lawyers, it belongs to clients; it is for clients to decide when the privilege can be waived and information disclosed.[1] Consequently, lawyers cannot choose to make public any communications with their clients, even if they believe it is in the clients' best interests to so do. As such, although there are some special circumstances in which lawyers might be required to reveal such information, the duty of confidentiality is strict and uncompromising.

The basis for this restriction is straightforward and uncontroversial: clients must be able to obtain full and frank legal advice and to confer with their lawyers without the fear that the basis of that communication will become public and be used against them. Clients should be able to speak with their lawyers in the full and uninhibited confidence that what is said will go no further. There is a zone of privacy around such communications that the law insists must be jealously guarded. Apart from protecting the clients' privacy, this confidentiality facilitates the

---

1   *Anderson* v. *Bank of British Columbia*, [1876] 2 Ch. D. 644 at 649 (C.A.), Jessel M.R. For a good general introduction to some of the broader evidence issues, see D.M. Paciocco & L. Stuesser, *The Law of Evidence* (Concord, Ont.: Irwin Law, 1996) at 132–52.

effective rendering of legal advice and assistance. In these situations, justice is said to be of more importance than truth. Or, to put it less bluntly, justice is better served by preserving the sanctity of certain relationships that are deemed to have sufficient social significance to outweigh the priority given to truth in the legal process. The classic statement of this justification is made by Lord Brougham:

> The foundation of this rule is not difficult to discover. It is not (as has sometimes been said) on account of any particular importance which the law attributes to the business of legal [practitioners], or any particular disposition to afford them protection, though certainly it may not be very easy to discover why a like privilege has been refused to others, and especially to medical advisers. But it is out of regard to the interests of justice, which cannot be upholden, and to the administration of justice, which cannot go on, without the aid of men skilled in jurisprudence, in the practice of the Courts, and in those matters affecting rights and obligations which form the subject of all judicial proceedings. If the privilege did not exist at all, every one would be thrown upon his own legal resources; deprived of all professional assistance, a man would not venture to consult any skilful person, or would only dare to tell his counsellor half his case.[2]

A good example is lawyers' responsibility in connection with settlement negotiations. Lawyers are under an obligation to keep all information and documents relating to settlement discussions confidential, in both informal communications and formal offers to settle. When it comes to trial advocacy, however, lawyers need to keep in mind the important distinction between facts and law. Although lawyers' duty to divulge facts and opinion is constrained by their confidential commitments to their clients, they have a definite duty to disclose all relevant legal authorities to courts or tribunals. Lawyers are responsible for ensuring that all legal authority that is "directly on point" is brought to the attention of the court. Moreover, they have an affirmative duty to mention binding authorities that are damaging to their clients' case and which have not been mentioned by their opponents (see IX, c. 2(h)).

The leading case on the lawyer-client privilege is *Descôteaux*. While this case involved the scope of the duty, and the circumstances in which lawyers might be under no duty to maintain confidentiality and might actually be required to disclose information received in confidence, Lamer J. offered a convenient statement of the privilege's reach:

---

2    *Greenough v. Gaskell* (1833), 39 E.R. 618 at 620–21.

In summary, a lawyer's client is entitled to have all communications made with a view to obtaining legal advice kept confidential. Whether communications are made to the lawyer himself or to employees, and whether they deal with matters of an administrative nature such as financial means or with the actual nature of the legal problem, all information which a person must provide in order to obtain legal advice and which is given in confidence for that purpose enjoys the privileges attached to confidentiality. This confidentiality attaches to all communications made within the framework of the solicitor-client relationship, which arises as soon as the potential client takes the first steps, and consequently even before the formal retainer is established.[3]

It is important to appreciate that this privilege applies only to those communications where the object of the interaction between lawyers and their clients concerns the seeking of legal advice: it does not apply to non-legal matters. While what counts as legal advice has been interpreted broadly by the courts and obviously covers most matters that relate to tax or business dealings, lawyers must understand and make sure that their clients appreciate that any communications that do not relate to legal affairs will not be privileged. Although they will fall under lawyers' general duty to keep all communications with their clients confidential, lawyers might be ordered by courts to reveal and disclose information that does not involve the giving of legal advice and assistance. Accordingly, lawyers must make it clear to clients when they are giving legal advice, as opposed to non-legal advice. Non-legal advice is not within the scope of the evidentiary privilege and will have to be disclosed in legal proceedings.[4]

In *Descôteaux*, an accused person had made an application for legal aid. The police sought to enforce a search warrant on a legal aid office to obtain a copy of an applicant's application form in order to establish if there had been fraud in the application. The Supreme Court determined that the financial information on the form was not privileged and that the lawyer who had received the information must disclose it. Apart from the fact that a misrepresentation of a person's financial position amounted to a criminal offence, it was held that the statement of financial affairs was not part of the lawyer's communications with the client over legal advice and therefore did not fall within the ambit of the rule. However, the Court did make clear that the other contents of the form were privileged and ought not to be disclosed to the police or anyone else.

---

3   *Descôteaux v. Mierzwinski*, [1982] 1 S.C.R. 860 at 892–93.
4   *Alfred Crompton Amusement Machines Ltd. v. Commissioners of Custom and Excise (No. 2)*, [1972] All E.R. 353 (C.A.).

This evidentiary privilege extends not only to the clients' communications with the lawyers' office assistants and colleagues but also comes into play even before there is an official retainer. In some situations, the duty of confidentiality might extend to keeping the identity of the client confidential. This issue will arise only in special circumstances where the clients go to the lawyer in order to preserve their anonymity. For example, where a person has committed a criminal offence and wants to seek advice before turning himself in to the authorities, the lawyer would be under an obligation not to reveal the identity or whereabouts of the person, unless there is a possibility that the client is likely to commit further offences.[5] Moreover, the lawyer's duty of confidentiality continues after the professional relationship with the client has ended and even after the client has died.[6] However, the courts have made an exception in the case of wills or other equitable arrangements where the validity or purpose of a testamentary disposition was in dispute. In such circumstances, the courts have insisted that the disclosure of such confidential information is in the interests of the deceased client and therefore is better disclosed than kept confidential.[7]

PROBLEM 22: At a social gathering, you run into a former client. You have both had a few drinks and he shares some sensitive information with you about a case he is presently involved in and for which he has hired the services of another lawyer. Do you have any duty to keep this information confidential?

PROBLEM 23: You are representing your client on a serious criminal charge. In the middle of the trial, you receive unsolicited communications and documents from one of your client's former business associates which contain very damaging information and evidence against your client. What should you do with the documents?

Special difficulties arise in dealing with confidentiality in the context of corporate lawyers' professional responsibilities. While it is clear that corporate counsel owe a duty to their client, it is not always obvious who constitutes "the client." Also, there is the difficulty of determining when lawyers are engaged in giving legal as opposed to non-legal advice; whereas the former is privileged, the latter is not, unless confidentiality is expressly claimed. For instance, if in-house counsel sends legal communications out on a legal letterhead, it is possible that non-legal advice produced on a page with legal letterhead may indicate an intention to

---

5   See *Thorson v. Jones* (1973), 38 D.L.R. (3d) 312 (B.C.S.C.).
6   See *Guay v. Société franco-manitobaine* (1985), 37 Man. R. (2d) 16 (Q.B.).
7   See *Geffen v. Goodman Estate*, [1991] 2 S.C.R. 353.

claim privilege. Moreover, the arguments in favour of confidentiality become complicated and harder to justify when considering the activities of certain corporations (see chapter 10). The rule of confidentiality is meant to protect the powerless by ensuring effective legal representation through open communication. Big corporations do not meet this idealistic definition and may be tempted to use the rule of confidentiality to conceal white-collar crime. It might therefore be more "just" to reconceive the application of the confidentiality rule: "an approach that balances the need for confidentiality and the need for disclosure might well permit or even require lawyers to disclose corporate illegality."[8]

## B. THE LITIGATION PRIVILEGE

Apart from the lawyer-client privilege that is sanctioned by the law of evidence, another evidentiary privilege exists — the general litigation privilege. As the name suggests, this privilege entitles and requires lawyers to keep confidential those communications that are made to them in the course of their professional efforts to litigate on behalf of their clients. The evidentiary privilege is both narrower and broader than the general lawyer-client privilege.[9] It is narrower in that, whereas the general lawyer-client privilege attaches to all communications whether in relation to litigation or not, the litigation privilege applies only to those matters that arise in the contemplation or the course of litigation. However, the litigation privilege is much broader in that it covers non-confidential communications between lawyers and third parties, and also material of a non-communicative nature (such as notes and records).

The most important and controversial aspect of this privilege is its application to "work product" or, as it is referred to in Canada, the "lawyers' brief." This privilege was first authoritatively explained in the American case of *Hickman*.[10] Following an accident in which people drowned, the owners of a tug employed a law firm to defend them against possible legal actions. One of its lawyers interviewed all the survivors. The plaintiff's lawyers later requested summaries of those interviews. The Supreme Court declined to order disclosure on the basis that such material was covered by the litigation privilege, even though those

---

8  See G. MacKenzie, *Lawyers and Ethics: Professional Responsibility and Discipline* (Scarborough, Ont.: Carswell, 1993) at 3-9. See also D. Luban, *Lawyers and Justice: An Ethical Study* (Princeton, NJ: Princeton University Press, 1989) at 182–83, and C.W. Wolfram, *Modern Legal Ethics* (St. Paul, Minn.: West Pub. Co., 1986) at 283–84.
9  *Wheeler v. Le Marchant* (1881), 17 Ch. D. 675 at 681 (C.A.), Jessel M.R.
10  *Hickman v. Taylor*, 329 U.S. 495 (1947).

interviewed did not provide such information on a confidential basis; the plaintiff's lawyers were free to interview the witnesses for themselves. Although there remains much debate about the scope of the rule and its potential for abuse, the litigation privilege is now firmly established as a feature of the Canadian professional landscape.

The rationale for the litigation privilege is different from the general lawyer-client privilege. Whereas the latter is directed towards the protection of a particular relationship and the protection of legal rights, the former derives from the adversarial system and is intended to facilitate that process. In short, without some sort of protection for the product of lawyers' investigations or ruminations, the adversarial incentive to pursue all possible lines of argument and inquiry might be hampered. Lawyers might not be as vigorous as they might otherwise be if the fruits of their labours were available to their opponents, and if unfavourable information that was generated had to be disclosed to opponents. Of course, while this might not always be a bad thing, there would be a definite temptation to free-ride on the efforts of adversaries. The rationale was neatly summarized by the Hon. Wilbur Roy Jackett:

> Turning to the "lawyer's brief" rule, the reason for the rule is, obviously, that, under our adversary system of litigation, a lawyer's preparation of his client's case must not be inhibited by the possibility that the materials that he prepares can be taken out of his file and presented to the court in a manner other than that contemplated when they were prepared. What would aid in determining the truth when presented in the manner contemplated by the solicitor who directed its preparation might well be used to create a distortion of the truth to the prejudice of the client when presented by someone adverse in interest who did not understand what gave rise to its preparation. If lawyers were entitled to dip into each other's briefs by means of the discovery process, the straightforward preparation of cases for trial would develop into a most unsatisfactory travesty of our present system. What is important to note about both of these rules is that they do not afford a privilege against the discovery of facts that are or may be relevant to the determination of the facts in issue. What is privileged is the communications or working papers that came into existence by reason of the desire to obtain a legal opinion or legal assistance in the one case and the materials created for the lawyer's brief in the other case. The facts or documents that happen to be reflected in such communications or materials are not privileged from discovery if, otherwise, the party would be bound to give discovery of them.[11]

---

11   *Susan Hosiery Ltd.* v. *Minister of National Revenue*, [1969] 2 Ex. C.R. 27 at 33–34.

The extent of this litigation privilege remains contested because, if interpreted too broadly, it can allow lawyers and clients to sweep up all relevant facts and opinions and claim confidentiality for them. The courts have resolved that the privilege applies only to those documents that are prepared with the dominant, although not the sole, purpose of submitting it to a legal adviser for advice and use in litigation. In the leading case of *Waugh*,[12] a Railway Board had the routine practice of requiring an internal report after any accident. The report ended with the words that "for the information of the Board's solicitor: this form is to be used by every person reporting an occurrence when litigation by or against the [Board] is anticipated." An employee's widow sought discovery of such a report in her action against the board. The House of Lords held that, notwithstanding the concluding words, the report had a dual purpose — for contributing to the railway's safety operations and the obtaining of legal advice. After canvassing various possibilities, it was decided that the report was not privileged because, while a substantial purpose was that of legal advice, this was not its dominant purpose. While the "dominant purpose" test has become the norm in Canada, there are still some jurisdictions that flirt with the test that the purpose need only be "substantial," and not "dominant," to be confidential.[13]

**PROBLEM 24: An insured's building is destroyed by fire. The insurer pays the claim and the building is rebuilt. On the basis of a report by an electrical engineer two days after the accident, the insurer commences a subrogated claim against your client a year later for negligently causing the accident by taking out the power supply to the building. The insurer claims privilege over the engineer's report on the basis that it engages an engineer only to determine whether a subrogated claim ought to be made against another party. What arguments would you make against the assertion of privilege?**

However, while the work product obtained is confidential, there are some situations in which lawyers might be obliged to disclose some aspects of that information or where the privilege will lapse:

- Most jurisdictions require that, in civil actions, the identity of persons interviewed or contacted must be disclosed to the other parties adverse in interest. This is especially the case when the situation involves experts' reports.
- The courts have made it clear that the privilege extends to communications and not to the facts communicated; parties cannot conceal a

12   See *Waugh v. British Railways Board*, [1980] A.C. 521 (H.L.(E.)).
13   See *Keuhl v. McConnell* (1991), 3 C.P.C. (3d) 22 (Ont. Gen. Div.).

fact by including it in communications to lawyers, nor can lawyers make certain facts confidential by including them in their work product. So, for example, taking copies of a document does not make the original confidential.[14]

- Unlike the lawyer-client privilege, the litigation privilege expires with the end of the litigation. Lawyers can reveal information that was produced during litigation, provided it was not from a client.[15]

# C. THE GENERAL DUTY OF CONFIDENTIALITY

Apart from the obligation to abide by the wish of clients to keep information confidential which is covered by the two evidentiary privileges, the professional rules impose on lawyers a series of compelling duties that concern the need to preserve confidentiality. Most important, lawyers have a clear and demanding obligation to "hold in strict confidence" all information that comes into their possession and knowledge while fulfilling their professional duties towards clients (see IV). They must not disclose such information to anyone else, use it to the clients' detriment, or take advantage of that information in any way. This duty arises both from lawyers' contract with their clients and also the professional duty placed on lawyers by the professional rules and the law generally. Again, it is, of course, a privilege held by clients and can only be waived with their consent. Consequently, to facilitate the giving and receiving of appropriate legal advice and assistance, lawyers must act in such a way as to ensure that there is "full and unreserved communication" between lawyers and clients (see IV, c. 1).

The evidentiary privilege and the ethical duty of confidentiality are not co-extensive. In particular, the ethical duty is based upon, but is more extensive than, evidentiary rules of lawyer-client privilege. Whereas the evidentiary rule applies only to legal advice given by the lawyer, the ethical rule embraces "all information concerning the business and affairs of the client," whether it is of a legal nature or not (see IV). The upshot is that, while clients can be confident that any information that arises in the course of providing legal advice and assistance will be secure against all challenges, other information might have to be disclosed by lawyers at the direction of courts. This disclosure will occur

---

14   *Ottawa-Carleton (Regional Municipality)* v. *Consumers' Gas Co.* (1990), 74 D.L.R. (4th) 742 (Div. Ct.).
15   *Meaney* v. *Busby* (1977), 15 O.R. (2d) 71 (H.C.).

only in exceptional circumstances. Nevertheless, lawyers should be aware that their duty of confidentiality covers all communications between clients and themselves: they are relieved of this duty only through the clients' waiver or a court order. Furthermore, the duty applies regardless of "the nature or source of the information or the fact that others may share the knowledge" (see IV, c. 2).

**PROBLEM 25: Your client is under investigation by Revenue Canada for suspected tax evasion. To frustrate the investigation, she asks you whether she should send all her financial records to you so you can claim that they are privileged as a confidential communication. What is your advice?**

The force and extent of this professional duty to preserve confidentiality are wide and exacting. Lawyers are under a "continuing" obligation to keep confidential any information that passes between themselves and their clients, even if they are only "casual" clients (see IV, c. 4). The duties concerning safekeeping of clients' property are connected to those governing confidential information; all papers, files, and property are also considered to be privileged information (see VIII, c. 5). If a third party attempts to seize information (including files and property), lawyers have a duty to "be alert to claim on behalf of clients any lawful privilege respecting information about their affairs" (see VIII, c. 6). In particular, lawyers "should avoid indiscreet conversations . . . and should shun any gossip" about their clients' affairs (see IV, c. 7). Moreover, even if the facts in question are "public knowledge," lawyers should avoid "speculation concerning the clients' affairs or business" (see IV, c. 8).

As part of reinforcing this extensive cordon of confidentiality, lawyers who testify as witnesses may not be asked, nor answer, questions posed to reveal confidential information, unless there has been a clear waiver by the clients. In circumstances where lawyers do not claim privilege, the court should refuse to hear such evidence. If lawyers are asked such questions, they must refuse to disclose such confidential information. Moreover, if lawyers do not appreciate the force of this obligation, the court should disallow such questions and refuse to hear any evidence that infringes the duty, even if neither side raises an objection.[16]

Based on lawyers' fiduciary duty to clients, lawyers are obliged to do more than refrain from using confidential information to the detriment of the clients. They must also be assiduous to ensure that they do not use such information to their own advantage or that of a third party. This obligation governs literary works or autobiographies by lawyers

---

16   See *Bell* v. *Smith*, [1968] S.C.R. 664.

(see IV, c. 5). The courts have made it clear that lawyers may be liable to account for using confidential information for their own benefit.[17] In a recent case, for example, a leading criminal lawyer was found liable in damages to a former client after the lawyer had been involved in the production of a television program about the client. Although there was no suggestion that the client had been misrepresented or that the knowledge was not already in the public domain, the lawyer was held to be in breach of his fiduciary and confidential duty to the client. As well as civil liability, lawyers who use confidential information to the disadvantage of their client or for their own advantage will run the real risk of being reprimanded by their professional body. For instance, an Ontario lawyer used confidential information about his client's sexual problems to initiate an affair with the client's wife. This behaviour led to civil and professional penalties.[18]

Finally, as well as those duties of confidentiality that arise in and from lawyer-client relationships, lawyers need to be aware that they might incur other duties to keep information confidential. In circumstances not involving legal advice or assistance, lawyers can come under a duty of confidentiality if there has been some perceived agreement between the lawyer and the confidant to keep the information confidential. In line with general evidentiary rules, this situation will occur where certain conditions are met: confidence was expected; confidentiality is essential to the relationship between the parties; the relationship is socially significant; and the injury would be greater than the benefits of disclosure. For instance, if a lawyer acted as a counsellor to a sexual abuse victim, it might be that the lawyer could be put under a duty not to disclose the information that passes between them.[19]

# D.   SCOPE AND LIMITS

Although the duty of confidentiality is strict and must be taken extremely seriously by any lawyer, there are limits to the scope of the duty. There are a number of situations in which lawyers will not only be entitled to relinquish their duty to clients but might also be required to do so. However, if disclosure of confidential information is required by

---

17   *McMaster* v. *Byrne*, [1952] 3 D.L.R. 337 (P.C.).
18   See *Szarfer* v. *Chodos* (1986), 54 O.R. (2d) 663 (H.C.).
19   See *R.* v. *S.(R.J.)* (1985), 45 C.R. (3d) 161 (C.A.). For a discussion of the circumstances in which a general duty of confidence will arise, see *R.* v. *Fosty* (*sub nom. R.* v. *Gruenke*), [1991] 3 S.C.R. 263.

law, lawyers must be "careful not to divulge more information than is required" (see IV, c. 13).[20] While these limits to the duty are varied, they are each based on a similar justification. Mindful that the general rationale for lawyers' duty of confidentiality is the need to enhance the effective exercise of legal rights, it would be wrong to allow the duty to operate in such a way as to subvert the administration of justice generally. In light of the possibility that lawyers might have to forgo their duty of confidentiality, it is imperative that lawyers explain the reach and limits of the confidentiality principle to clients before any delicate or incriminating information is divulged.

There are a number of situations in which lawyers are required to break their duty of confidentiality. Of course, lawyers must be sure they have reasonable grounds to reach the appropriate conclusions. In such situations, lawyers have no choice, and the obligation shifts from preserving confidentiality to disclosing information. They will breach the professional rules if they do not reveal the information and, where applicable, they might actually commit a criminal offence themselves in the process:

- Confidential information may be disclosed if lawyers have a reasonable belief "that a crime is likely to be committed," but disclosure becomes mandatory only if the "anticipated crime is one involving violence" (see IV, c. 11). Also, this duty of disclosure is triggered by the existence of a reasonable belief that "a dangerous situation is likely to develop at a court facility." In such a situation, lawyers assume a responsibility to "suggest solutions" to deal with the problem (see IV, c. 12). Obviously, lawyers must not assist clients in planning unlawful acts, and lawyers have a public responsibility to prevent harm.
- The duty of confidentiality does not extend to communications that are themselves criminal. Because the general basis of the duty is the facilitation of the administration of justice, it would defeat the purpose if the duty was extended to cover lawyers who aided and abetted criminal or illegal activities. The leading authority is *Descôteaux*. The police sought to enforce a search warrant on a legal aid office to obtain a copy of an applicant's application form in order to establish if there had been fraud in the application. The Supreme Court held that the client could not claim that the information was privileged and that the lawyer must disclose such information; "communications that are in themselves criminal or that are made with a view to

---

20   See M.H. Freedman, "Solicitor-Client Privilege under the Income Tax Act" (1969) 12 Canadian B.J. 93.

obtaining legal advice to facilitate the commission of a crime" are not
privileged and need not be held in confidence by lawyers.[21] Indeed,
in such circumstances, lawyers have a positive duty to disclose such
information to the authorities.

- While confidentiality does not extend to information about future
  crimes and to communications that are criminal in themselves, it
  does cover information about past crimes. However, the privilege
  does not apply to physical objects, such as stolen property or weapons used in crimes; these are not treated as "communications." Nevertheless, lawyers must keep confidential any communications that
  take place with the client over such objects.

- Of course, a lawyers' duty to retain the confidentiality of their clients'
  communications can be abridged by rules of law or by judicial order.
  There are a few of these situations: discovery and evidence rules.
  However, lawyers must be sure that disclosure is mandated rather
  than merely encouraged before they breach their clients' confidences,
  even if the communication is to do with non-legal matters. For
  instance, in *Solosky*, the Court decided that the legislation governing
  prisoners' communications should take precedence or, at least, mod-
  ify the lawyer-client privilege.[22]

**PROBLEM 26: Your client is charged with a minor assault offence. In the
course of a pre-trial interview, he tells you that he committed a particularly
heinous crime for which another person is being tried and is likely to be convicted. What can you do? What should you do?**

While the duty of confidentiality is indeed important, there is a real
sense in which it can in certain circumstances result in a sense that the
confidentiality tail is wagging the professional dog. As William Simon
expresses it, "[W]hy do we value the improvement in legal advice to the
client that confidentiality facilitates above the prevention of injustices
to others that confidentiality inhibits?"[23] It is important therefore that
lawyers think hard about the extent to which the duty of confidentiality
might be limited by situations where the consequences of upholding the
duty lead to greater substantial injustice than breaching it. In so doing,
lawyers will appreciate that a limit on a principle is not the abnegation
of that principle or its perversion. These considerations will be particularly pertinent in those situations where lawyers can choose to breach

---

21   See *Descôteaux*, above note 3 at 893.
22   *Solosky v. Canada*, [1980] 1 S.C.R. 821.
23   W.H. Simon, *The Practice of Justice: A Theory of Lawyers' Ethics* (Cambridge, Mass.:
     Harvard University Press, 1998) at 55.

their duty of confidence. These circumstances are infrequent and, although disclosure is permissible, lawyers are well advised to think seriously about exercising such a considerable entitlement. It might be in their own and future clients' interests to adopt this course where all other avenues of approach have been tried and the end to be achieved warrants the heavy-handed means to be used.

- Lawyers can disclose information revealed in confidence by clients if it is necessary to defend themselves against accusations of malpractice (see IV, c. 10). The reason for allowing the lawyer self-interest exception to the confidentiality rule is to inhibit clients from using the rule to the detriment of their lawyers. However, because the resort to this exception may be very harmful to the clients' interests, it is difficult to assess how much information is necessary to be disclosed. In *Piercy*,[24] a client challenged a lawyer's fees while matrimonial litigation was pending. In defending himself at the assessment, the client's lawyer had to disclose information about the chosen strategy; this information later came to the attention of the client's wife and her counsel. The client was considered to have waived his right to privilege by commencing the assessment proceedings and, therefore, could not stop his wife from using the information against him.

- Lawyers can also disclose information if necessary to collect fees or defend themselves against accusation of malpractice (see IV, c. 10). Again, lawyers should be slow to resort to such a draconian sanction against their clients.

- Lawyers can and sometimes must disclose certain confidential information or communications to advance the public interest. For instance, it has been held that lawyers are required to reveal confidential information where it might allow an accused person to establish his or her innocence.[25] Also, an interesting situation arises where lawyers subsequently discover that they have been unwittingly used by their clients to perpetrate a fraud or some other wrongdoing. In a recent English decision, the Court of Appeal held that lawyers might be able to disclose these facts to the victims, but only under the authority of a court order.[26]

PROBLEM 27: A single parent seeks your legal advice on a housing matter. He brings his young children to your office and, during your meeting, they become boisterous. The parent becomes very angry and aggressive towards

---

24   *Piercy v. Piercy* (1990), [1991] 75 D.L.R. 299 (B.C.C.A.).

25   See *R. v. Stinchcombe*, [1991] 3 S.C.R. 326.

26   *Finers v. Miro*, [1991] 1 W.L.R. 35 (C.A.).

them. The children begin to cry and one says fearfully, "Daddy, you're not going to tell me to take my clothes off and sleep in your bed, are you?" What do you do?

Finally, the scope of the confidentiality rule can and, on occasion, should influence the identity of future clients who can be represented and the nature of that representation. This matter concerns potential conflicts of interest (see chapter 8). For instance, lawyers should refrain from employment that would require them to disclose the confidential information of one client to another (see IV, c. 6). In situations where lawyers are retained by more than one client in the same matter, lawyers must advise the clients that "no information received in connection with the matter from one can be treated as confidential so far as any of the others is concerned" (see V, c. 5).

# E. WAIVER AND DISCLOSURE

As well as those situations where lawyers are required or entitled by law to disclose confidential communications between clients and themselves, such information may be disclosed at the authorization of clients. The clients are the "holders" of the privilege and it is their entitlement to waive the privilege and disclose the information. Such a waiver must be clear, freely made, and informed; the clients must realize that the choice is entirely theirs and must appreciate the consequences of any waiver.[27] Although it will be best for the lawyer if the waiver is express and in writing, a waiver can be implied. While a valid waiver can be express or implied, lawyers should act on implied waivers only in the clearest of circumstances. Indeed, it might be good practice to obtain such consent in writing where possible. However, lawyers have implied consent to disclose information when working in consultation with partners, associates, and other firm staff. In such circumstances, lawyers are "under a duty to impress" upon those working on the file the importance of confidentiality and must "take reasonable care to prevent" disclosure (see IV, c. 9).

Whether there has been an implied waiver will depend on more than the holder's intentions. Mindful that a holder will seldom after the alleged fact of waiver concede that there was an intention to waive, the courts have also taken into account overall considerations of fairness

---

27   *Kulchar v. Marsh*, [1950] 1 W.W.R. 272 (Sask. K.B.), and *R. v. Perron* (1990), 54 C.C.C. (3d) 108 (Q.C.A.).

and consistency in the particular circumstances. For example, selective disclosure is discouraged. Courts have regularly accepted that, where clients agree to disclose part of a privileged communication that is favourable to their cause, it will be assumed that they have impliedly waived the privilege to the entire communication; otherwise, the privilege could be used affirmatively to misrepresent facts and further muddy the truth-finding process. An implied waiver of privilege can occur when clients disclose information to a third party. Once clients have waived their privilege, it is generally not possible to reclaim privilege.[28] In trial situations, trial judges are obliged to ensure that lawyers who disclose confidential information have obtained an express waiver from their clients.[29]

PROBLEM 28: You act for the defendant in a civil action. Documents intended for the plaintiff are sent to your office. You open and begin reading them before you realize that they were intended for the plaintiff. Can you rely on the information? Must you reveal the fact that you have seen the documents to the plaintiff? Would it matter how the documents came to be sent to you?

Although lawyers might not be able to reveal information that is confidential, it might be the case that, as a result of the receipt of confidential information from clients, they do have to take certain steps. Even if clients tell their lawyers about responsibility for past crimes, lawyers cannot reveal that information; the exception covers information only about future crimes and communications that are criminal in themselves.[30] However, lawyers cannot ignore such information in deciding how to continue to represent such clients as a result of that information. Where clients reveal past criminal activities to lawyers, this will put certain restrictions on the kind of legal assistance and advocacy in which lawyers can engage. In short, lawyers cannot breach the duty of confidentiality and disclose the information, but they will not be able to run certain defences or lines of argument on behalf of the clients. Indeed, lawyers might feel a compulsion to withdraw in such circumstances. Lawyers must inform clients of such consequences in order that the clients can make an informed decision about what to do. Indeed, it will be good professional practice to inform some clients as part of the overall and early discussion with them, before they have said anything about their situation, what the confidentiality principle does and does

---

28   *London Trust & Savings Corp.* v. *Corbett* (1994), 24 C.P.C. (3d) 226 (Ont. Gen. Div.).
29   See *Geffen*, above note 7.
30   See *R.* v. *Bennett* (1963), 41 C.R. 227 (B.C.S.C.).

not require lawyers to do. In particular, lawyers ought to outline the exceptions to the confidentiality rule concerning when lawyers may disclose or be compelled to disclose information. To fail to provide such initial advice might well be in breach of the broad duty to provide competent advice to clients.

**PROBLEM 29:** Your client tells you the whereabouts of some incriminating tapes in a series of criminal transactions. You locate the tapes and listen to them. You hand them over to your client who, against his express promise to you, destroys them. What should you do? When your client is charged, the police wish to question you about the tapes. Should you reveal the content of your communications with your client? Would it make a difference if he was no longer your client?

The difficulty of what lawyers should do when they are told confidential information that severely compromises their relationship with their clients is most acute in criminal cases. In particular, this raises the "perjury dilemma" (see chapter 9). There are also a number of significant difficulties that can arise in civil cases. Mindful that the duty of confidentiality is only one aspect of lawyers' general duty to their clients and that there are other competing and occasionally higher duties to the courts (see chapter 6), lawyers cannot proceed with "business as usual." For instance, when their clients tell them that they have lied, lawyers cannot engage in any strategy that suggests or is premised on the fact that such a statement is true. Indeed, in some circumstances, it might be incumbent on lawyers to withdraw from the case. However, if they do withdraw, they are still bound to keep confidential any information that the clients have told them (see chapter 5). Also, it is important that, when withdrawing, lawyers do not do anything that will inadvertently reveal confidential information or prejudice the clients' case.

**PROBLEM 30:** You act for a plaintiff in a civil action. At the examination for discovery, your client makes certain statements that are inconsistent with what she had told you previously. Following the discovery, your client tells you that the version she gave under oath on the discovery is false. What do you do? What difference would it make if she told you before the discovery? What would you do if this occurred in the middle of the trial or only after judgment had been given for your client for a substantial amount in damages?

When lawyers do withdraw from cases or files, they should cooperate with the successor lawyer. Nevertheless, any "confidential information not clearly related to the matter" should be disclosed to the new lawyer only with the "express consent" of the clients (see XII, c. 9). On a similar basis, if, in the course of holding public office, lawyers acquire confidential information, official or otherwise, about a person, they may not represent adverse parties in matters where the information could be used to the disadvantage of the person about whom the lawyer has received information (see IV, c. 14).

# F.  CONCLUSION

The duties and responsibilities of lawyers to preserve the confidentiality of their clients' communications are both strict and confusing. Although lawyers are expected to observe a very high degree of confidentiality, it is not always easy to ascertain exactly in what circumstances that obligation arises and what are its limits. Moreover, the ethical and popular pressure to divulge confidences when it is in the public interest is very strong. The highly publicized incidents involving the videotapes in the Paul Bernardo case have brought this complexity to the fore and, in the process, have raised questions about the rationale and range of such a privilege. Moreover, this *cause célèbre* has pointed out the confusion and indecision in the legal profession over the correct course to follow in such circumstances. Nevertheless, lawyers must recognize that, in fulfilling their duty of zealous partisanship to their clients, they will have to impose and defend a strict zone of secrecy around their clients' affairs and communications.

# CHAPTER 8

# CONFLICTS OF INTEREST: SCREENS AND SILENCES

It is imperative that, in entering into professional relationships with clients, lawyers do not act in such a way as to place themselves in a position where the interests of their clients might be taken advantage of or compromised. This is part and parcel of lawyers' overall fiduciary duty and their particular role as a zealous partisan for their clients' interests and affairs; lawyers' professional, economic, and personal interests can undermine their independence and judgment and threaten the integrity of the lawyer-client relationship. However, lawyers have traditionally not been as sensitive as they might to the complex and unanticipated circumstances in which conflicts of interest might arise. While there is little to suggest that lawyers have operated willy-nilly in actual or potential conflict situations, the legal profession did not take such possibilities as seriously as it might have done. However, in recent years, the need to flag and avoid conflict situations has come to the forefront of the profession's attention. Both individually and collectively, lawyers have now become much more attuned to the possibilities of conflict situations arising. Indeed, one might almost conclude that they have become overconcerned, to the extent that the full and reasonable provision of legal services is being adversely affected.

In this chapter I will survey the nature and extent of the prohibitions that have developed around conflicts of interest. There are three situations in which potential conflicts of interest might arise: acting for two parties; acting against former clients; and a clash between the clients' and the lawyers' own interests. Each of these is exacerbated by the recent rise of large law firms in which lawyers are not always sure about the identity, let alone the interests, of many of their colleagues' clients. In each situation, the requirement to avoid conflicts of interest flows both from the duty to be loyal to the client and from the duty of confidentiality. As part of their fiduciary duty to their clients, lawyers must ensure that they avoid potential as well as actual conflicts. While in many cases it will be sufficient to inform clients of potential conflicts and seek their express approval to continue acting as their lawyer, there will be occasions on which lawyers will be expected to withdraw. Unfortunately, the doctrine surrounding conflict situations arose in simpler times and in simpler circumstances than the conditions of contemporary professional practice. Consequently, the doctrinal and ethical challenge is to adapt the basic principles to the more complex problems and possibilities that now arise.

## A. LAWYERS' OWN INTERESTS

The basic rules that frame an actual conflict of interest and what lawyers must do in such situations can be traced back to lawyers' general duty to act as a zealous partisan on behalf of their clients and their interests. As the imposition of a fiduciary on lawyers to their clients suggests, it is essential that clients are able to trust their lawyers. Without an appropriate degree of trust, the professional relationship is severely compromised. In the same way that clients should have no doubt that their lawyers will hold all communications between them in the strictest confidence, so should they be completely assured that their lawyers will not engage in conduct that jeopardizes the clients' interests or otherwise impairs their lawyers' ability to act with only their clients' interests foremost in their minds. It is clearly not in clients' interests to have their lawyers representing other clients who are adverse in interest to them and/or who might benefit from their lawyers' disclosure of confidential information. Also, on the basis of the fiduciary relation between lawyers and clients, lawyers are not to take advantage of or benefit from information that is received from clients, even if it would not disadvantage the clients.

In discussing conflicts of interest, the obvious place to begin is with a sense of what might be considered a conflict. The professional rules insist that lawyers must be "as free as possible from compromising influences," which are characterized as anything that would "affect adversely the lawyer's judgment, advice or loyalty" to the clients, actual or prospective (see V, c. 1 and c. 2). When dealing with a potential conflict of interest between lawyers and their clients, it is important to remember that it is not only the lawyers' personal interests that are to be taken into account but those of associates. For these purposes, "associates" has a wide definition; it includes spouses, children, and relatives "living under the same roof," legal partners, trusts or estates in which the lawyer acts as trustee or has a "substantial beneficial interest," and corporations of which the lawyer is a director or in which the lawyer controls "a significant number of shares" (see VI, c. 3). While the rules are silent on the issue of less formal relationships, lawyers would be wise to disclose any intimate relations they have or had with other lawyers who might have some interest or connection to the file. Also, the prohibitions on lawyer-client conflicts that implicate the personal interests of lawyers stretch to both the financial and the romantic interests of lawyers.[1]

**PROBLEM 31: You run into one of your clients at a social function. You spend the night together. In the morning, she tells you that her company is in real difficulty and needs to get out of its union commitments. You tell her that another one of your clients has become adept at "union-busting" and might be able to help her. Have you done anything that is professionally wrong?**

Indeed, apart from the general admonition, there is ample illustration of the specific circumstances that lawyers must be sure to guard against to avoid conflicts of their personal interests with those of their clients. For instance, lawyers should not enter into debtor-creditor relationships with clients; they should not borrow money from clients (unless that is the client's business); and lawyers should not lend money to clients except when it is to advance clients' expenses in legal matters (see VI, c. 4). Lawyers with interests in joint business ventures may represent the venture against third parties, but not as between the business venture and the joint venturers (see VI, c. 5). Even if they are not normally lawyers' clients, people are to be treated as clients for these purposes if they "reasonably feel entitled to look to lawyers for guidance and advice" in respect of the particular transaction under consideration; the normal lawyer-client fiduciary obligations will apply. In all these situations, lawyers carry the considerable burden of establishing that people with whom they engage in business transactions or exchange proprietary and pecuniary interests are not the kind of people who might reasonably be thought to be "looking to the lawyer for guidance and advice" (see VI, c. 6).

---

1   *Szarfer v. Chodos* (1986), 54 O.R. (2d) 663 (H.C).

In particular, lawyers who wish to enter into business transactions with clients or otherwise exchange proprietary or pecuniary interests are placed under exacting duties (see VI). They must ensure that they fulfill three substantial conditions:

- The transaction must be "fair and reasonable" and its terms must be fully disclosed to clients in writing. In fulfilling their duty to disclose, lawyers must meet a high standard. The courts have treated such a lack of candour as tantamount to evidence of bad faith on lawyers' parts. Mindful that they are in a fiduciary relationship, lawyers will be required to repay all profits to their clients.
- Clients must be advised to take independent legal advice and be given a reasonable opportunity to do so. In particular, if lawyers receive a substantial gift from clients under an instrument drawn up by the lawyer, the common law presumes that undue influence is present and there can be no rebuttal unless the clients had independent and competent legal advice.[2]
- Clients must consent in writing to the transaction. Without such written consent, the transaction will be considered to be in violation of the rules and the client will be entitled to relief.

Lawyers cannot be involved in outside interests, such as business or investment consulting and property management, without making it clear that they are not acting in a professional capacity; this is especially so where the outside interest involves the practice of another profession. Indeed, provincial laws establish to what extent it is possible to be concurrently members of other professions. When involved in legal transactions where they also have personal interests, lawyers must disclose these personal interests and whether they are acting in a personal or a professional capacity (see VII, c. 4). If they are involved in outside interests, they must be careful to make sure they are not doing so as lawyers and that any monies received are deposited only in the lawyers' trust accounts for work done in a professional capacity on behalf of the outside interest (see VII, c. 5). Moreover, where lawyers do have such outside interests, it is supposed to be the kind of undertaking that is compatible with the practice of law, in the sense of being "honourable" by not detracting from the status of the legal profession and not being the type of outside interest that might give rise to a potential conflict of interest between lawyers and clients (see VII, c. 6). However, in reality, there is little that has been sanctioned; lawyers have become rock stars, loan sharks, and muck-raking journalists with impunity.

---

2   *Trusts & Guarantee Co. v. Hart* (1902), 32 S.C.R. 553.

**PROBLEM 32:** An old law school pal and lawyer seeks your assistance. He has entered into a business venture with three non-lawyers who contributed considerable sums to buy into the project; they did not consult lawyers and relied on your friend's legal advice. As chief executive, he has given himself the right to receive an annual bonus whose amount is entirely at his own discretion. He intends to pay himself a very large amount, which will exhaust the venture's resources. He wants to know what is likely to happen. What do you tell him? What would you do if he offered you a share of his bonus on the condition that you defend him against any resulting legal claims?

When lawyers hold public office, they must not let personal interests conflict with their discharge of their official duties. If lawyers also engage in private legal business or hold public office on a part-time basis, they must make sure there will not be conflicts between official and legal duties. However, circumstances will occur in which an unforeseen conflict arises between their public and their private obligation. It is clear that "official duties must prevail" in such situations. Again, the personal interests of lawyers also include the interests of lawyers' relatives, professional associates, partners, and clients (see X, c. 2). Lawyers in public office who foresee potential conflicts of interests must "declare such interests at the earliest opportunity" and must not take any further part in any "consideration, discussion or vote with respect" to such issues (see X, c. 4). However, where it becomes apparent that it will no longer be possible to continue to discharge public duties without becoming entangled in future and unavoidable conflict situations, lawyers must withdraw entirely from such duties (see XII, c. 4).

It has been suggested that lawyers can have a conflict of interest with clients in regard to certain forms of compensation for work done.[3] When lawyers work on an hourly rate of payment, the interests of clients can be diametrically opposed. It is in the interest of lawyers to work the maximum hours possible, whereas it is in the interests of clients for lawyers to work the minimum hours possible. In some circumstances, clients may be better served by lawyers working fewer hours and concentrating on negotiating a settlement, but lawyers may better serve themselves by working more hours and downplaying efforts at settlement. In those situations where work is done on a contingency fee basis, interests may conflict, but in an opposite way: lawyers will want to settle quickly because they will make the same fee regardless of time spent on a case (see chapter 5). Furthermore, because of their superior knowledge and

---

3   G. MacKenzie, *Lawyers and Ethics: Professional Responsibility and Discipline* (Scarborough, Ont.: Carswell, 1993) at 12-4.

experience, lawyers always have a distinct edge over clients in bargaining over the terms of a contingency fee arrangement. In response to the potential conflict of interest in the circumstances and conditions under which contingency fees can be accepted, regulations exist that are designed to protect clients by placing limits on allowable percentages and by conferring on clients the right to have any fees taxed.

**PROBLEM 33: A long-time client brings her elderly and frail father to the office and asks you to draft a new will for him. She insists on staying with her father to help him and ensure that "he gets it right." The father tells you he wants to leave all his estate to your client, who also urges her father to transfer a considerable part of the estate to her now for tax purposes. What do you do?**

# B.  MULTIPLE CLIENTS

Conflicts include the "duties and loyalties" of lawyers (and their partners and professional associates) to any other clients of their own or their law firm's, even those involved in unrelated matters. Because these duties include the "obligation to communicate information," lawyers must make complete disclosure to clients about conflicting interests that exist or are likely to arise (see V, c. 3). Before lawyers can be retained by multiple clients in the same matter, lawyers must inform clients that they have been asked to represent other parties in the matter and that no information will be held confidential between the parties. Lawyers must advise clients that in the event of an unresolvable dispute, lawyers may have to withdraw as counsel of one party or all of them. Lawyers must disclose to clients if there is a pre-existing and continuing relationship with one of the parties, and they should advise other clients to seek "independent representation" (see V, c. 5).

Upon disclosure, lawyers can continue to act for clients who consent (see V, c. 3 and c. 4). In some circumstances, clients may decide it is in their own best interests to retain their original lawyers; they have developed a good relationship with them and rely on their lawyers' understanding of their affairs, which might have developed over a long period of time. As in all of these situations, however, such consent must be informed and unequivocal to be effective: clients must be fully apprised of all relevant concerns and considerations before they can be expected to approve of certain courses of action that might implicate potential conflicts of interest. It is, of course, preferable if that consent is in writing. Whereas the Americans impose a strict standard of informed consent, the English courts have been less rigorous.[4]

---

4    *Clark Boyce v. Mouat*, [1993] 4 All E.R. 268 (P.C.).

The Canadian position is that, while written consent is preferable, it is not essential (see V, c. 5). Nonetheless, even after obtaining consent, lawyers should not act for multiple parties when it is "reasonably obvious" that their interests "will diverge as the matter progresses" (see V, c. 5). For instance, there are some common situations in which lawyers should particularly be on their guard about possible conflicts: co-accuseds in criminal cases, co-plaintiffs in tort cases, insureds and their insurers, parties named as beneficiaries under wills or trusts, and construction lien and bankruptcy claimants.

The most compelling of these situations is where lawyers are asked to represent co-accuseds. The benefits of joint representation include reduced costs for co-accuseds and, especially with regard to "white collar crime," the possibility that one lawyer who represents a large number of people involved will be able to control any investigation better. However, the courts have decided that it is an accused's constitutional right, under section 7 of the *Charter*, to be represented by counsel who is not hamstrung by conflicts of interest.[5] In particular, lawyers should not put accused clients in situations where lawyers might not be able to render effective service to one accused client if the best trial strategy is likely to be an attempt to shift blame to another accused client. While co-accuseds can waive their constitutional right, the courts are reluctant to hold that a defendant did so knowingly and voluntarily. The validity of a waiver "is dependent upon it being clear and unequivocal that the person is waiving the procedural safeguard and is doing so with full knowledge of the rights the procedure was enacted to protect and of the effect the waiver will have on those rights in the process."[6] Accordingly, in the case of criminal co-defendants, lawyers should develop a list of potential conflict matters which could arise and which should be discussed with each client. These might include trial strategy, plea bargaining, and confidentiality.

Lawyers should not advise multiple clients on "contentious issues" that arise between the clients. When these situations arise, they should usually refer both clients to other lawyers. However, providing the parties agreed beforehand, lawyers can continue to work for only one client, while referring the other to another lawyer. If the issue "involves little or no legal advice" and the clients are "sophisticated," the clients "may settle the issue by direct negotiation in which the lawyer does not participate" (see V, c. 6). However, it is permissible for lawyers to arbi-

---

5    *R. v. Silvini* (1991), 5 O.R. (3d) 545 (C.A.).
6    See MacKenzie, above note 3 at 22-2.

trate or settle disputes among multiple clients who submit to such a process (see V, c. 7). Of course, there can be conflicts of interest between parties without there being any contentious dispute; this occurs frequently in real estate transactions between vendors and purchasers or between mortgagors and mortgagees. In such situations, lawyers should advise their clients that it is advisable to obtain separate representation (see V, c. 10). Provided that there has been full disclosure, clients can agree to be represented by the same lawyer. However, where lawyers are asked to represent multiple parties in a transaction where it appears that they have similar interests, a conflict may still exist or arise. For example, co-purchasers of real property and persons forming a partnership or corporation might begin with shared and unopposed interests, but matters might arise and information be forthcoming that warrant a reconsideration. In such circumstances, notwithstanding earlier consent, lawyers are obliged to reopen the conflicting questions with their clients (see V, c. 11 and cc. 4–5). It is more common for lawyers to represent multiple parties in transactions than in litigation. Litigation is much less predictable, and it is less disruptive to engage another lawyer in the middle of a transaction than a trial.[7]

Whenever disputes take shape over conflict problems, the burden lies squarely on lawyers to prove that they acted in "good faith," that there was "adequate disclosure," and that the clients' consent was obtained (see V, c. 13). In making any decision as to whether to act on behalf of multiple parties to a transaction, lawyers would be well advised to consider three interrelated issues:[8]

- What is the kind of relationship that exists between the clients? When parties have an established and continuing relationship, it is often in both their best interests to try to resolve disputes, and the arrangement of a shared lawyer might facilitate a mutually satisfactory outcome.
- What are the strategic interests of the clients? If it is the kind of situation in which each of the parties stands only to gain at the other's expense, it is unlikely that joint representation will be in the interests of either party. However, if both parties stand to gain by cooperation and compromise, it is likely that sharing the same lawyer will increase the likelihood of avoiding a protracted wrangle.

7   C.W. Wolfram, *Modern Legal Ethics* (St. Paul, Minn.: West Pub. Co., 1986) at 356–57.
8   *Korponey v. Canada (A.G.)*, [1982] 1 S.C.R. 41 at 49, and *R. v. Clarkson*, [1986] 1 S.C.R. 383 at 394.

- What are the nature of the services to be performed? There is less chance of conflicts of interest arising when lawyers are asked only for legal advice so that the parties can inform themselves and seek to resolve the problem themselves. It will, of course, be a different matter if lawyers are asked to take an active role in helping parties manoeuvre for a dominant position.

If parties with coinciding interests are involved in litigation in which they are included as adverse parties for purely formal reasons, it is acceptable for lawyers to represent both parties. However, lawyers can only represent both spouses in an uncontested divorce if all matters concerning custody, access, maintenance, and the division of the parties' property were previously settled by negotiation or litigation in which each party had independent legal representation. Furthermore, when co-parties consent (after adequate disclosure) to representation by the same lawyer, that lawyer may be disqualified only in the event of an actual conflict rather than a potential one. For instance, in an inquest into a fatal police shooting, a lawyer was disqualified from acting on behalf of the Metropolitan Toronto Police Services Board and the five officers involved in the shooting, even though he had the consent of all co-parties, because the coroner ruled that there was a conflict of interest.[9] Acting on behalf of both employers and employees listed as co-defendants may give rise to the same concerns.

**PROBLEM 34: A corporate client that you represent is being sued for nuisance for polluting the surrounding water supply at one of its plants. The likely cause of the pollution is the failure of the site manager to follow the designated disposal procedures. The manager is a sizeable shareholder in the company and a client of your firm, but not one of your clients. What course should you and the firm follow?**

Finally, conflicts can arise when one client's case requires the lawyer to argue a certain point of law, which, if accepted, would have an adverse impact on the interests of the lawyer's other client in a different case. Even in such circumstances, lawyers must disclose such possibilities to their clients and continue only if they obtain informed consent. However, no professional problem is involved in lawyers arguing different sides on a point of law from case to case. While it might detract from the lawyer's argument to be arguing one side of a doctrinal problem in the morning and the other side in the afternoon, there is no professional

---

9    *Booth v. Ontario (Coroner) (sub nom. Booth v. Huxter)* (1994), 16 O.R. (3d) 528 (Div. Ct.).

problem, as it is for the courts, not the lawyer, to decide what is the applicable law. In such circumstances, lawyers must be especially careful to ensure that they have brought all relevant authorities before the court on both occasions. To do otherwise would put them in breach of their overriding obligation to the courts (see chapter 6).

## C. FORMER CLIENTS' INTERESTS

One of the most difficult conflict situations that arises concerns the circumstances, if any, in which lawyers or their law firms can act against former clients. Lawyers who have represented clients in one matter should not act against them "in the same or any related matter." This restriction applies to situations in which they are required to take a stance where they might "be tempted to breach the Rule relating to confidential information." Lawyers may act against former clients in "fresh and independent matters wholly unrelated" to any previous work (see V, c. 8). As usual, "clients" will include clients of the law firm (even where lawyers have never handled clients' affairs) and those clients of other lawyers associated with the first group of lawyers, where there is an appearance of practising in partnership or association, even where no such arrangement may actually exist (see V, c. 9). Also, the conflict rules kick in with regard to those people for whom, after a brief consultation, lawyers decline to act on their behalf. In one case, a firm was disqualified from acting on a defendant's behalf because a lawyer in the firm had held a ten-minute consultation with the plaintiff before litigation, even though the lawyer involved swore that no confidential information had passed between them.[10]

These rules are not simply specific to a particular transaction but can have a continuing impact. For instance, if a lawyer has represented a borrower, it is unacceptable to represent a lender in future dealings with the borrower because confidential information about the borrower's financial position might have been divulged. This duty is triggered not by actual evidence of conflict, but by the possibility of conflict. A particular difficulty is that it is not always obvious that there might be a conflict; lawyers might not be aware of certain information that would trigger the awareness of a conflict. However, there is a very strong duty on lawyers to take all reasonable steps to ensure that no

---

10   *Popowich v. Saskatchewan*, [1995] 6 W.W.R. 314 (Sask. Q.B.), reversed on other grounds [1996] 1 W.W.R. 215.

conflict arises. Indeed, in most situations that give rise to conflicts of interest, lawyers will carry a heavy burden of responsibility as compared with their clients.

In many conflict situations, a number of competing values are in play: maintaining the integrity of the legal profession and justice system such that clients and the public at large will have confidence that they operate to the highest levels of professional probity; ensuring that clients can have the widest possible choice and discretion in selecting lawyers to represent them such that they are not deprived of their chosen lawyer without very good cause; and facilitating the mobility of the legal profession such that lawyers are not unduly hampered in their ability to advance their careers or to practise where and with whom they want. The thrust of these policy arguments in conflict situations is neither clear nor decisive. While it is crucial to ensure that conflicts and the resulting dissemination of confidential information do not occur, it is also important not to place too onerous a restriction on clients in their choice of lawyers, or lawyers in their choice of practice. The injustice and disruption caused by genuine conflicts do not always outweigh the expense and inconvenience to clients and lawyers, especially when the action or dealing is well advanced.

In recent years, the rise of megafirms has tended to exacerbate some of these already difficult conflict problems. Indeed, in the past couple of decades, law firms have become so large that all the common problems of large-scale bureaucracies have surfaced. Most significant in this area is the general complaint that the right hand not only does not know what the left hand is doing but might not actually be aware of the existence of certain digits on the left hand. Although the solution is to create greater and better incentives for law firms to improve their overall administration and coordination of firm activities, the professional rules are still predominantly premised on the understanding that the avoidance of conflict problems (and almost all other ethical and professional challenges) is the responsibility of individual lawyers. Nevertheless, while there has been a significant trend towards larger firms, the majority of lawyers still practise in partnerships of ten or less. Indeed, outside metropolitan areas, the vast bulk of lawyers are so employed.

Whether in small or large partnerships, the Canadian legal profession has begun to take much more seriously the problems that might and do arise in situations where there are conflicting interests between lawyers and their former clients. In particular, there have been numerous cases that have involved motions to remove the opposing party's lawyers from the record on the ground that those lawyers had earlier acted for the moving party. Since the late 1960s, two divergent lines of authority emerged to deal with these situations. One line developed and applied a narrow "probability of real mischief" test which required that real conflict and prejudice would almost certainly occur if the lawyer was allowed to continue to take part in transaction or litigation. Another line of authority opted for a broader test in which it had only to be demonstrated that there was a "possibility of prejudice" or "appearance of impropriety" in order for the lawyer to be removed. Whereas the former led to few lawyers being removed from the record, the latter more readily led to the disqualification of lawyers on the basis of conflict of interest.

## D. THE MARTIN CASE

In 1990 the Supreme Court of Canada was presented with the opportunity to provide an authoritative determination of the applicable standard in the case of *MacDonald Estate* v. *Martin*.[11] The facts of the case were typical of much modern legal practice. Martin retained law firm A to represent him in an accounting action against Gray, who was represented by law firm B. Kristen, a young lawyer, worked extensively on Martin's file with a senior partner: she was privy to many confidences disclosed by Martin. A couple of years later, Kristen moved to law firm C, which another two years later merged with law firm B. After her move to law firm B, Kristen had no involvement with Gray's file, though the dispute with Martin was still continuing. Martin's new counsel brought an application to have law firm B removed as lawyers for Gray. Kristen and senior members of law firm B filed sworn statements that no discussions had or would take place between Kristen and firm members in respect to the Martin/Gray case. While the trial court initially granted the application to have the lawyer and her law firm removed from the record, the Manitoba Court of Appeal reversed that decision.

The Supreme Court of Canada was unanimous in supporting Martin's application to have law firm B removed, but divided 4 to 3 in its reasoning. The leading judgment of the Supreme Court was given by Sopinka J. After a thorough review of American and Commonwealth jurisprudence, he contended that, because proof of prejudice will not be readily available, the "probability of mischief" test was insufficiently demanding. Instead, he concluded that a disqualifying conflict of interest would arise where a reasonably informed person would be satisfied that use of confidential information would occur. It is a demanding test.

---

11   *MacDonald Estate v. Martin*, [1990] 3 S.C.R. 1235.

Once lawyers have received confidential information in a lawyer-client relationship and that information is relevant to the matter at hand, lawyers are in a conflict if there is a risk that it will be used to the prejudice of that former client:

> In my opinion, once it is shown by the client that there existed a previous relationship that is sufficiently related to the retainer from which it is sought to remove the solicitor, the court should infer that the confidential information was imparted unless the solicitor satisfies the court that no information was imparted which could be relevant. This will be a difficult burden to discharge. Not only must the court's degree of satisfaction be such that it would withstand the scrutiny of the reasonably informed member of the public that no such information passed, but the burden must be discharged without revealing the specifics of the privileged communication. Nonetheless, I am of the opinion that the door should not be shut completely on a solicitor who wishes to discharge this heavy burden.[12]

Once it has been determined that the lawyer did receive confidential information, it is automatic that the lawyer cannot act against the former client: no guarantee that the information will not be so used is valid or acceptable. This is the case because the lawyer might well be dissuaded from using information legitimately acquired in order to prevent the appearance of indiscretion in the preservation of confidential information and also because the former client would always feel at a disadvantage in the transaction or litigation. In the particular circumstances of *Martin*, Sopinka decided that, as the junior lawyer had actively worked on the very case on which her new firm was acting against the former client, she was ineligible to be involved in the case. Furthermore, he also held that the law firm was in conflict, as insufficient steps had been taken to rebut the strong inference that confidential information had or might be disclosed (see below).

Although Sopinka's test has a certain general appeal, its problems arise from the fact that Sopinka seems to have based his approach on the unrealistic assumption that legal practice throughout Canada is carried on under similar circumstances and arrangements. As I have argued, the professional practice of Canadian lawyers is characterized by its diversity in both organization and operation (see chapter 3). Indeed, against this background, it has been suggested that Sopinka's test is both too strict and not strict enough. It is too strict in that clients

---

12   *Ibid.* at 1260–61.

in small communities might be precluded from having the lawyer of their choice and be effectively obliged to have a lawyer who, all things considered, they would prefer not to have. Also, the mobility of young lawyers would be seriously hampered, and the viability of law firm mergers could be severely compromised.

Conversely, others have insisted that Sopinka's test is not strict enough because lawyers can too easily arrange their affairs in such a way as to get around potential conflict situations. In response to this possibility, Cory J. advocated a much stricter test in his dissenting opinion on behalf of the minority. Where a lawyer actually receives confidential information and later joins another law firm that is acting for those opposing the interests of the former client, an irrebutable presumption that lawyers who work together will share confidential information is triggered: "[T]o those who are not members of the legal profession, it must appear that the opportunities for private discussion are so numerous that the disclosure of confidential information, even if completely inadvertent, would be inevitable."[13] However, the strictness of Cory's approach raises almost as many problems as it seeks to resolve. For instance, any client who is obliged to change lawyers will suffer considerable financial loss, be delayed in pursuing the case, and lose the benefit of the lawyer's experience and knowledge of his or her affairs. In a contemporary world of mega-mergers, Cory may have allowed his zeal for protecting clients to blind him to the adverse effect it might have on those very same clients: he throws the vulnerable baby of client choice out with the unethical bathwater of conflicts.

In his leading opinion in *Martin*, Sopinka J. went to considerable pains to answer the pressing and significant question of what are the circumstances in which a lawyer's colleagues and associates in the law firm will be disqualified from representing clients against the former client of that lawyer. Unlike the actual lawyer previously retained, Sopinka did not believe that disqualification of other lawyers should be automatic once it was shown that there was confidential information at risk. However, more was required than a simple affidavit by lawyers declaring that no disclosure had occurred. After drawing attention to the changing face of the legal profession in terms of the tendency to larger and larger firms, he concluded that it was less clear whether automatic disqualification should follow:

---

13   *Ibid.* at 1266–67.

I am not convinced that a reasonable member of the public would necessarily conclude that confidences are likely to be disclosed in every
case despite institutional efforts to prevent it. There is, however, a
strong inference that lawyers who work together share confidences. In
answering this question, the court should therefore draw the inference, unless satisfied on clear and convincing evidence, that all reasonable measures have been taken to ensure that no disclosure will
occur by the "tainted" lawyer to the member or members of the firm
who are engaged against the former client. Such reasonable measures
would include institutional mechanisms such as Chinese Walls and
cones of silence.[14]

This *Martin* presumption is very difficult to rebut because lawyers
must not only show that no information was disclosed in the previous
matter that would be relevant in the current matter but do so without
divulging to the court any confidential information that was received in
the former case. In order to satisfy their burden, lawyers must effectively
prove beyond a reasonable doubt that no relevant confidential information was exchanged. On the facts of *Martin*, Sopinka came to the decision that, while there was no reason to doubt the sworn statements by
the participants that no confidential information had been disclosed,
insufficient measures had been taken to rebut the strong inference of
disclosure. No general process of screening had been implemented by
the firm, and there was no evidence that potential dangers or difficulties
had been brought to the new lawyer's attention when she joined the
firm. Accordingly, Sopinka J. held that no member of the law firm as
well as the particular lawyer herself could avoid a conflict situation and,
therefore, could not take any further part in the matter.

Mindful that the rule prohibiting lawyers from acting against former
clients is for the protection of the interests of both the current and the
previous clients, clients will be denied the opportunity of disqualifying
former lawyers who had acted on their behalf in related matters if there
is an unreasonable delay in bringing such motions. In one case, two
years' delay after the realization that there was a potential conflict was
held to amount to acquiescence.[15]

---

14   *Ibid.* at 1262. These are general terms used to refer to any device that is intended to
     prevent communications among members of an organization.
15   *Ramsbottom v. Morning* (1991), 48 C.P.C. (2d) 177 (Ont. Gen. Div.).

PROBLEM 35: You have recently joined a large metropolitan firm of lawyers. Before that, you worked at a local small firm for a couple of years. You discover that your new firm is engaged in litigation with clients of your previous firm. While you did not work on their file, you know they were clients when you were there. What should you do? Would or should it make any difference if you had moved from a large to a small firm?

The majority and minority judgments were both unpersuaded by assurances that confidential information had not been disclosed. The majority held that the presumption that a lawyer would share confidential information could be rebutted if the firm could show that successful measures, such as "Chinese walls" or "cones of silence," were taken to isolate the lawyer. Indeed, in an unusual step, Sopinka J. called on the Canadian Bar Association and provincial law societies to develop effective screening devices to be used as national standards. In response, the CBA made several recommendations for physical (e.g., office location and file access) and non-physical (e.g., written policies and sworn undertakings) screening mechanisms in both litigious and non-litigious matters.[16] As well as giving paramount weight to the value of maintaining integrity in the profession and the legal system, the CBA was alert to the possibility that too strict an approach might encourage lawyers to use disqualification as a tactical weapon and thereby deprive some clients unfairly of their chosen lawyer or law firm. Mindful that the public interest must be put above the private interests of lawyers, the CBA concluded that the desire to guard against the possibility of impropriety should not become so single-minded as to ignore the adverse effects of a preventative regimen that is too harsh.

In light of these concerns, the CBA made several recommendations about the kind of screening mechanisms that law firms should implement. In all, the CBA proposed thirteen guidelines that law firms might follow in developing appropriate schemes. Of these, three were considered absolutely essential to the viability and efficacy of any screening process:

- the screened lawyer should not participate in the current representation;
- the screened lawyer should not disclose confidential information relating to the prior representation; and

---

16  Canadian Bar Association, *Conflict of Interest Disqualification: Martin v. Gray and Screening Methods: Report of the Canadian Bar Association Task Force on Conflict of Interest* (Ottawa: The Association, 1993). In response to these recommendations, a special committee of the Federation of Law Societies drafted a new rule that has been adopted in Ontario and is under consideration by other provinces.

- no member of the new law firm should disclose confidential information relating to the current matter or the prior representation with the screened lawyer.

Other guidelines included the need to inform current and former clients of the measures adopted to provide adequate protection of everyone's interests and to take efforts to obtain the former client's consent to the new firm's representation. Also, law firms are urged to pay attention to the administrative steps that need to be taken to monitor the effectiveness of such screening measures. While the CBA's recommendations are not without merit, they do little more than restate the goal to be achieved rather than provide concrete suggestions of the means to be employed; this is particularly the case with the three guidelines that are designated as essential. Also, little attention is paid to the difficult matter of what steps are to be taken to discover whether conflict situations have or will occur: it is one thing to respond to a conflict situation when it arises, but entirely another matter to identify conflict situations before they occur.

## E. THIRD PARTIES' INTERESTS

Canadian rules of conduct have not yet fully explored the conflicts of interest arising out of legal relationships with non-clients. One example of such a conflict would involve lawyers being retained by clients who are acting on behalf of mentally incompetent individuals or others . Lawyers have a duty to the clients who retain them, but it is unclear how to define the nature of the duty owed to the third party in such cases. One situation that commonly arises is when lawyers' fees will be paid by non-clients. For example, parents will often take responsibility for fees incurred for work for their children, and employers may reimburse lawyers for legal expenses done on behalf of their employees. However, lawyers must make sure that they protect the interests of their clients to the exclusion of all others, including those non-clients who pay their fees. Also, in class actions, there is potential for conflicts of interest between class representatives and other class members. In the event of subclasses with conflicting interests, different lawyers should act on behalf of each subclass. In class actions, conflicts between lawyers and clients over compensation may develop and, again, the onus is on lawyers to keep their clients (and others who might erroneously perceive that lawyers are acting on their behalf) fully aware of potential and actual conflicts that might arise.

One set of circumstances that can often give rise to potential and actual conflicts of interest is when there are claims under an insurance policy. The existence and terms of liability insurance policies can often conflict with the interests of lawyers and their clients. For instance, lawyers must be sensitive to the possibility that, if the amount of any claim is in excess of policy limits, it might be in the best interests of the insurer to reject a settlement offer, but in the best interests of the clients to settle at that time and for the amount offered. Under most policies, the insurer has the right to determine the nature and force of any defence argued and, most important, to decide on what terms a settlement of the insured's claim might occur. Obviously, lawyers must not represent the insured, if they are retained by the insurer and involved in planning a defence on behalf of the insurer against the insured's claims under the insurance contract. When insurers know of reasons to deny coverage, it is incumbent on lawyers in any communications with the insured to give a clear and explicit warning that information in this matter cannot be maintained as confidential. In particular, lawyers should not disclose in such circumstances that they are working in the interests of the insurer. While insurers must defend the insured's claims, they do not have to provide coverage. Consequently, if an insurer disputes coverage, a conflict of interest will arise and the insured can retain independent counsel at the insurer's expense. Finally, if an insured client is a defendant and is related to the plaintiff, lawyers must advise them against colluding with the plaintiff at the considerable risk of the client losing insurance protection.[17]

## F. CONCLUSION

Few issues of ethical and professional responsibility have become as troublesome as conflicts of interest. This is particularly the case with situations that involve acting against former clients. However, when all is said and done, the Supreme Court has made more of a meal out of the problem of whether lawyers can ever act against former clients than was necessary. The professional rules make it reasonably clear that lawyers must avoid not only actual and potential conflicts of interest, but also situations that might create the appearance of jeopardizing the duty of confidentiality to their clients. Accordingly, it is incumbent on lawyers not to put themselves in situations where they might be obliged to do

---

17 See MacKenzie, above note 3 at 5-14.

just that. In particular, this means that lawyers have a clear professional responsibility not to move to law firms against which they are currently litigating. Also, mergers of law firms should involve the abandonment of conflicting files. Either way, it seems vitally important that the burden of discontinuance should not fall entirely on the shoulders of the discontinued firm's client.[18] The control and avoidance of conflicts ought not to be at the expense of client choice. After all, conflict rules are intended to benefit clients, not penalize them.

---

18   H.P. Glenn, *MacDonald Estate v. Martin*, "Case Comment" (1991) 70 Canadian Bar Rev. 351 at 358.

# CRIMINAL LAWYERS: PUTTING UP A DEFENCE

If the legal profession at large suffers from bad press, the criminal bar is in a dire predicament. Indeed, the theory and practice of legal ethics in criminal defence lawyering are seen by many to present in its worst light the professional ethic that permits lawyers, as John Stuart Mill put it, to "frustrate with their tongues." These general concerns usually crystallize in the most pressing question that criminal lawyers have to face: "How can you defend someone whom you know to be guilty?" While many criminal lawyers have become inured to the issue and its implicit moral censure, the question is still an important one and needs to be addressed squarely. However, when unpacked, there is not really one question that criminal lawyers must face, but three separate questions that demand very different responses. The first question, "How *can* you defend someone whom you know to be guilty?" speaks to the broad moral question of criminal lawyers being party to criminals going free and being at large to commit further crimes. The second question, "How can *you* defend someone whom you know to be guilty?" addresses the issue of why a particular individual chooses to commit his or her professional life to criminal defence work. And the third question, "How can you *defend* someone whom you know to be guilty?" goes to the methods and tactics that criminal lawyers can legitimately use to defend those people whom they believe to be guilty.

In this chapter, I intend to provide a framework within which to develop answers to these difficult questions. As usual, those answers are not always obvious or universal. In the first section, I introduce the basic challenge that criminal lawyers face and analyze the different and not-so-different circumstances under which they operate. The second section examines the duties and responsibilities of criminal lawyers and sets the scene for understanding the limits that might be placed on those duties. In the third section, I explore how far criminal lawyers can or might go in arguing a defence for their clients. The fourth section concentrates on the thorny issue of the limits that exist around raising a "false defence" and, in particular, the problem of what to do when lawyers believe that their clients are going to or have committed perjury. In the fifth section, I canvass the different role of prosecuting counsel and inquire into the ethical responsibilities that this involves. Finally, I look to the interesting ethical challenges for defence and prosecution lawyers in engaging in the common practice of plea bargaining.

## A. THE CRIMINAL LAWYER

The ethical history of criminal lawyering is populated by a cast of colourful characters. At one end of the spectrum lies the ennobled image of Clarence Darrow and, at the other, are the more dubious personas of contemporary figures such as Johnnie Cochrane and F. Lee Bailey. The public have a love-hate relationship with defence lawyers. While as a group they tend to be the butt of much criticism, individual lawyers seem to be championed by those who have benefited from their services. There is a tendency to associate defence lawyers with their accused clients, and so impute quasi-criminal behaviour or unsavoury character onto defence counsel. As one popular critic observed, there is "a post-Simpson belief that defence lawyers are little more than flamboyant actors delivering an incredible narrative to a gullible audience." This ambivalence about the role and function of criminal lawyers extends to much of the legal profession, who tend to look down on them as being engaged in a grubbier existence than the other branches of professional practice. Nevertheless, criminal lawyers fulfill a crucial role in the legal process. Their mixed reputation is simply the price to be paid in pursuing their chosen style of practice.

Of course, there are probably as many reasons for becoming a criminal lawyer as there are criminal lawyers. However, for present purposes, they can be reduced to stock characters.[1] Each of them can help us to

---

1   These are freely adapted from B.A. Babcock, "Defending the Guilty" (1983) 32 Cleveland St. L. Rev. 175.

understand something about criminal lawyers themselves as well as the different rationales for why it is ethically acceptable to defend the guilty.

- *The Garbage Collectors*: The basic credo of these figures is that "it is a dirty job, but someone has to do it." Although it needs no more rationale than that, these criminal lawyers occasionally resort to the grander theme that, by protecting criminals, people are protecting themselves: one day you might be the one caught up in the criminal process and you will be more than grateful that such bottom-dwellers exist.

- *The Legalist*: Something of a world-weary cynic, these figures maintain that there is no truth and that all facts are contingent and indeterminate; it is simply the luck of the draw as to who gets charged and convicted. By way of rationale, they insist that it is not the duty of lawyers to establish the facts; this is the official task of judges. Moreover, criminal trials are about legal guilt, not moral culpability. It is better that ten guilty people go free than one innocent person be found guilty.

- *The Che Guevara*: Driven by a political passion, these figures believe that most criminals are themselves victims, whether as members of particular groups (e.g., oppressed minorities) or as individuals (e.g., battered women). Moreover, the conditions of imprisonment are themselves so indefensible and horrible that lawyers perform important political work when they prevent more people being damaged further by such shameful conditions. Righting wrongs, they are bent upon protecting the besieged individual against the ravages of a tyrannical state.

- *The Mother Teresa*: These figures are committed to presenting a more caring face of the legal process and society. They contend that, being largely from disadvantaged social classes, accused persons will benefit from having a defender who will treat them with respect and demonstrate that the community does care about their plight. This will be rehabilitative, whatever the outcome of the case. If the Che Guevara lawyer is driven by rage and indignation, the social worker is inspired by a sustaining belief in the underlying virtue of the legal process.

- *The Show-Boater*: For these colourful figures, the name of the game is personal excitement, not social mission. Criminal work is considered way more dramatic than other run-of-the-mill legal work. Lawyers get a buzz from their involvement in such a high-stakes game and get to be in the action sooner than in other forms of litigation. And, most important, they occasionally win against the odds and bask in the reflected glory of their achievements — celebrity is the ultimate prize.

Whatever the particular reason professionals have for becoming criminal lawyers, they fulfill an important social function. Unlike many other lawyers, they are frequently asked how they can do what they do: "How can you devote your considerable talents and energies to the cause of many undeserving people when there are so many other opportunities to do good in the world?" Isn't there a deeper duty to society to see that justice is done? Most lawyers develop an indifference to whether their clients are guilty or not and take refuge in the professional pleasure of a job well done. Others point out that the criminal justice system is flawed and geared towards the bureaucratic processing of guilty pleas, so the real question is less "Why do you represent the guilty?" than "Why don't *you* defend the guilty?" In the words of Lord Eldon, criminal defence lawyers are seen to be the ultimate servants of a free society who "lend [their] exertions to all, [themselves] to none. The result of the cause is to [them] a matter of indifference."[2]

At the root of this popular challenge to criminal lawyers is the foundational assumption that criminal trials are about truth, and that lawyers' professional efforts tend to obscure the search for truth rather than facilitate it; criminal lawyers are more devoted to criminals than to the law. The best response is that, while prosecutors have a duty to ensure that the truth is exposed in court, defence counsel have no such duty. The constraints and requirements of "role morality" have their greatest salience in this area (see chapter 3). It is argued that criminal lawyers have a very different mission from uncovering the truth; they are committed to doing all they can to ensure that their accused client is acquitted and that the state does not exercise its considerable powers of punishment without respecting the rights of those it proceeds against. It is contended, therefore, that it is not truth that is the heart of the criminal trial, but the broader and more nuanced question of when the power of the state can be used to punish people for their actions. Consequently, while there might be a general public concern with whether the accused "did it," the focus of defence lawyers must be more limited and fixed on the legal guilt of their accused clients. In an adversarial system, each accused person is entitled to have his or her own champion whose loyalty is to the cause of the accused and to no one else. Nevertheless, the fact that an accused person is entitled to as strong a defence as possible does not translate into an invitation to counsel to do anything and everything to avoid conviction. As Simon puts it, there is a very important dif-

---

2    *Ex. parte Lloyd* (1822), Mont. 70n. at 72 [noted in the case of *Ex. parte Elsee* (1830), Mont. 69].

ference between "as good an opportunity to prove one's innocence (and to vindicate one's intrinsically valuable procedural rights) and the quite different notion of as good an opportunity to escape conviction."[3]

Accordingly, the responsibility of criminal defence lawyers is specific and specialized: they must take all possible steps to raise a reasonable doubt about the client's innocence. Many rights are given to the accused that are independent of their guilt or innocence, and it is for defence lawyers to ensure those rights are respected. In line with such a responsibility, the critical challenge is to establish what the ethical limits are on the methods and strategies that can be used to achieve that goal. This inquiry is particularly pointed when the client's goals are inconsistent with the truth. Defining the limits on what lawyers can and should do in such circumstances is at the heart of this chapter: Can defence lawyers undermine the credibility of Crown witnesses who are likely telling the truth? Can they object to the admissibility of evidence that they think is probably truthful? Can they raise alternative explanations for the alleged crime when they have little faith in their veracity? Can they allow their clients to commit perjury? In each of these situations, all lawyers should be careful not to assume that if they can, they should. There is a very important ethical distinction between what others might consider acceptable and whether you yourself should engage in such conduct. Because you can do something does not mean that you should or must do it.

It is for each lawyer to determine what it is he or she will and will not do in defending clients accused of criminal behaviour. The essence of what it means to act as an ethical professional is not to be found in unthinking imitation of customary practices; ethical lawyers will develop a mode of practice on which they have critically reflected and for which they are willing to take personal responsibility. It is incumbent on any lawyer to establish such limits in accordance with the relevant professional rules. Nevertheless, such codes offer only general advice and mark the absolute limit of what can be done in the name of defending one's client. Moreover, criminal lawyers who wish to deviate from the customary practices of the profession have the very clear duty to ensure that their clients are aware of their personal approach to lawyering. It would be grossly unfair for lawyers to spring on clients at trial that they were not prepared to take certain steps in their defence. Accordingly, the importance of an initial interview with the client in

---

3   W.H. Simon, *The Practice of Justice: A Theory of Lawyers' Ethics* (Cambridge, Mass.: Harvard University Press, 1998) at 181.

which both the lawyer and the client share their expectations and concerns — about confidentiality, trial tactics, cross-examination techniques, and the like — cannot be emphasized enough as the basic building block of any ethical approach to legal practice.

Before proceeding to examine the duties of criminal lawyers and the limits that might be placed on their exercise, it is worth mentioning again the significance of the decision to take someone on as a client. As explained, the traditional line on client selection is that lawyers are neither under any obligation to take unpopular cases nor ethically compromised by the moral (un)worthiness of their clients' causes (see chapter 5). However, for many criminal lawyers, it is a matter of principle that they should accept all requests for legal assistance, no matter how unpopular or unjust, because any other course would deprive people of their rights and usurp the function of the jury or judge. Under the Rules, lawyers should not exercise the right to decline employment "if the probable result would be to make it very difficult for a person to obtain legal advice or representation." Furthermore, lawyers should not decline simply because the "cause is unpopular or notorious," "powerful interests or allegations of misconduct and malfeasance are involved," or they have a "private opinion about the guilt of the accused" (see XIV, c. 6). Also, if lawyers do refuse to accept someone as a client, they have an obligation to assist that person to find the services of another competent lawyer (see XIV, c. 4).

However, while the need to ensure that all persons receive adequate legal representation is a compelling systemic imperative, it does not follow that it must be a personal injunction for all criminal lawyers. There is no irresistible reason why the lawyer who provides legal assistance has to be you. As well as being affected in their choice of clients by their area of expertise and the clients' ability to pay, criminal lawyers are entitled to represent only those clients or causes that they are prepared to justify as being more rather than less beneficial for society. Because there might be all manner of reasons why particular lawyers are prepared to defend particular accused persons, this allows lawyers a wide range of choice, as long as they are willing to accept personal responsibility for that choice and to justify it, at least to themselves. Of course, this recommendation should not be seen to suggest that lawyers should be taken as endorsing their client's case or cause; it is only intended to speak to their ethical responsibility for the work they do.

PROBLEM 36: You are asked to represent persons who are charged with a serious assault. Although you have strong reason to believe they are guilty of the offence charged and of other even more serious offences, there is a "technicality" readily available to help them escape a prison term. Do you accept the case?

PROBLEM 37: You have been a regular supporter of the pro-life/pro-choice cause for several years and have donated (anonymously) significant money to its fund-raising campaigns. You are asked to defend a person who is accused of a serious offence in relation to an assault on a leader of your favoured cause. What would you do? Why?

# B. DUTIES AND LIMITS

Criminal lawyers are subject to exactly the same duties and responsibilities as any other lawyers. In general, it is the duty of defence lawyers to do all they can to seek an acquittal for their clients by "fair and honourable means, without illegality," and, in doing so, they treat the court with "candour, fairness, courtesy and respect" (see IX, c. 1). This general injunction pulls in a number of different directions and places a considerable burden on defence counsel to ensure that they are all taken seriously: they have to juggle the competing obligations to their clients, the courts, and the profession generally. However, because the circumstances in which they operate are significantly different from those of other lawyers, they have a different attitude and approach to the practice of criminal law. The balance between their various obligations takes on a different character and tilt. The dominant duty, to which the others function as limits, is well expressed by Lord Reid, who said that advocates are expected "fearlessly to raise every issue, advance every argument, and ask every question . . . which [they think] will help [their clients'] case" and "to obtain for [their] clients the benefit of any and every remedy and defence which is authorized by law."[4]

In seeking a viable path through this thicket of competing obligations, the professional Rules offer considerable guidance. While the list of permitted and prohibited conduct is intended to apply to all lawyers, the following guidelines have particular relevance for the criminal lawyer:

- Lawyers must not "knowingly" assist clients to do anything they consider to be "dishonest or dishonourable" (see IX, c. 2(b)).
- Lawyers must not "knowingly" assist in any fraud, crime, or illegal conduct in dealing with the court (see IX, c. 2(e)). It amounts to the criminal offence of perjury for lawyers to counsel false evidence (see *Criminal Code*, ss. 22 and 120).

---

4   *Rondel v. Worsley*, [1969] 1 A.C. 191 (H.L.(E.)) at 227; *Canadian Bar Association Code of Professional Conduct* (Ottawa, Ont.: Canadian Bar Association, 1988) at chapter 9, commentary 1.

- Lawyers can interview "any potential [Crown] witnesses" whether under subpoena or not, provided that they disclose their identity and interest. Where those persons are legally represented, the consent of their lawyers is required (see IX, c. 6).
- Lawyers should "never waive or abandon" their clients' legal rights without the clients' "informed consent." This means that all possible defences should be fully considered and brought to the attention of clients (see IX, c. 7).
- Lawyers must not assist, encourage, or instruct their clients to commit crimes or other illegal conduct. At all times, they "should be on guard against becoming the tool or dupe of an unscrupulous client" (see III, c. 7).
- Lawyers may disclose confidential information if they have a reasonable belief "that a crime is likely to be committed," but disclosure becomes mandatory only if the "anticipated crime is one involving violence" (see IV, c. 11). This duty to disclose is also triggered when a lawyer develops a reasonable belief that "a dangerous situation is likely to develop at a court facility." In such a situation, a lawyer is to inform those responsible for security, and is supposed to "suggest solutions" to deal with the problem (see IV, c. 12).
- Lawyers "shall not stand bail" for an accused client, unless there is a "family relationship," in which case lawyers should not represent the accused person (see XIX, c. 9).
- Lawyers should be "courteous and civil to the court" and their adversaries in all proceedings. While rude and disruptive behaviour might not amount to contempt of court, it can still be grounds for disciplinary action (see IX, c. 14).
- Lawyers must advocate their clients' cases "within the limits of the law" and, if clients insist on courses of action that would "breach" the rule, lawyers should withdraw from the case (see IX, c. 4).
- Lawyers must follow local rules governing communication with witnesses. However, it is considered "improper" for lawyers to communicate with their witnesses while they are being cross-examined (except by leave of the court) (see IX, c. 16).
- Lawyers should not advise, threaten, or bring about a criminal prosecution "to secure a civil advantage for the client" and, conversely, should not "procure the withdrawal of a prosecution" in return for money or property (see III, c. 9).

PROBLEM 38: As a junior lawyer in a large firm, you are assigned to the file of a national chemical corporation. After extensive research, you reach the conclusion that the client is in clear disregard of relevant environmental legislation. However, your senior partner informs you to write to the client saying that the area is legally doubtful and, in any event, it is unlikely that the enforcement agencies will discover the breach. What should you do?

The major source of difficulty for criminal lawyers flows from their general duty of confidentiality to clients. It is extremely difficult to balance this fundamental obligation against the oft-repeated duty to treat the court with candour. Indeed, a prominent commentator, Monroe Freedman, has suggested that it creates "the lawyer's trilemma — the lawyer has a duty to know everything, to keep it in strict confidence, and to reveal it to the court."[5] In resolving this conundrum, Freedman opted clearly and controversially for the position that the duty of confidentiality should be paramount. He went so far as to argue that defendants should be able to testify, even when their lawyers know their clients will offer perjurious testimony. His rationale was that, without such a possibility, the guarantee of confidentiality would ring hollow and the interests of individual clients would be sacrificed for social expedience. Of course, many Canadian commentators disagree with the uncompromising pro-accused position. However, Freedman's arguments provide the framework for contemporary debate over the limits to which criminal lawyers can go in seeking to serve their accused clients.[6] Three particular situations merit extended discussion: the limits on the kind of defences that can be run, the consequences that follow from the lawyers' realizations that the clients are guilty of the offence charged, and the options available to defence lawyers when their clients insist on giving perjured testimony. Each of these situations presents lawyers with difficult ethical choices and is subject to special professional rules. The next two sections deal with these situations.

One instance where this competition between competing duties of client confidentiality and court candour has caused considerable misunderstanding is in regard to physical evidence. Confidentiality attaches only to communications between lawyers and clients, and not to the physical evidence itself. If lawyers come into possession of articles they know will make up physical evidence in a case, they cannot destroy or conceal them. Such evidence must be handed over to the police or the appropriate authorities. However, lawyers are obliged to take all efforts to keep confidential the source of the evidence that is turned over to the police. To preserve confidentiality as best as possible in such circumstances, the most

---

5   M.H. Freedman, "Professional Responsibility of the Criminal Defence Lawyer: The Three Hardest Questions" (1966) 64 Michigan L. Rev. 1469.

6   See G. MacKenzie, *Lawyers and Ethics: Professional Responsibility and Discipline* (Scarborough, Ont.: Carswell, 1993) at 7-2.

desirable course is to turn over the physical evidence to an intermediary (e.g., Law Society), which could then pass the evidence to the police without revealing who or where it came from. Nevertheless, this duty to disclose confidential information is very limited in scope and applies only to physical evidence that can reasonably be considered to be the instrumentalities of crime (e.g., weapons or equipment) or the proceeds of crime (e.g., stolen money or property). Moreover, while criminal lawyers must advise clients not to destroy or conceal evidence themselves, lawyers cannot disclose such communications to anyone about the fact of destruction or the location of concealment.[7]

PROBLEM 39: Your client is accused of a series of particularly savage murders. He tells you that he videotaped the events and that the tapes are hidden at his house. When the police have searched unsuccessfully for the tapes at your client's house, he instructs you to pick up the tapes. What do you do? Would it make any difference if the client gave you the tapes in your office? Or if it was a set of your client's diaries rather than videotapes? Or if he claimed that the tapes would help to at least reduce the charges against him, if not exonerate him?

# C. MAKING A DEFENCE

There is a general duty on lawyers not to participate in the deception of the court by "offering false evidence" or by "suppressing what ought to be disclosed" (see IX, c. 2(e)). However, this duty has to be read against specific provisions that speak to the predicament of defence counsel in a criminal trial. The duty of defence counsel is to "protect" the accused. In defending their clients, lawyers can use "all available evidence or defences . . . not known to be false or fraudulent" (see IX, c. 10). Lawyers should also inform their clients that "admissions . . . may impose strict limitations on the conduct of the defence," as lawyers are prohibited from calling evidence they "believe to be false" and can only challenge the "admissibility" and "sufficiency" of the Crown's evidence after the accused has made such an admission (see IX, c. 11). These general provisions need to be fleshed out and placed in a more informative context.

---

7    See E.A. Cherniak, "The Ethics of Advocacy" (1985) 19 L.S.U.C. Gazette 145.

There are two aspects to any criminal defence: one concerns defence counsels' approach to the Crown's case against the accused, and the other involves the nature and tactics of any affirmative case presented by the defence itself. The limits to what criminal lawyers can do in each of these situations might well be substantially affected by whether lawyers believe that their clients are telling the truth. However, for this to become an operative factor, lawyers have to have more than a suspicion that their clients are guilty or not: they must be convinced that clients not only committed the alleged crime but have no viable defence. Even when clients confess to their lawyers, this is not always irrefutable evidence of their legal guilt; the state might have used improper methods to obtain evidence or it might simply not have enough evidence to meet the requisite standard of proof. In particular, the fact that clients tell inconsistent stories about the relevant facts is certainly insufficient to ground a belief in the accused clients' guilt. In many circumstances, lawyers cannot really claim to *know* that their clients are guilty; there may be a host of extraneous reasons for clients seeking to take responsibility for the crime. Also, it is not the criminal lawyers' job to decide whether clients are deserving of punishment. Their task is to raise a reasonable doubt in the judge and/or jury's mind: it is not to prove the innocence of the accused. Baron Bramwell put it squarely when he stated that "a man's rights are to be determined by the court, not by his attorney or counsel. . . . A client is entitled to say to his counsel, 'I want your advocacy, not your judgment: I prefer that of the court.'"[8] Accordingly, lawyers should be slow, but not unwilling, to reach the conclusion that their clients are guilty and thereby tie their own and the clients' hands in presenting a vigorous and successful defence.

In many circumstances, few ethical issues will arise for resolution, and lawyers will proceed to offer a vigorous defence of the clients' case. However, ethical issues will come to the fore when lawyers are impelled to raise a so-called false defence as part of their duty to force the prosecution to prove its case beyond a reasonable doubt. This situation can arise in a number of circumstances: where lawyers make arguments or lead evidence that is intended to convince the court that facts established by the Crown and known to the defence lawyer to be true are not true, or that facts known to the defence lawyer to be true are false. This turn-around can be done by cross-examining truthful Crown witnesses to discredit their evidence, and also by the presentation of evidence that is itself false or evidence that is not itself false, but is used to bolster a

---

8    *Johnson v. Emerson* (1871), 6 L.R. Exch. 329 at 367.

false theory of the accused's innocence. Is there ever a right to present a false case? And, if lawyers can, whether they should?[9]

Most commentators agree that there is an important difference between challenging the prosecution's case in a vigorous manner and putting forward affirmative and alternative accounts on behalf of the accused (such as an alibi or a fabrication). Assuming that lawyers do not believe that their accused client is guilty or lying (and the two may not be the same), lawyers have a wide licence to put the Crown's case to a stiff test to ascertain whether it can get over the official hurdle of reasonable doubt. There is little doubt that challenging is a proper and indispensable part of the lawyer's role. As the Rules state, lawyers are entitled to rely on all available defences, including "so-called technicalities not known to be false or fraudulent." Also, they can proceed "notwithstanding the lawyer's private opinion as to credibility or merits." Accordingly, while defence counsel are limited to acting with fairness and courtesy, they can cross-examine Crown witnesses to undermine their credibility even if defence counsel knows they are telling the truth, and they can object to admissibility of evidence even if they believe it is more likely than not to be truthful. However, there may well be limits to the vigour that criminal lawyers can use that flow from their general professional responsibility to moderate their zealousness (see chapter 6). Robust challenges to Crown evidence are entirely acceptable, as all that needs to be done to secure an accused client's acquittal is to raise a reasonable doubt. Moreover, it might well be the case that the prosecution's witnesses have been coached.

PROBLEM 40: Your client is charged with the attempted poisoning of his wife. The evidence is overwhelming that, at the relevant times, he was responsible for the preparation of their meals. His wife and her mother, who lived with them, are the only Crown witnesses. Although you have no direct evidence or any proof at all, you decide that the best course of action would be to discredit the mother's evidence by revealing her very murky past and to suggest that she might have been responsible for the poisoning. Is this an acceptable way of proceeding? What else might you do? Would it make any difference to your decision if, at the first day of trial, your client had broken down and confessed to you.[10]

---

9   For a good debate on the limits of criminal advocacy which covers most of the argumentative manoeuvres, see S.I. Subin, "The Criminal Lawyer's 'Different Mission': Reflections on the 'Right' to Present a False Case" (1987) 1 Georgetown J. of Legal Ethics 125, and J.B. Mitchell, "Reasonable Doubts Are Where You Find Them: A Response to Professor Subin's Position on the Criminal Lawyer's 'Different Mission'" (1987) 1 Georgetown J. of Legal Ethics 339.

10  See C.K. Allen, "R. v. Dean" (1941) 57 L.Q.R. 85.

PROBLEM 41: Your client is charged with theft. While she admits that she was in the relevant building at the time of the offence, you strongly believe her protestations of innocence. Should you cross-examine a prosecution witness who accurately identified your client as being in the building at the time of the offence about her defective vision?

Opinion is much more divided over the limits that surround the choice to put forward affirmative and alternative accounts on behalf of the accused (such as alibi or fabrication) when the accused's lawyer knows that they are more than likely false. Some maintain that defence lawyers should not put hypothetical and certainly not false arguments before the jury: good faith challenges to the Crown's case and the assertion of true defences are the limit to the criminal counsel's advocacy on behalf of the accused. The rationale is that, to do otherwise, lawyers will unfairly and inappropriately subvert the search for truth. While a goal of the criminal justice system is to ensure that only the guilty are convicted, it does not follow that this goal is enhanced by allowing lawyers to use any device that encourages a verdict that is known to be false. In Canada, this view is confirmed by the Rules, which prohibit defence counsel from relying on evidence or defences that are "known to be false or fraudulent" (see IX, c. 10). Again, much will hinge upon lawyers' decision and standards for determining when something is "known" to be false or fraudulent.

PROBLEM 42: Your client is charged with assault. The victim testifies that it took place at 9:00. Your client has a cast-iron alibi for 9:00, but your client has told you that the assault actually took place at 9:30. Can and would you use the alibi evidence to acquit your client? Would it make any difference if your client had told you that he was involved in the assault, but it was a justified act of self-defence?

The timing of any confession by clients to lawyers or the confirmation of lawyers' beliefs about the accused's guilt will be very important. There is a difference between such a realization occurring before or during trial. The bottom line is not that lawyers need automatically to withdraw, although they are entitled to do so if it is before the trial, provided that the client is not unfairly prejudiced and is able to find another competent lawyer. However, if lawyers do continue in such circumstances, restrictions are placed on the kind of defence that can be run for accused clients. While defence lawyers can challenge the Crown's evidence or its witnesses' credibility, they cannot present any affirmative defence to the charge and, as the next section explains, they most certainly cannot allow their clients to take the stand and connive in their untruths. Of course, in all these circumstances, criminal lawyers are under an obligation to inform their clients of the lawyers' responsibilities so they can decide whether they wish to dismiss them as their lawyers and retain another. If lawyers are dismissed, they still owe their former clients a duty of confidentiality such that they cannot share their knowledge or suspicions with anyone else, particularly the new lawyer, unless the client expressly consents (see IV, c. 4 and c. 9). However, the former client's new lawyer will likely be alerted to some problems by the very circumstances in which they were retained.

**PROBLEM 43: Your client is a homeless person. After much bureaucratic aggravation, you manage to obtain welfare benefits for him. A couple of months later, you receive strong evidence from an impeccable source that your client has lied and probably would not have received benefits if he had not lied. What do you now do?**

In conclusion, it can be said that it is far from easy to draw a black-and-white distinction between true and false defences, even if it were possible for lawyers to know with any great certainty what is and is not true in matters of intent, motive, and so on. As the rules state, it is the duty of criminal counsel to raise reasonable doubts in the mind of the judge or jury. Even if they know the prosecution evidence to be true, they are still "entitled to establish the evidence given by each individual for the prosecution and argue that the evidence taken as a whole is insufficient to amount to proof that the accused is guilty of the offence charged." However, defence lawyers "should go no further than that" (see IX, c. 11). Controversially, this might still allow for putting alternative possibilities before the court that the counsel knows are false, but without asserting the truth of those alternatives. It is vital to remember that defence counsel do not have to prove what did or did not *in fact* happen: all they have to do is raise a reasonable doubt in the minds of the jury about the case brought by the Crown against the accused. Rather than undermining truth and the system's capacity to uncover it, criminal lawyers raise doubts in order to question the legitimacy of the government's power to punish the accuseds for their alleged behaviour. Consequently, in raising various alternative possibilities, criminal counsel are not arguing about whether certain facts are true or false, but they are challenging the ability of the prosecution to meet the legal standard required of them before the court is entitled to register a conviction against the accused and impose sanctions.

**PROBLEM 44: You represent the accused in a theft case. An important issue for the jury is whether the accused was caught in the rain when the offence allegedly occurred. At the relevant time, the accused was seen entering a building with a wet hat and coat. Although you know that it was raining and the accused got wet in that way, can you enter evidence or suggest to the jury**

that the accused might have become wet because a nearby fire hydrant went off unexpectedly in the street?

# D. THE PERJURY PROBLEM

Are there any limits to raising false defences? Most answer in the affirmative and insist that lawyers cannot be involved in permitting their clients to commit perjury. The first issue is to determine on what basis it is reasonable for lawyers to assume that their clients are going to commit perjury. Mindful that the negative consequences of such belief by the client's lawyer will likely be significant for the client, the standard cannot be too low. Consequently, before lawyers assume that their clients are about to commit perjury, they should have actual knowledge rather than only good grounds for belief. As the Rules put it, lawyers must be "convinced that the admissions are true and voluntary" (see IX, c. 11). Even when clients tell their lawyers expressly that the evidence to be presented is false, lawyers should take steps to confirm that the clients' statements are true (that what they say in testimony will be false). In other situations, particularly where the belief is based on the clients telling their lawyers inconsistent accounts of what happened, lawyers should be cautious about leaping to the perjurious conclusion. As Justice Stevens said, "a lawyer's certainty that a change in his client's recollection is a harbinger of intended perjury . . . should be tempered by the realization that, after reflection, the most honest witness may recall (or sincerely believe he recalls) details that he previously overlooked."[11] Accordingly, if lawyers have any doubt about whether their clients are going to give perjurious testimony, there is no duty not to lead such evidence.

Once lawyers have actual knowledge that their clients are going to commit perjury, what are they supposed to do? The first step counsel must take is to make all possible efforts to dissuade the client from this course of action. Whatever other action lawyers ultimately take, this step is imperative. Next, there are several options open to the lawyer: proceed as if nothing has happened and allow the client to testify; ask the client to make a narrative statement to the court as regards that part of the testimony believed to be perjurious; inform the court of the client's intention to lie; or withdraw from the case. Each of these options are not without difficulty and a couple are fraught with serious drawbacks:

---

11   *Nix v. Whiteside*, 475 U.S. 157 at 190–91 (1986).

- *Proceed as normal*: Freedman reasons that to prevent clients from testifying serves only to penalize the client for being candid with counsel and devalues the importance of confidentiality and the right against self-incrimination. As well, if lawyers prevent the client from testifying when they know that the client intends to lie under oath, they will not only be breaching their duty of confidentiality by acting upon information disclosed in confidence but will be doing irreparable damage to the client's interests. However, Freedman does not advocate counselling a client to give false testimony; rather, he agrees that there is an onus on lawyers to try to dissuade the client from such a course of action. At the end of the day, he insists that the decision is up to the client and that lawyers must follow their clients' wishes.[12]
- *Narrative statement*: This proposal is followed in some American states. The accused takes the stand and is sworn, but the lawyer does not perform the usual mode of direct examination. Instead, counsel should invite the accused to make a narrative statement to the court. While this course has some obvious attractions as an attempt at compromise, it tends to tip the court off to the problem and jeopardizes the accused's right to put forward the defence of choice.
- *Inform the court*: This approach is a form of whistle-blowing and requires lawyers to break their duty of confidentiality to their clients. Condemning the knowing use of perjury by lawyers, the U.S. Supreme Court has held that lawyers must inform the court of a client's intention to lie, if all their efforts to dissuade the client have failed.[13] The problem, of course, is that this tactic not only renders somewhat hollow the client's right to confidentiality but also has the effect of breaching the accused's right against self-incrimination.
- *Withdraw*: Although the Rules permit withdrawal in certain circumstances, the reality is that this reaction is ill-suited to meet the demands of the situation. Except where lawyer and client have lost all confidence in each other and are unable to continue in a professional relationship, this option seems unhelpful and can be potentially devastating to the client's interests. The dangers are summed up by a Florida appellate court:

---

12   Freedman, above note 5 at 1475–78.
13   See *Nix v. Whiteside*, above note 11, and D. Luban, *Lawyers and Justice: An Ethical Study* (Princeton, NJ: Princeton University Press, 1989) at 197–201.

If withdrawal were allowed every time a lawyer was faced with an ethical disagreement with the accused, the ultimate result could be a perpetual cycle of eleventh-hour motions to withdraw. . . . In addition, new counsel might fail to recognize the problem of fabricated testimony and false evidence would be presented to the court; or, perhaps, the defendant might eventually find an attorney who lacks ethical standards and who would knowingly present and argue false evidence.[14]

The Canadian response to this dilemma involves a combination of these options and embraces a number of the difficulties attendant on each course of action. Lawyers must not "call any evidence that, by reason of the [clients'] admissions, the lawyer believes to be false" and they cannot "knowingly attempt to deceive or participate in the deception of the tribunal" (see IX, c. 11 and c. 2(e)). If lawyers know that their clients are making false statements under oath and do nothing to correct it, their silence "indicates, at the very least, a gross neglect of duty."[15] If clients persist in their intention to give perjurious testimony after their lawyers' best efforts to dissuade them, lawyers have no alternative other than to "withdraw or seek the leave of the court to do so" as promptly as possible and with a minimum of prejudice to their client (see IX, c. 4). Once lawyers inform the court that they are withdrawing from a case, judges cannot order them to continue to act as counsel for an accused, nor can the court ask lawyers about "their reasons for withdrawing." However, judges should only allow defence counsel to withdraw during trial if all efforts at persuasion have failed and there is no significant prejudice to the accused.[16]

Also, lawyers have a duty to inform the court about false evidence that has been inadvertently introduced by them when, for example, clients give unexpected false testimony. In such circumstances, lawyers are required to breach their confidentiality to clients (see IX, c. 3). However, some criminal commentators suggest an alternative approach which recommends that counsel should not make disclosure to the court, but should continue examining their clients in such a way as to elicit truthful answers and thereby correct the false evidence. In summing up, lawyers would then emphasize only the latter evidence. The attraction of such an alternative is that it would allow lawyers to avoid drawing attention to the false evidence and reduce any prejudice to clients by not revealing confidential communications between clients and

---

14   *Sanborn v. State*, 474 So.2d 309 at 314 (3d Dist. C.A. 1985).
15   *Re Ontario (Crime Commission)*, [1963] 37 D.L.R. (2d) 382 at 391 (C.A.), McLennan J.A.
16   *Dunkley v. R.*, [1995] 1 All E.R. 279 (P.C.).

themselves.[17] Again, in all these cases, lawyers would save themselves and their clients a lot of trouble and disappointment if they covered such matters in an initial interview (see chapter 5).

PROBLEM 45: Your colleague's client is an Aboriginal person and is accused of the murder of a police officer. There are serious questions about the validity of the client's confession to the police, and the Crown's overall case seems very weak. Your colleague seeks your advice. She tells you that the client has confessed his guilt to her and that, as a result, she intends to tell the judge in open court that she has been placed in the worst dilemma in her professional career and ask to withdraw from the case. What advice do you give her?[18]

# E.  THE CASE FOR THE PROSECUTION

The role of the Crown is very different from that of defence counsel. The task of prosecuting lawyers is less adversarial than their defence counterparts. They are more a part of the justice system and have a different set of responsibilities. In most provinces, it is the police who make the decision to lay charges. However, in British Columbia, Quebec, and New Brunswick, it is crown attorneys who make that decision; they must base their decision on a "substantial likelihood of conviction" test combined with a consideration of the public interest.[19] However, once charges have been laid, prosecutors have the sole carriage of the case and it is their responsibility to determine whether to continue with charges, when to drop them, in what circumstances to accept a plea bargain, what tactics to use at trial, and whether to stay proceedings. In fulfilling these responsibilities, the duty of prosecutors is not to seek convictions, but to remain neutral. This duty places them at odds with the adversary system. Nonetheless, at least in theory, the role of prosecutors excludes any notion of winning or losing, since they have a quasi-judicial obligation.

Insofar as a prosecutor has a client, it is the public. It is most definitely not the victim. Consequently, prosecutors play a dual role: they must seek convictions for the guilty and, at the same time, guard against the wrongful convictions of the innocent; they must balance the duties of advocate and administrator. These different roles and responsibilities

---

17   B. Finlay, "The Conduct of Lawyers in the Litigious Process: Some Thoughts" in E. Gertner, *Studies in Civil Procedure* (Toronto: Butterworths, 1979) at 27–28.

18   See *Tuckiar v. The King* (1934), 52 C.L.R. 335 (H.C. of A.).

19   MacKenzie, above note 6 at 6-3.

were made clear by Rand J. in *Boucher*, where Crown counsel had used inflammatory and vindictive language in his jury address to express his personal opinion that the accused was guilty:

> It cannot be over-emphasized that the purpose of a criminal prosecution is not to obtain a conviction, it is to lay before a jury what the Crown considers to be credible evidence relevant to what is alleged to be a crime. Counsel have a duty to see that all available legal proof of the facts is presented: it should be done firmly and pressed to its legitimate strength but it must also be done fairly. The role of prosecutor excludes any notion of winning or losing; his function is a matter of public duty than which in civil life there can be none charged with greater responsibility. It is to be efficiently performed with an ingrained sense of the dignity, the seriousness and the justness of judicial proceedings.[20]

As with defence lawyers, the professional rules offer considerable guidance in helping prosecution lawyers to meet their ethical responsibilities. While the list of permitted and prohibited conduct is intended to apply to all lawyers, the following guidelines have particular relevance for the prosecuting counsel:

- As part of their overall commitment to ensure that justice is done, prosecutors are not entitled to lead evidence or make suggestions that are based on factual assumptions that they have reason to doubt. Unlike defence counsel, they must pursue only a line of argument they have some basis for believing to be true. For example, it is inappropriate for the Crown to suggest that an accused and the owner of a car were one and the same person when they had some reason to believe they were not.[21]
- Lawyers in general, and prosecutors in particular, may interview "any potential [defence] witnesses," but may do so only through and with the consent of their lawyers if they are "professionally represented" (see IX, c. 6).
- The abiding duty of prosecutors "is not to seek a conviction," but to present all "credible" and "relevant" evidence to the court so "that justice may be done through a fair trial" (see IX, c. 9).
- Prosecutors fulfill a "public function," which must be carried out "fairly" (see IX, c. 9).

---

20   *Boucher v. R.*, [1955] S.C.R. 16 at 23–24.
21   *R. v. Hay* (1982), 70 C.C.C. (2d) 286 (C.A.).

An important case on prosecutorial ethics is the recent decision in *Stinchcombe*. A former secretary of a lawyer, charged with fraud and theft, was interviewed by police; defence counsel was informed of the existence of the statement, but not its content, and requests for disclosure were refused by the police and trial judge. The Supreme Court of Canada allowed the accused's appeal against conviction on the basis that the prosecution were under a duty to disclose all relevant evidence to the defence. The Crown operates as a guardian of the public interest and is authorized to ensure that justice is done. It is not the goal of the Crown to secure a conviction at all costs. Nevertheless, the Crown does have a discretion over whether the evidence is relevant and must exercise it in good faith. Apart from the existence of any legal privilege that attaches to relevant evidence, information should not be withheld if there is a reasonable possibility that this restriction will impair the right of the accused to make full answer and defence. As Sopinka J. made clear, all relevant statements must be disclosed:

> All statements obtained from persons who have provided relevant information to the authorities should be produced notwithstanding that they are not proposed as Crown witnesses. When statements are not in existence, other information such as notes should be produced, and, if there are no notes, then in addition to the name, address and occupation of the witness, all information in the possession of the prosecution relating to any relevant evidence that the person could give should be supplied. . . . If the information is of no use then presumably it is irrelevant and will be excluded in the discretion of the Crown. If the information is of some use then it is relevant and the exercise of the determination as to whether it is sufficiently useful to put into evidence should be made by the defence and not the prosecutor.[22]

The Crown ought to make initial disclosure of all and any relevant evidence as early as possible and certainly before the accused is called upon to elect the mode of trial or to plead. The obligation to disclose will be triggered by a request from the accused's counsel. Most important, the material that is disclosed must make no distinction between inculpatory and exculpatory evidence; it is all disclosable. If the Crown fails to disclose relevant evidence, the accused's counsel must bring this fact to the trial judge's attention at the earliest opportunity so that any prejudice can be remedied without there having to be a new trial. Counsel cannot delay, once they learn of the failure to disclose, in the hope that they can

---

22   *R. v. Stinchcombe*, [1991] 3 S.C.R. 326 at 345–46.

use this at a later date to the accused's better advantage; this is an unethical practice and one that is severely frowned upon by the courts.

For most commentators, the role of prosecuting lawyers is an exception and one that proves the general rule that lawyers are to participate in legal proceedings in an adversarial manner. However, it might be worth asking whether the peculiar role of prosecuting lawyers might have something to offer by way of example to other lawyers, civil and criminal. Its emphasis on the need to operate in a dual capacity as both a partisan advocate and as a court administrator could offer the basis for a whole reconception of criminal lawyers' roles generally. For instance, it might be argued that such a broadened perspective might better guide defence counsel in deciding what to do by way of cross-examination of Crown witnesses or of asserting affirmative defences. Whatever individual lawyers are encouraged to do, it is imperative that criminal clients are informed beforehand about any non-conventional views or approaches that the defence lawyer might have in mind. To do otherwise would reduce clients to mere convenient tools in the hands of their lawyers (see chapter 2).

## F. PLEA BARGAINING

Criminal trials are the exception, not the rule, in criminal law; alternative dispute resolution is the daily diet of the criminal bar. The vast majority of cases are completed without a trial and after a plea bargain has been struck between the Crown and the accused. Plea bargaining is a process whereby inducements are exchanged for cooperation by both sides of the bargaining table: the prosecution secures a plea of guilty from a defendant, in exchange for providing some form of leniency in the charge and/or recommended sentence. The basic deal is that defendants give up the right to go to trial and the chance for an acquittal, and the Crown forgoes the opportunity for a stiffer sentence in exchange for a lighter one, thereby obtaining convictions without lengthy, expensive, or uncertain trials. It is estimated that approximately 95 percent of criminal charges do not make it to trial. The most common form of a plea bargain occurs where an accused has been charged with numerous offences associated with the commission of one or more crimes, and the Crown agrees to drop all or most of the minor charges in exchange for a guilty plea to the more serious charge. Other forms of plea bargaining include the Crown's use of summary conviction procedure rather than indictable procedure in offences where the Crown has a choice; promises not to apply for sentences of detention; promises not to charge friends or family; promises not to mention aggravating circumstances of the offence or the accused's criminal record; or promises to accept a plea to a lesser charge for evidence against another person.

The pros and cons of plea bargaining are beyond the scope of this book, but the problems of legal ethics and professional responsibility are not and they fall squarely within its mandate. The pressures on both prosecution and defence to reach a satisfactory plea bargain are very strong and create a breeding ground for unethical practices. The prosecution's need to use its limited resources efficiently and to register an acceptable rate of convictions, and the defence's desire to lessen an accused's punishment, can combine to prompt lawyers to reach deals that are problematic both in terms of substance and the methods used to achieve them. In short, lawyers might be tempted to put their own professional concerns above those of their clients and society generally. Some of the common problems include:

- Given that the legal preparation and undertaking of a full trial is a lengthy and expensive process, plea bargaining offers defence counsel an easy and cost-effective means to reduce the cost of trial work.
- Any deal reached is entirely suspect and unconscionable because bargaining usually occurs in a coercive environment in which the defendant has little choice. Occasionally, an innocent defendant might plead guilty.
- In situations where witnesses are not available or *Charter* considerations arise, the utilization of plea bargaining by the prosecution goes directly against "justice." By side-stepping standards of proof and due process in a criminal setting, the justice system is brought into disrepute.
- The circumstances surrounding an alleged offence might encourage an innocent accused to plea bargain. Mistaken witnesses or prior criminal records may pressure accuseds into accepting an offer from the Crown, out of fear they will otherwise receive a severe sentence if they go through a trial maintaining their innocence.
- The regularity of the practice might be thought to result in police and prosecutors overcharging at the initial point of an investigation. Knowing the likelihood that plea bargaining will become an option, this practice provides the Crown with increased leverage in negotiations.

The usual response to these alleged abuses by both defence lawyers and prosecutors is that all plea bargains have to be approved by the court; it is counsel's professional responsibility to obtain the best deal they can in the circumstances. Although it is absolutely clear that judges are not bound by the terms and conditions of a plea bargain reached by counsel,[23] defence lawyers are required to ensure that any proposed guilty plea does not compromise the public or the clients' interest (see IX, c. 12). While they cannot upset the dropping or reduction of charges by Crown counsel, judges do have the last word on sentencing. However, the reality is that, while the court's discretion remains unfettered, judges do not discard such agreements lightly or without good reason. Moreover, the Crown can repudiate such an agreement only where the accused has substantially misrepresented the factual basis for such a bargain, and can appeal a sentence only if it is revealed to be grossly insufficient in light of recently discovered facts; it is not bound by individual prosecution lawyers in the absence of personal instructions or involvement by the attorney general.[24] The position of convicted persons is similar; they will be permitted to appeal only where they can show that they did not understand their basic rights, or where the Crown has acted fraudulently in obtaining their consent (such as by withholding evidence).

Notwithstanding these judicial checks, it is imperative that both defence lawyers and the prosecution engage in modes of bargaining that ensure that the resulting plea is both fair and efficient, in that overly strategic or exploitative bargaining is reduced. Various guidelines have been developed by the Rules and the courts to accentuate the advantages of plea bargaining and to curb its disadvantages by improving the balance of information available to each side, by clarifying when such deals can be avoided, and by stipulating what judges can and cannot do in response to such agreements.[25] Insofar as they pertain to matters of legal ethics, the following considerations ought to be followed by lawyers in making plea bargains:

• *Counsel must have been present and have acted candidly in negotiating a plea bargain.* There is considerable responsibility on both counsel to ensure that there is an adequate exchange of information. In particular, Crown counsel must reach an agreement only where the likelihood of a conviction is, at least, possible, even if improbable at trial. In this sense, it is important to distinguish between proof and truth. Both counsel should inform accuseds that judges are not bound by sentencing recommendations, but that they can hold accuseds to their guilty plea.

---

23   See *R. v. Naraindeen* (1990), 75 O.R. (2d) 120 (C.A.).
24   See *R. v. Crneck* (1980), 30 O.R. (2d) 1 (H.C.).
25   See, for example, *R. v. Turner*, [1970] 2 All E.R. 281 (C.A.).

- *Judges ought not to participate in negotiations.* To preserve their impartiality and neutrality, judges ought not to be involved in bargaining as this would undermine their capacity to pass judgment on the fairness of the deal achieved. This places an even higher onus on the lawyers to exercise due diligence. Moreover, if any meeting does occur, both counsel must be present, and it is the duty of defence counsel to disclose the fact of such a meeting to accuseds and inform them of what took place.
- *The Crown should consult victims and/or their intimates.* It is important that the victims should play some role in the disposition of incidents in which they were involved. As always, Crown counsel must represent the broader public interest. However, this does not mean that victims hold a veto; it is the Crown's ultimate duty to assess if the general administration of justice is best served by proceeding to trial or not.
- *Judges must be satisfied that the accused's consent to a plea bargain is voluntary and informed.* Accused persons are free to reject the agreement at any time before entering an actual plea; they must be given an opportunity by judges to acknowledge that they willingly and knowingly waived standard constitutional rights and protections in a clear and unequivocal manner and that they understand that the agreed sentencing recommendations might be rejected. This means that defence counsel must have been absolutely candid and up-front in their dealings with their clients, particularly with regard to assuring clients that they have complete freedom of choice to plead guilty or not guilty. In particular, they must, after thorough investigation, have advised the accused that an acquittal is "uncertain or unlikely," have warned the client about the possible consequences of a guilty plea, and received clear and preferably written instructions from the client (see IX, c. 12).
- *The Crown should be able to repudiate a bargain before trial only in the rarest of circumstances.* This rejection should occur only if the continued honouring (or dishonouring) of the deal will bring the administration of justice into disrepute and the accused's future position is not irreparably prejudiced (i.e., inculpatory statements from plea negotiations must not be used against accuseds).
- *Appeals should only be allowed in exceptional cases.* For obvious reasons, each party should be able to challenge the after-the-fact validity of the negotiated plea only in special circumstances. This might occur, for the Crown, where the sentence is grossly inadequate and new undisclosed facts have arisen, and, for defendants, where there has been deception that was relied upon in waiving their rights unknowingly.

PROBLEM 46: Your client appears to you to be in an extremely tight corner. While you are reasonably convinced that your client is not guilty of the offence charged, the evidence is stacked against her. In light of the fact that she has a lengthy list of prior convictions, you worry that an unsuccessful "not guilty" plea will result in your client serving a long prison sentence. What would you do? Would and could you ever advise an innocent person to plead guilty?

# G.  CONCLUSION

The challenges to the criminal bar in meeting its ethical and professional responsibilities are difficult and many. It is relatively easy for counsel to drift into a professional stance that ducks questions of ethical significance and settles on an amoral indifference to such issues. In answering the people's nagging query, "How can you defend someone whom you know to be guilty?" criminal lawyers can continue to do a good job for their accused clients and remain ethical persons. As I have tried to suggest, there is no need to abandon the moral realm: criminal lawyers are both required to justify what they do as much as anyone else and entitled to rely on a range of ethical justifications that set them apart from their less harried colleagues. Like all other lawyers, criminal lawyers must be able to accept responsibility for what they do by reference to an ethical argument. The most compelling of professional responsibilities is to take an ethical stand and to be accountable for it: there can be no better or other approach.

# CHAPTER 10

# BEYOND THE GENERAL PRINCIPLES: SPECIAL SITUATIONS

A recurring theme of this book is that there are no absolutes when it comes to ethics generally and legal ethics particularly; what will and will not amount to a satisfactory fulfillment of professional responsibility is a contextual matter. Up to this point, aside from those involving criminal lawyers and prosecutors, the general ethical duties and professional responsibilities that I have dealt with apply to all lawyers. However, how these general principles and guidelines work themselves out in actual situations will vary considerably. Accordingly, this chapter takes four specialized areas of legal practice and explores the ethical challenges that arise. The first section deals with corporate lawyers and asks if there is any difference between in-house counsel and outside lawyers. In the second section, the expanding role of alternative dispute resolution in legal practice necessitates a closer scrutiny of the ethical problems facing negotiators and mediators. The third section tackles the special demands that are placed on those lawyers who devote their professional lives to the plight of the disadvantaged and downtrodden. Finally, the fourth section looks at the different circumstances in which government lawyers function and the problems they must resolve. Throughout the chapter, the emphasis is on the ethical details of these special situations as they relate to general principles and guidelines.

# A. CORPORATE LAWYERS

In any discussion of ethical and professional responsibilities, it must be stressed that a corporation is considered a separate entity and has a distinct legal identity from those who own it or run it. Corporate lawyers must always remember that they work for the corporation itself and owe their primary duties and allegiance to it, and not to any of its officers, shareholders, employees, or other connected persons (see VI, c. 3). Lawyers acting for organizations can represent their constituents, as long as they are in accordance with the rules and commentaries concerning conflicts of interest (see V, c. 12). While they may assume duties to the corporation's agents, their duties to the corporation are paramount and, if there is a conflict, the duty to the corporation must prevail. Consequently, corporate lawyers are well advised to obtain express clarification in their retainers about who has authority to instruct them on the "client's" behalf. They should inform agents of the corporation that, in the event of a conflict of interests, they will be representing the corporation as a whole and that individual agents should seek independent representation (see V, c. 5). Although difficulties can arise when lawyers become involved in the operations of related companies, there is less likelihood of a conflict when it involves a wholly owned subsidiary or a sister corporation of the primary corporate client rather than when there is a minority interest in an affiliated company.

Nevertheless, there are situations where corporate lawyers should be particularly on their guard against possible conflict problems:

- When lawyers are asked to represent multiple parties in a transaction where it appears that the parties have similar interests, a conflict may still exist. A typical example is where there are "persons forming a partnership or corporation" (see V, c. 11). In such circumstances, corporate lawyers must be sure to disclose to all parties the possibility of conflicts (see V, c. 4 and c. 5).
- The duty of corporate lawyers to shareholders will depend on the size of the company and the number of shareholders. For example, in derivative proceedings, shareholders may bring an action on behalf of the corporation against the alleged misconduct of those controlling directors and officers who normally instruct the corporations's lawyer.[1] While such derivative proceedings do not automatically require separate representation, lawyers should alert all interested parties to the conflict risks and remind everyone that the lawyers' primary

---

1   See *Vadecko International Inc.* v. *Philosophe* (1990), 1 O.R. (3d) 87 (Gen. Div.).

responsibility is to the company. Directors and officers not named in the allegations of impropriety can retain and instruct counsel on behalf of the corporation. If this is not feasible, the court can assign independent counsel to represent the interest of the corporation.

• These potential conflict problems arise in other situations where lawyers represent organizations. A typical example occurs in the case of unions and allegations of wrongdoing against union leaders. Lawyers acting for such organizations can represent their constituents, as long as they are in accordance with the rules and commentaries concerning conflicts of interest (see V, c. 12).

The duty of confidentiality does not translate easily into the corporate context. First, the customary justification for confidentiality — that, without it, clients would not be candid with their lawyers and, therefore, not fully vindicate their own legal rights — does not apply to the realities of corporate organization. Corporations have little choice other than to involve their lawyers in important corporate decision making. Indeed, a large part of such sensitive material might actually flow from the lawyers' office. Second, a corporation has little need to protect its dignity, but only its economic reputation; the need for confidentiality in such circumstances is much less compelling. While this comment is not meant to suggest that corporate counsel's duty of confidentiality should be non-existent, it is intended to highlight the possible reason for curtailing the extent and inviolability of that duty in the corporate context. Rather than enhance the Rule of Law, it might work to shield white-collar crime or misconduct from public exposure. These problems are thrown into sharp relief by the difficult question of who is the lawyers' client. In particular, it must be established to whom corporate counsel owe their duty of confidentiality: Is it the directors, the executives, the shareholders, or the employees? The courts have had little difficulty with deciding that communications to lawyers from anyone who has some control over the company's decision-making process is a privileged communication. However, there has been less clarity over whether communications from lower-level employees are privileged.

A leading case is the decision of the American Supreme Court in *Upjohn*.[2] A multinational company initiated an internal inquiry into alleged corrupt practices by its foreign subsidiaries. At a later date, the tax authorities sought access to the information generated as a result of the company voluntarily disclosing questionable payments. The American Supreme Court was aware of the danger of creating "a broad zone

---

2    *Upjohn Co. v. United States*, 449 U.S. 383 (1981).

of silence over corporate affairs," but extended the litigation privilege to cover such information. In a much-criticized decision, it was held that the duty of confidentiality is in play beyond dealings with those who actually control the corporation (managers and directors) and encompasses all those employees who disclose to the lawyers any information whose subject matter is the employees' duties of employment. However, such employees are in a very exposed position. While counsel cannot disclose any communications to the government, they are at liberty and must, if requested, reveal such information to the company's managers, as they are also holders of the privilege and are free to waive it on the corporation's behalf. Consequently, the *Upjohn* test can have the unfortunate effect of giving enormous power to employers, who can take advantage of whatever information employees give to company lawyers. As one critic has observed, the underlying problem with this decision is that, by elevating "litigation shenanigans to a principle," the courts have allowed the exception (of confidential privilege) to consume the rule (disclosure of facts to establish the truth).[3]

In Canada, the courts have tended to give the lawyer-client privilege a similarly broad ambit of operation. For instance, in *Mutual Life*, it was decided on an audit that the company's lawyer was not obligated to hand over to Revenue Canada at its request most documents that were in the lawyer's possession.[4] As well as granting privilege to all legal communications between the lawyer and the management and employees of the company, the court extended confidentiality to all legal communications between the lawyer and employees of a wholly owned subsidiary, since the management of the two companies was closely connected. Privilege also extended to communications about law in foreign jurisdictions and to documents exchanged between other employees which commented on privileged legal communications. However, in line with the traditional doctrine, communications between the lawyer and management or other employees about business matters were not privileged, nor were documents simply received and filed by the lawyer if they were not directly related to legal matters. Accordingly, corporate lawyers must make it clear when they are giving legal as opposed to non-legal advice.[5]

---

3   D. Luban, *Lawyers and Justice: An Ethical Study* (Princeton, NJ: Princeton University Press, 1989).

4   See *Mutual Life Assurance Co. of Canada* v. *Canada (Deputy A.G.)* (1988), 28 C.P.C. (2d) 101 (Ont. H.C.).

5   *Alfred Crompton Amusement Machines Ltd.* v. *Commissioners of Custom and Excise (No. 2)*, [1972] All E.R. 353 (C.A.).

In some situations, it can be useful to distinguish between two different kinds of corporate lawyers: the in-house counsel and the outside lawyer. There have been efforts to argue that the circumstances and conditions of employment are sufficiently dissimilar to warrant different duties and responsibilities. Nonetheless, despite the fact that in-house counsel may lose a certain independence by becoming too closely linked with the mentality and goals of their corporate employers, the obligations on in-house counsel and outside lawyers are the same.[6] However, there has been a necessary willingness to appreciate that their different circumstances might be taken into account in their application. For instance, while Canadian jurisprudence is silent on the issue, it is likely that the refusal of house counsel to comply with instructions that would involve violating the rules of professional conduct cannot be considered just cause for dismissal. The major difference in terms of professional responsibility is how the conflict-of-interest rules are to apply to in-house counsel if they engage in moonlighting. This can occur when in-house counsel are asked by their employer to represent them in a matter with another party, especially if that other party is an employee. In matters between the employer and employees, lawyers should inform the employees that as in-house counsel they will not be acting on their behalf and that the employees should obtain independent legal representation. If asked by employers to act for both parties, lawyers should be guided by the appropriate Rules (see V, c. 5, and chapter 5).

When in-house counsel moonlight, they would do well to follow several guidelines if they are to avoid conflict-of-interest problems and fulfill their professional responsibilities fully:[7]

- counsel should seek the employer's consent before working for any other clients;
- outside work should not be allowed to impinge on work for their corporate employers;
- work done for private practice must still meet high standards, and counsel must be available to private clients, but not on company time;
- counsel should only accept work that they are qualified to execute;
- counsel should obtain their employer's permission to perform work for private clients during company time on company premises;

6   See *U.S. Steel Corp.* v. *United States*, 730 F.2d 1465 (Federal C.A. 1984).
7   See G. MacKenzie, *Lawyers and Ethics: Professional Responsibility and Discipline* (Scarborough, Ont.: Carswell, 1993) at 20-5, paraphrasing a paper by S.E. Traviss, "Issues of Professional Responsibility: Obligations of Counsel," which was delivered to the Law Society of Upper Canada Continuing Education Program on Law for the Company Counsel in Toronto on 25 February 1988.

- counsel who moonlight must make full payment of errors and omissions insurance (lawyers who work only as in-house counsel do not have to pay these premiums); and
- counsel must abide by all the rules governing Law Society filing and record keeping which are expected of lawyers in private practice.

A pervasive problem for corporate lawyers is the extent of their obligation to advise their corporate clients about not only the legality of their behaviour but also its ethical propriety. For many, this is no problem at all: the role of the corporate lawyer is to do what is best for corporate business and to keep the company on the right side of the law. Whatever the corporation's management might think, however, corporate lawyers are first and foremost lawyers, and they are subject to the ethical responsibilities imposed by the professional Rules. Consequently, it remains incumbent on corporate lawyers to follow lawful courses of action and to reject plans that are ethically dubious. It is all lawyers' general duty to avoid "dishonourable or questionable conduct" and, in particular, "to be on guard against becoming the tool or dupe of an unscrupulous client" (see II, c. 7). While this obligation might seem naive to some, it is surely appropriate that, if lawyers (and, therefore, their corporate employers) are to receive the benefits that flow from being lawyers, it is only fair and appropriate that they should be held to its perceived disadvantages.

This tension between in-house counsel's role as a member of the corporation and as a lawyer begins to have strong practical implications when counsel knows that the corporation is acting or planning to act unlawfully. As in all situations, there is a fine balance to be maintained between protecting lawyer-client confidentiality and upholding the law. The practice of whistleblowing is a sensitive one and raises broad ethical issues. However, it is clear that corporate lawyers are entitled to breach their duty of confidentiality "if the lawyer has reasonable grounds for believing that a crime is likely to be committed." It becomes a "mandatory duty" only if "the anticipated crime is one involving violence" (see IV, c. 11). This means that the Rules permit, but do not demand, disclosure. Furthermore, the entitlement extends only to future crimes, not past ones. As such, there can be no better situation to emphasize the need for lawyers to develop and hone a professional sense of moral judgment: the Rules are an occasion for the exercise of moral judgment, not a substitute for it. In reaching any decision on whether to whistleblow, corporate lawyers should take some initial steps. After informing the employees involved in writing that their activities are illegal and making all efforts to dissuade them from such conduct, corporate lawyers should report the unlawful activity to those who have overall responsibility for the company's operation, including, if necessary, the board of directors. If these efforts are unsuccessful, corporate lawyers must decide if they are prepared to go public and resign over the issue. At all times, lawyers should put everything down in writing and obtain confidential guidance either through the Law Society or other senior members of the legal profession.[8]

**PROBLEM 47: You are in-house counsel for a large manufacturing company. There have been several serious accidents involving one of its products. Internal memoranda that you have reviewed make it clear that the product is negligently designed. Also, you have told the board of directors that the company would have little chance of defeating well-advised legal actions. After much debate, the company decides that it is more economically efficient to keep the product on the market, not to recall any products sold, and to pay off legal claims as and when they occur. You are instructed to engage in vigorous efforts to settle such cases as expeditiously, quietly, and cheaply as you can. What do you do?**

**PROBLEM 48: As an in-house lawyer, you are asked to negotiate a settlement with one of the company's employees who was injured in a work-related accident. You know that if the employee was represented by a lawyer, she could likely get at least double the amount being offered. What should or can you say to the employee?**

# B. ALTERNATIVE DISPUTE RESOLUTION

Dissatisfaction with the adversary system by both lawyers and clients has led to a vast increase in both the willingness to explore and the actual incidence of alternative methods of dispute resolution. ADR's touted virtues are that it can help to resolve disputes in a cheaper, quicker, more participatory, and less aggressive way. Indeed, many jurisdictions are now enacting rules and legislation that require some form of ADR activity before or during litigation. However, although much of the impetus for a shift from litigation to ADR derives from a desire for alternatives to lawyers and their adversarial mentality, it is almost inevitable that lawyers will continue to play a dominant role in the future practice and development of ADR. As such, the challenge to adapt ethical standards to ADR practices will be paramount. Of course, ADR has always been a staple feature of most lawyers' practice in the form of negotiation: the wiles of bargaining must be learned by all law-

---

8   See MacKenzie, *ibid.* at 20-12.

yers and regularly exercised. Other forms of ADR — mediation and arbitration — are relatively new to most lawyers. Moreover, because they require lawyers to play a very new role, such ADR initiatives require a new approach to matters of appropriate professional responsibility and raise compelling ethical issues.

The professional Rules are very quiet on the ethics of negotiation, in that they tend to concentrate on advocacy matters. To remedy this, a separate Code has been drafted that awaits final approval (see appendix B). Not surprisingly, this code is typically vague and sweeping in its injunctions, leaving lawyers with considerable discretion in how to proceed. However, some important points have been clarified. For instance, if mediators hold private sessions (breakout meetings, caucuses) with a party, "they shall discuss the nature of such sessions with all parties prior to commencing such sessions" (see VI, c. 3). Also, mediators who are lawyers shall not represent any parties to the mediation (see VII, c. 4). Moreover, before any mediation commences, it is incumbent on the mediator to make a written agreement with the parties which includes terms about the confidentiality of communications and documents; the right of the mediator and the parties to terminate or suspend mediation; fee expenses, retainer, method of payment, and what, if any, fee there is for cancellation, lateness, or delay; and the fact that the mediator is not compellable as a witness in court proceedings by any parties to the mediation (see X).

Under the Rules, lawyers have a duty to advise and encourage clients to settle disputes "whenever possible on a reasonable basis." This includes discouraging clients from engaging in "useless" litigation (see III, c. 6). Even after litigation has begun, lawyers should still actively encourage clients to settle if the case "can be settled fairly" (see IX, c. 8). Also, it is clear that the general prohibitions against engaging in conduct that is "dishonourable or questionable" apply to settlement negotiations (see I, c. 3). Apart from these vague directives, lawyers are left to their own ethical sensibilities. This absence of formal regulation ought not to be interpreted by lawyers as a signal that "anything goes." Lawyers must decide for themselves what they are and are not prepared to do under the guise of settlement negotiations. Again, the importance of meeting with clients and sharing expectations cannot be too strongly and frequently emphasized.

Nevertheless, lawyers are not entirely left to their own devices. There are a variety of legal obligations that constrain and guide lawyers' approach and conduct in settlement negotiations. The fact that most negotiations take place on a "without prejudice" basis means that both lawyers are expected to retain the confidences of the other party as well as their own clients'. Lawyers can only make or accept offers to settle on instructions and authorization from clients; the terms of the retainers will be important in determining the authority of lawyers to settle disputes. However, once an opposing lawyer makes an offer to settle, lawyers are entitled to assume that the opposing lawyer has been sanctioned by his client to settle on such terms and conditions. Also, as a contract, all settlements are subject to all the basic substantive doctrines on misrepresentation, mistake, and duress. In dealing specifically with lawyers' conduct in negotiations, it has been held that a court may refuse to enforce a settlement in four situations where[9]

- there was a limitation on counsel's authority to settle that was communicated to the opposite party;
- there was a misapprehension by the lawyer of the client's instructions or of the facts, of a type that would result in injustice or make it unreasonable or unfair to enforce the settlement;
- there was fraud or collusion; or
- there was an issue to be tried as to whether there was such a limitation, misapprehension, fraud, or collusion in relation to the settlement.

Apart from these general stipulations, many lawyers believe that, as in love and war, all is fair in negotiating. But what are the rules of engagement in negotiating? Does anything go, or are there limits to what lawyers should be able to do on behalf of their clients? In particular, is it ever acceptable for lawyers to lie in order to gain the negotiating upper hand? Indeed, are lawyers required to lie occasionally for the good of their clients?

Charles Curtis maintained that there was a simple and obvious answer. Not only is a lawyer to "treat outsiders as if they were barbarians and enemies" but "there will be situations in which a lawyer may be duty bound to lie for his client."[10] The negotiating table might well be one of those perverse situations in which it is not only ethically justifiable, but it might actually be morally mandated. The basic logic behind this uncompromising stand is that the role of lawyers is to act as champions for their clients, not moral consciences. The prime ethical mandate is "do what you can to help friend and harm enemy, as long as you stay within the law." If this requires lawyers to lie, then they should do so (as long as they are not under oath). The lie is not the lawyer's, but the system's; lawyers are actors in an institutional drama scripted by cli-

---

9    *Hawitt v. Campbell*, [1983] 148 D.L.R. (3d) 341 (B.C.C.A.).
10   C.P. Curtis, "The Ethics of Advocacy" (1951) 4 Stanford L. Rev. 3.

ents, not themselves. Of course, many will instantly recoil at such a suggestion. They will think that Curtis is more compromised than uncompromising; he has gone too far in his depiction and defence of lawyers as latter-day champions for unscrupulous barons. Lawyers are not only mercenaries but are also, in the medieval metaphor, moral knights who fight for a (moral) cause as well as for (immoral) clients.

Yet the insistence that lawyers should never lie for their clients is a little hard to sustain. Most people accept that telling a lie is not always a sin; it depends on circumstances and consequences. Lying to save lives seems not only excusable but desirable. Moreover, it is the rare (and perhaps bad) lawyer who does not "stretch the truth" in negotiations. The real problem is not simply whether it is ever acceptable for lawyers to lie in negotiating, but what are the types, limits, and situations in which lawyers are entitled to engage in conduct that others might consider lying. On closer inspection, even those who claim to be unwilling to lie for clients appear to do so on a regular basis; their prosaic practice belies their principled statements. If a client informs you that you should settle for anything over $100,000, you presumably lie when you respond to the other side's opening offer of $50,000 with the line that "my client will not accept less than $150,000."

An obvious response to such a charge is that there is a difference between acceptable negotiating strategy (bluffing and exaggeration) and outright lying. Lying amounts to more than stating that something is true or false when you know it is not. It also demands that an intentional false statement be expected to mislead the other side. On this basis, your negotiating partner is unlikely to accept all your statements at face value; negotiating is a game whose essence is bluff and counter-bluff. In many cases, the use of more impersonal and less categoric language will finesse the problem. Instead of asserting that "my client will not accept less than $150,000," you could say that "an offer nearer to $150,000 would be more reasonable." Also, as with all negotiating, there is a strong strategic (if not moral reason) not to lie: if you get found out and cannot back up your claim, you will be perceived as a bad negotiator. A good negotiator must retain credibility, and "lying" regularly is no way to do that.[11]

However, the line between so-called bluffery and outright lying is shifting and very thin: context will be vital. For instance, there is a tricky question of whether it is acceptable to include the "false" demand

---

11   J.J. White, "Machiavelli and the Bar: Ethical Limitations on Lying in Negotiations" (1980) A.B.F. Research J. 926.

in order to drop it later in the negotiations as a concession and sign of good faith. Also, there remains the thorny problem of whether it is possible to lie by omission: Is it always ethical to fail to reveal a relevant and important piece of evidence or law? Of course, denying the existence of such evidence is another matter entirely. An instance that seems to cross the line and move the lawyer into unethical territory is agreeing to perpetuate a client's lie. It might be one thing to keep quiet about certain matters, but it is another thing to actively connive to mislead. While it is acceptable to begin negotiations with a high demand, it is much more dubious to sustain a claim for settlement on the basis of a client's vastly exaggerated assessment of damage. However, even here, some might argue that it is for the other lawyer to be satisfied with the merit or worth of a claim. Also, further ethical pressure is added to the negotiating process when one of the parties is represented by a lawyer and the other is not (see chapter 6).

**PROBLEM 49: Your client tells you that he has discovered he is HIV-positive (which has not developed into full-blown AIDS) from a botched injection by his doctor. He requests you to negotiate a settlement on his behalf. Negotiations proceed quickly and the doctor's lawyers seem willing to settle for a sizeable amount. Shortly before finalizing the settlement, the client informs you that he has had a second medical examination that has revealed conclusively that he is not HIV-positive. However, he insists that he still wants you to continue the negotiations on the basis that he is HIV-positive and to take the settlement on offer. What should you do?**

Perhaps the best answer to the issue of "lying in negotiations" is that the negotiator's primary duty is to be fair. Obviously, some situations demand a high degree of integrity; this involves not lying about those matters that (you believe) the other side would also not lie about. But it does not demand an absolutist commitment to always telling "the whole truth and nothing but the truth." As with the litigation process itself, justice between the parties ought to be the abiding ambition of the system. Of course, the adoption of this standard can be very self-serving and allows all kinds of dubious conduct, but it seems the only sensible and reasonable solution. For good and bad, legal ethics are simply the ethics of lawyers writ large. To demand more is naive; to expect less is irresponsible. Ultimately, the legal profession is only as good as the people who comprise it. It is not better rules, but better people, that will enhance the standards of ethical lawyering.

The ethical challenges in mediation are of a very different character. Most areas of legal disputes are amenable to ADR approaches, but mediation has become well established in family law, partnership terminations, company mergers, and restructuring. A preliminary (and controversial) inquiry is whether ADR, or at least certain aspects of ADR, constitute the practice of law. If so, the practical implications of such matters as conflicts of interest, confidentiality, and legal liability need to be carefully considered. The answer is surely that lawyers will be assumed to be acting in a lawyering capacity unless there is some explicit agreement to the contrary. It is a duty of lawyers to ensure that they do not engage in business "that makes it difficult to distinguish in which capacity the lawyer is acting." Moreover, even if they are acting in a non-legal capacity, they are still under a clear obligation to adhere "to standards of conduct as high as that [the] Code requires of a lawyer engaged in the practice of law" (see VII, c. 4). Also, if lawyer-mediators are bound by the professional Rules, suitably adapted, there is the converse question of whether non-lawyers who act as mediators might be engaged in the unauthorized practice of law. Common sense suggests that the act of mediation is not always and only part of legal practice and, provided mediators do not hold themselves as lawyers, such persons are not engaged in the unauthorized practice of law.

There is no bar to lawyers engaging in mediation, but they must be sure that they abide by the rules about acting for multiple parties (see chapter 5). For instance, a lawyer can act to settle a dispute between two or more clients "who are *sui juris* and who wish to submit the dispute to the lawyer" (see V, c. 7). Some law societies have developed special rules designed to govern lawyer-mediators. The main thrust of these rules is to ensure that the clients are aware of the different consequences that might follow from engaging lawyers to act as mediators. The primary problem results from the fact that lawyers-as-mediators are putting themselves into a very different role from that normally assumed; it requires them to be non-adversarial and neutral. Moreover, it means that they will have two clients, not one, and, while their clients might not be completely adverse in interests, they will not necessarily share exactly the same expectations and interests. If lawyers are to become mediators, it is especially important that they meet with both clients to establish their expectations and to inform them about the lawyers' professional obligations about conflict of interests and confidentiality. In particular, before undertaking the task of mediator, lawyers must satisfy themselves that there is a sufficient parity between the two clients in terms of their relative capacity to make and, as important, not make decisions. Because they are unable to advise each client separately on the merit of any particular outcome, lawyer-mediators should avoid situations where mismatched parties (as in certain matrimonial situations) are involved. Occasionally, it might be appropriate to accept the role of mediator, provided that each client obtains independent counsel, even if this solution does somewhat defeat the purpose of mediation in the first place. In all circumstances, lawyer-mediators should have professional responsibility for the overall fairness of the process and its results.[12]

Lawyers who mediate also face significant uncertainties over how their ADR work will affect future assignments for their law firms and how the rules of confidentiality will apply. Because this is a very new and burgeoning area of practice, there has been little definitive work on the precise obligations on ADR lawyers. Nevertheless, a number of important issues concerning conflicts of interest and confidentiality are beginning to become clearer:

- On conflict, lawyers should not agree to mediate where they acted for one of the parties in another unrelated matter, unless there is no chance that this experience will affect the lawyer's neutrality and that all parties to the mediation give informed consent.[13] A number of issues are still in need of clarification: Is a law firm barred from representing a party because one of its lawyers served as mediator in a matter involving the potential client? When is an individual lawyer's conflict imputed to their firm? And are screens appropriate to protect against broad disqualification?
- As regards confidentiality, while the communications that pass between lawyer-mediators and the parties are confidential, they are not covered by the evidential rule of solicitor-client privilege, since the lawyer-mediator is acting in a neutral capacity. Again, it is preferable for lawyers and parties to the mediation to determine beforehand in an agreement what the nature and limits of confidentiality are. This agreement will be mandatory under the new code (see X). In this regard, the words of Farley J. on arbitration apply with equal force to mediation:

> I believe that it is obvious that if the ADR process entered into is along the mediation philosophy structure that it will be appreciated that the best and most productive results re dispute resolution will be achieved generally if such process involves a degree of confidentiality. This of course is subject to some exceptions such as when the parties agree that in a mediation of public policy issues there is a positive requirement for public exposure. . . . In other instances public

---

12   See J.L. Maute, "Public Values and Private Justice: A Case for Mediator Accountability" (1991) 4 Georgetown J. of Legal Ethics 503.
13   See A.J. Pirie, "The Lawyer as Mediator: Professional Responsibility Problems or Profession Problems?" (1985) 63 Can. Bar Rev. 378.

exposure may induce a very negative reaction — e.g, if outsiders can be observers, then some (depending on their relationship to the parties involved) may become "cheerleaders," "advisors without the benefit of the facts" or "advisors without the discipline of having to live with the end result of the mediation." Unwanted pressure may thus be applied to one or more of the participants. Similarly a volunteer advisor-type may give "free" advice (e.g., "Don't settle; take him to court; you've got an absolute winner!") when the hidden agenda of this officious intermeddler is to foment disruption, harass the other side or pursue his own interests. Allow me to observe that it would be unusual for anyone to feel obliged to conduct all his negotiations (including those to settle disputes) in a fishbowl.[14]

However, while the solicitor-client privilege does not apply, there is some level of confidentiality that attaches to those communications that are genuinely in the course of settlement. This privilege is subject to a number of exceptions: the communications must be part of a good-faith effort to settle disputes or differences; the communication for which privilege is claimed must be integral to the settlement process and not incidental to it; and the privilege will not apply in situations where the validity or nature of the settlement is in dispute.[15]

## C. POVERTY LAWYERS

In light of the empowered role and elevated status of lawyers in society, the hired-hand image is a very humble representation of what lawyers do and what people experience in their dealings with lawyers. As stated in chapter 2, a particular fallacy that is contained within the image of the lawyer-as-hired-hand is the belief that legal practice is much the same for those who serve disenfranchised people and those who work for more privileged clients; it is simply a matter of following different rules. Not only is access to legal services obviously disparate but the needs of the poor require a very different kind of lawyering. Treating all clients the same will do little to alleviate the situation of poorer people. Unlike those of more privileged people, the problems of the poor are continuing and systemic rather than sporadic and particular; legal problems do not arise so much in the otherwise smooth course of their life,

14   *887574 Ontario Inc.* v. *Pizza Pizza Ltd.* (1994), 35 C.P.C. (3d) 323 at 328–29 (Ont. Gen. Div.).

15   See P.M. Perrell, "The Problems of Without Prejudice" (1992) 71 Can. Bar Rev. 223.

but constitute and define much of their life. Whereas advantaged clients want their lawyers to use the system to remedy a discrete conflict, disenfranchised clients want their lawyers to change the system so they can escape life's continual round of legal difficulties and bureaucratic hassles.[16] Apolitical engagement in social struggles through law is a luxury few poverty lawyers and their clients can afford.

The first problem for poor people in pursuing their legal claims is finding a lawyer who is willing to take them on as clients. The fact that they are poor and, therefore, unable to afford legal services is an obvious barrier. As previously discussed and criticized, while lawyers are collectively encouraged to participate in legal aid plans, referral services, pro bono work, and public education programs to help make legal services more accessible and understandable to the "inexperienced," there is no duty on individual lawyers to do so (see chapter 5, and XIV, c. 5). However, there is an obligation on lawyers who decide not to act on behalf of someone after a consultation meeting "to assist in finding" another lawyer "without charge" (see XIV, c. 4). Needless to say, these moral inducements have not managed to bridge the gap in the quality of service available to the rich and the poor. Indeed, it can also be argued that the Rules' restrictive approach to advertising, solicitation, and contingency fees has further exacerbated the problem of unequal access to justice.

Assuming that a poor person is able to obtain legal services, a second problem concerns the role and tactics that so-called poverty lawyers should adopt. Too often, well-intentioned lawyers succumb to the temptation to treat poor clients as having the same problems and, therefore, requiring the same kind of legal assistance as rich clients. In particular, many lawyers are too quick to shift into a litigation mode of thinking. Little serious consideration is given to the real risk that courts and the legal process at large are part of the problem and will neutralize efforts at transformation and change. While litigation will not always be avoidable or co-optive, the courts are only occasionally the emancipatory and empowering institution that many lawyers and commentators claim. As such, progressive scholars must look for better and different ways to empower disadvantaged groups and clients. In effecting such a proposal, two approaches might be taken. The first step is to raise the critical consciousness of lawyers by disabusing them of their ingrained habit of resorting to the courts as the transformative forum of choice. They must become more sensitive to the debilitating effect of the extended involvement of courts in civic life. Second, progressive law-

---

16   See S. Wexler, "Practicing Law for Poor People" (1970) 79 Yale L.J. 1049.

yers must develop a posture of strategic scepticism towards the efficacy of even limited use of litigation in the struggle for social justice. The history of social struggle suggests that the prospect of significant social change through litigation is, as one American judge so colourfully put it, "a teasing illusion like a munificent bequest in a pauper's will."[17]

The key issues for those devoted to improving the lot of the oppressed and downtrodden are to determine what substantive changes will best achieve that objective, how those measures can be implemented most effectively, and which institutions can best carry through on that agenda. Mindful that the details and priorities of a progressive politics must be the continuing subject of healthy debate and respectful disagreement, there must also be a willingness to use a diversity of strategies to effect progressive change and to resort to a variety of institutional sites. However, it is important that such tactical calculations are sensitive to the prevailing realities of social power and economic ordering. Some of the appropriate questions to ask about rights are posed by Elizabeth Schneider:

> Does the use of legal struggle generally and rights discourse in particular help build a social movement? Does articulating a right advance political organizing and assist in political education? Can a right be articulated in a way that is consistent with the politics of an issue or that helps redefine it? Does the transformation of political insight into legal argumentation capture the political visions that underlie the movement? Does the use of rights keep us in touch with or divert us from consideration of and struggle around the hard questions of political choice and strategy?[18]

As well as perpetuating the idea that justice comes from a judicial act of *noblesse oblige* rather than a popular action and struggle, a dependence on litigation will dissipate much valuable energy that could be better used elsewhere. Direct citizen involvement is always to be preferred to litigation. At the heart of any progressive campaign for social justice, there must be a firm commitment to the development of popular coalitions, so that the disenfranchised can become part of their own empowerment. For instance, in responding to the plight of the homeless, those very people can be involved as paid consultants and workers in the planning

---

17  *Edwards v. People of State of California*, 314 U.S. 160 at 186 (1941). For a much fuller exploration and defence of these claims, see A.C. Hutchinson, *Waiting for Coraf: A Critique of Law and Rights* (Toronto: University of Toronto Press, 1995) at 175–82.

18  E.M. Schneider, "The Dialectic of Rights and Politics: Perspectives from the Women's Movement" (1986) N.Y.U. Law Rev. 589 at 622–23.

and (re)building of affordable housing and public amenities so that, once such homes are created, they might be able to pay their way in their cooperative management and maintenance. In particular, poverty lawyers should consider shifting from less of an individual-centred and rights-based approach to more of a group-based and power-oriented program that will facilitate this ambition. In this way, it might become possible to "recognise and accommodate the political importance of process over legal goals and build links with communities whose perspectives" are not usually or easily represented in the litigation.[19]

Apart from abjuring the instinctive tendency towards litigation, lawyers might doubt their capacity for useful involvement qua lawyers. However, they would be wrong. Lawyers have an important role to play in such efforts. While it will involve a reorientation of what is traditionally understood to be the primary skills of lawyering, a revised legal practice will still call upon many of the peculiar talents of lawyers for sophisticated organization and sound planning. The model of the good corporate lawyer can be appropriated and given a community-based twist. In facilitating the establishment of community institutions, lawyers can enhance the cooperative's capacity to make informed decisions about its own development and activities; they can nurture a democratic culture and organizational structure that meets the needs and wishes of its members. In this way, the lawyer becomes a public part of the civic community rather than a private adversary of it.

In their pioneering scholarship and practice, Gabel and Harris suggest that any strategy to help poor people must not simply take (and leave) the legal system as it is but should seek to challenge and transform the process itself; the courts and lawyers are as much a part of the problem as the solution.[20] They propose several tactics that lawyers might adopt to advance the interests of poverty clients. These proposals are intended to apply to run-of-the-mill personal injury cases as to high-profile political cases. They include:

- *The disruption of the state's attempt to individualize cases by locating the common political thread that runs through them.* As part of a continuing effort to reconceptualize cases so as to emphasize rather than downplay their ideological structure, lawyers should select and litigate cases in order to politicize the operation of the legal system. For

19   S. Razack, *Canadian Feminism and the Law: The Women's Legal Education and Action Fund and the Pursuit of Equality* (Toronto: Second Story Press, 1991) at 57.

20   P. Gabel & P. Harris, "Building Power and Breaking Images: Critical Legal Theory and the Practice of Law" (1983) 11 N.Y.U. Rev. of Law and Soc. Change 369.

instance, criminal lawyers might take cases that reveal the tendency for the criminal process to routinize certain crimes and the prosecution of particular groups, or civil lawyers might organize tenants to oppose the whole regime of landlord-tenant law.

- *The concentration on efforts to build community organizations.* In the spirit of anti-hierarchical activism, lawyers should remember that they must resist the temptation to take over the case. Mindful that their ultimate responsibility is to do away with poverty, the lawyers of poor clients must help poor people to help themselves; there is little permanent progress if poor clients win the battle, but have no real idea about how to fight the next battle in the continuing war against poverty.
- *The politicization of courtrooms and other "legal" public spaces that are presently pervaded by a technical and bureaucratic mentality.* Lawyers should challenge the symbolic power of the courts, over time presenting themselves and their clients in a less formal and impersonal way. This process need not involve acts of contempt or disobedience, but it can include challenges to petty protocols (e.g., clothing and demeanour) and the insistence in presenting clients and themselves as real and different people.
- *The deprofessionalization of the lawyer-client relationship.* Lawyers should ensure that they develop a relationship of genuine equality and mutual trust with their clients. They must disabuse themselves of the notion that they are neutral and objective participants in an inherently just exercise. Also, they must try to educate their clients so they are able to act occasionally for themselves and become empowered in the process.

Needless to say, such an approach and tactics are not guaranteed to endear lawyers to the legal establishment. Indeed, if they did, poverty lawyers can assume that they are not as successful as they might think. But efforts to engage in transformative lawyering will likely involve poverty lawyers in a style of practice that offends many established lawyers and will oblige them to sail very close to the ethical wind, at least as understood by more traditional practitioners. Indeed, some maintain that such an alternative approach to legal ethics and professional responsibility — one that actually puts the interests of clients above those of the profession and the legal system — is entirely unethical and warrants the removal of such lawyers from the profession. A particularly tough response on political activism through lawyering is made by a former Law Society treasurer and judge, George Finlayson, who said:

> [I]t is one thing to speak out in favour of a cause, it is another to use clients as a means of promoting that cause. Here the client is not being

represented. Here the client is the victim of what the lawyer considers to be a matter that is worth fighting for. . . . There is no reason why [an environmental concern, for example] should not be passionately expressed. But it is no function of lawyers who have such a view to actively attempt to thwart public projects by advocating public protests, instituting frivolous court proceedings, arguing procedural delays and employing confrontation tactics before regulatory bodies.[21]

In light of the dubious moral character of much standard practice, however, it is difficult to interpret activist opposition as unduly obstructionist and reactionary. Accordingly, in the circumstances of poverty lawyering, the whole notion of legal ethics needs to be reoriented. As the government's hostility to legal aid increases and lawyers' willingness to engage in pro bono work decreases, the issue of what amounts to professional responsibility should be urgently revisited.

PROBLEM 50: You are approached by a couple of tenants in a large urban building. They want to get their plumbing fixed. The landlord is a corporation that has a deserved reputation for keeping its many properties in bad repair. You know from experience that you can help the two tenants by threatening the landlord with legal action. However, you know this will do little to help the many other tenants in the same predicament. What could you do in this situation to help both your clients and the other tenants?

PROBLEM 51: A rich client wants you to take a class action against the city to force it to take care of its homeless citizens. It is a condition of payment that her identity remain strictly confidential. She suggests that you arrange for someone to distribute leaflets to homeless people announcing that there will be a meeting, at which food and clothing will be available, to consider the possibility of a legal action. At the meeting, you provide all those who sign up as potential class members with food vouchers for a local restaurant. Are there any problems with carrying out any of these actions?

# D. GOVERNMENT LAWYERS

Lawyers in public office must continue to maintain the same high standards expected of lawyers in private practice because their position "is in the public eye" and, therefore, "the legal profession can more readily

---

21   G.D. Finlayson, "The Lawyer as a Professional" (1980) 14 L.S.U.C. Gazette 229 at 232, 233–34. For a provocative account of one lawyer's effort to politicize legal practice, see P. Rosenthal, "The Toronto Nuclear Weapons Trials: A Look Back to the Future" (1991) 10 Windsor Yearbook of Access to Justice 194.

be brought into disrepute" by misconduct (see X, c. 1). As part of this expectation, lawyers "should not appear professionally" in front of official bodies of which they are members, but they can appear professionally before committees of some official bodies, as long as the lawyers are not members of those specific committees (see X, c. 5). Although American courts have placed a higher standard on government lawyers, the tendency of Canadian courts is to hold them to a similar standard as lawyers in private practice.[22] When acting as prosecutors, the special duties that arise in criminal cases are in play (see chapter 9).

When lawyers hold public office, they must not let personal interests conflict with official duties. If lawyers also engage in private legal business, they must make sure there will not be conflicts between official and legal duties. However, in case of an unforeseen conflict, it is clear that "official duties must prevail." Personal interests of lawyers include those of lawyers' relatives, professional associates, partners, and clients (see X, c. 2 and c. 3). Lawyers in public office who foresee potential conflicts of interest must "declare" them at the "earliest opportunity" and must "take no part in any consideration, discussion or vote with respect" to such issues (see X, c. 4). Once they have acted in an official capacity in respect of "any persons or interests," lawyers should not represent those parties "in the same or any related matter." If lawyers were members of official bodies at the time certain rulings were made, they should not advise clients on such rulings (see X, c. 6).

Information acquired in the course of holding public office must be maintained as confidential even after lawyers have ceased to hold such positions (see X, c. 7). Discreditable conduct in public office affecting lawyers' integrity may lead to disciplinary action (see X, c. 8). On leaving public office, lawyers should not accept employment connected to matters with which they would have had "substantial responsibility or confidential information" while in office, to avoid the "appearance of impropriety." In such matters, lawyers may act in a professional capacity on behalf of the public body for whom they worked (see XIX, c. 3). Lawyers who practise together in government departments are allowed to share confidential information. Also, lawyers who have obtained "confidential government information about a person" while serving in public office may not represent a client (other than their former public employer or agency) with adverse interests, where "the information could be used to the material disadvantage of that person" (see IV, c. 14). Finally, conflicts of interest may be imputed to the government department

---

22 *Everingham v. Ontario* (1992), 88 D.L.R. (4th) 755 (Div. Ct.).

based on the conflicts of interest of one of the lawyers. When moving between private practice and public service, the relevant rules about conflicts apply (see chapter 8).

## E. CONCLUSION

In this chapter, I have sought to explore four situations — corporate, poverty, government, and ADR lawyering — in which the general principles come into play and operate in a slightly different way than might normally be expected. While lawyers engaged in these specialized pursuits face a series of different challenges, they are still bound by the general rules and responsibilities that apply to all lawyers. As with all lawyering dilemmas, the special circumstances of the particular context are vitally important in prompting individual lawyers to determine what is and what is not the most responsible and ethical course to follow. In short, the conditions of practice may be different, but the challenge is the same. Whether one is a corporate lawyer or a poverty lawyer, and whether one is involved in ADR work or government enforcement, the ethical impetus ought to be a common enterprise — to develop a professional *modus vivendi* that respects the pushes of the institutional expectations and the pulls of individual conscience.

# CONCLUSION: TAKING IT PERSONALLY

In this short book, I have sought to challenge many of the prevailing misunderstandings that pervade discussions on legal ethics and to make good on present shortcomings in professional responsibility. As I stated in the introduction, the book is intended to be both a critical primer on the current approaches to professional responsibility and a call to ethical arms. I reject the traditional image and defence of the ethical lawyer as hired hands (as well as more recent alternatives) because they are based on a flawed set of assumptions about the operation of law and the practice of lawyering in contemporary Canada. Mindful that the homogeneity of lawyers is beginning to be replaced by a more diverse professional personnel, I have found the unifying theme for the book in the challenge that a fragmented society and legal profession holds for the development of a transformed practice of professional responsibility and legal ethics. Accordingly, in place of the traditional exposition, I seek to offer a more compelling and workable account of lawyering. The result is, I hope, a sensible contribution to an important task that should be appreciated and shared by all lawyers, both personally and collectively: the development of an ethically satisfying and professionally responsible approach to legal practice. In this final chapter, therefore, I will trace some of the broader implications for future developments and innovations, especially in regard to the study and training of young lawyers.

# A. INSTITUTIONAL CHANGE

Although almost all lawyers share a general agreement on the need to engage in ethical conduct and responsible professional behaviour, there is very little agreement on what that means or demands in situations of moral complexity. The traditional vision of lawyering tends to be as much a way to finesse the hard questions of practice as a tool to confront and grapple with them. While the idea of professionalism ought not to be a reliable guide to lawyers, this does not imply that its content and orientation must be unchanging; "it makes sense to view professionalism not as a fixed ideal, but rather as an ongoing struggle."[1] In many ways, the Rules do little service in the day-to-day practice of lawyers as a result of their generality and vagueness: ethical problems are often too complex and subtle to lend themselves to formulaic resolution. While there is still need for a disciplinary regime, there must also be an improved process of education and continuing training as well as important changes in the structural imperatives of legal practice.

The first step in developing an ethically satisfying and professionally responsible approach to legal practice is that, if legal practice is to play a more transformative and socially responsive role in society, it must first transform legal practice itself. At present, despite the traditional insistence to the contrary, lawyers and lawyering march as much to the beat of their economic interests as those of their clients; lawyers do what their clients want as much and so long as it is in the lawyers' overall interests. As I have tried to show, this approach is effected in myriad ways and is often done in the name of social justice (see chapter 5, on access to legal services). However, exploring the possible means for their institutional transformation — loss of monopoly and self-regulation, socialized legal services, and so on — is well beyond the scope of this book. Nevertheless, there are three primary obstacles to the realization of a truly ethical and responsible legal practice:

- Lawyers are trained to see law and its institutions as just and necessary structures. While there is no suggestion that lawyers must become unappeasable critics of the legal order, they ought to be more encouraged to question the extent to which present legal and doctrinal arrangements serve the community and social justice generally.

---

1    D.L. Rhode, "The Professionalism Problem" (1998) 39 W. & M. L. Rev. 283 at 325. See also P.J. Schlitz, "Legal Ethics in Decline: The Elite Law Firm, the Elite Law School, and the Moral Formation of the Novice Attorney" (1998) 82 Minn. L. Rev. 705 at 713–18.

- There is a professional discipline of political neutrality. While there is no obligation on lawyers to become overtly political in their selection of clients and strategies, they ought to become more attuned to the impact that their professional efforts have upon the allocation and exercise of power in society.
- The social organization of the profession and its continuing lack of real diversity in membership marginalize any alternative or challenging modes of lawyering. As well as redoubling efforts to broaden the demographic base of the legal profession, it is vital to ensure that young lawyers are introduced to less traditional and uniform visions of lawyering: variety can be the spice of legal life.[2]

If there is to be some substantial progress in overcoming these obstacles, changes will be required not only in the legal profession but also in the way legal education is carried out. Law schools and the professoriate must accept their share of the blame for the profession's continuing state of affairs. One obvious place to start is the dismal performance of law schools in taking legal ethics and professional responsibility seriously. Only four schools presently have a compulsory course in legal ethics: Dalhousie, Alberta, Manitoba, and New Brunswick. Such courses should not be exercises in indoctrination, in which students are introduced to and asked to internalize prevailing views and values. Rather, it would be important to teach students about existing rules and attitudes, but also to strive to place the work of lawyers in a historical, social, and political context, so that students will be able to develop a critical intelligence and sense of judgment about issues of professional responsibility and legal ethics. Indeed, a thorough and responsive approach to the teaching of legal professional responsibility will need to draw upon an eclectic range of resources that include the philosophical insights of Kant and Wittgenstein, the popular TV series of Ally MacBeal and *Street Legal*, the political writings of MacKinnon and Arthurs, and the trial techniques of Eddie Greenspan and Ken Murray.

In a cogent article, Jocelyn Downie canvasses three main arguments in favour of compulsory education in legal ethics:

- Whether they like it or not, law schools do train students for legal practice. As part of their contribution to meeting obligations that arise from the public trust in the legal profession, law schools can make good on the promise of law to achieve justice. The present silence

2   See S. Scheingold, "The Contradictions of Radical Law Practice" in M.E. Cain, *Lawyers in a Postmodern World: Translation and Transgression* (New York: New York University Press, 1994) at 265.

on legal ethics is deafening and informs students that professional responsibility is not really important.

- Students can learn valuable practical skills in legal ethics courses that will help them throughout their professional career. Moreover, law schools themselves will benefit from the incorporation of ethical debate into their community life, and their overall study of law might be enriched.

- While many lawyers will never encounter many of the legal problems that they study in their substantive courses, all lawyers will at some time in their career be obliged to confront and resolve difficult ethical dilemmas. Other professions, like medicine, take the responsibility to instruct and sensitize their student members to the ethical challenges they will face in practice.[3]

As part of this general overhaul, one important initiative will be to institutionalize and accelerate the diversification of the legal profession. Instead of paying lip-service to the idea, there must be aggressive and sustained efforts to open up the legal profession to the many different groups that presently face significant barriers to entry. Indeed, some of those changes have already taken place, and it is for the professions' ruling bodies and establishment to recognize and accommodate that fact. It is already impossible to proceed on the basis that there is such an entity as *the lawyer*, a fungible professional model that can stand in for and represent the rest of the profession. There are many different kinds of lawyers and ways of lawyering: small firms, large firms, sole practitioners, urban practices, rural practices, generalist firms, specialist firms, female firms, ethnic firms, and so on. It flouts social reality to pretend that legal regulation or instruction can be based on anything but plural and multiple visions of legal practice.

Of course, in spite of the diversity in forms of business organization and delivery of legal services, the legal profession is still a privileged and élite profession that is largely populated and dominated by white, middle-aged men of old European stock. In the same way that the cultural and ethnic diversity of Canada has changed, so must the legal profession reorganize itself to reflect this pragmatic fact of social living. It is not, as many established lawyers believe, that there are "special" groups and soci-

---

3   J. Downie, "A Case for Compulsory Legal Ethics Education in Canadian Law Schools" (1997) 20 Dal. L.J. 224. A starting place for such improvements is contained in the recommendations of a recent report of the A.B.A., titled "Teaching and Learning Professionalism: Report of the Professionalism Committee" (Chicago: American Bar Association, Section of Legal Education and Admissions to the Bar, 1996).

eties whose interests must be recognized and whose members must be absorbed into the legal profession. The truly special group in the Canadian legal profession is the one that has controlled its affairs and self-image for decades. Effective transformation will only occur when that group is willing or obliged to relinquish its hold on power. The only real changes in the system will come when the composition, demographics, and life-experience of lawyers change and their different view of what it is to be a lawyer is not simply tolerated, but actually begins to displace or transform the regnant images that have been nurtured by the dominant group in society and falsely heralded as neutral in operation and design.

At the heart of my pragmatic proposal, therefore, is an insistence that what is required is the development of a fresh approach to legal ethics that is both sensitive to the changing shape and style of modern legal practice and, at the same time, demands that lawyers aspire to a more diverse and critical self-image. In developing such a proposal, the central question is whether it is ever acceptable that lawyers might, can, or should act in a professional capacity in such a way that it would be contrary to their own moral values. My answer is that there ought to be a special and symbiotic relation between personal morality and professional expectations. As part of this pragmatic project, I have made a series of recommendations for change and revision. The most important are as follows:

- There must be a shift of emphasis from professional regulation to personal responsibility. The ambition is not to promote a particular set of ethical outcomes or inculcate a specific mode of professional responsibility. It ought to be to challenge students and lawyers to develop a professional *modus vivendi* of their own that constructs as it constantly challenges and reworks an appropriate professional attitude and practice.
- In the same way that there is no one or unchanging way to be a good person, there is no one or unchanging way to be a good lawyer. Each and every lawyer must be capable of developing a style and substance of lawyering that incorporates a continuing dialogue — with oneself, clients, other lawyers, other professionals, and the community at large — about what counts as good lawyering. In many so-called hard cases, there is rarely an obvious or incontestable path to follow.
- The professional Rules do not and cannot relieve lawyers of the continuing responsibility to exercise their own professional and moral judgment about the appropriate course to follow. Unthinking compliance with the specified Rules does not guarantee that lawyers will develop a sense of ethical judgment: professional morality is more than law-abiding conformity. This does not mean that the Rules have

no place in any appreciation of legal ethics and their actual improvement; they are an important resource in discussion and decision making, but they are not a decisive or determinate play-book that relieves lawyers of the personal responsibility to develop an ethical style and substance of legal practice. As I try to stress throughout this book, the Rules are only a starting point or resource in the broader debate about appropriate ethical behaviour: they act as the outside limits within which debate can and must occur.

- All lawyers and students must justify their sense of professional responsibility through their actions rather than justify their actions by reference to the ideals of professional responsibility. If the legal profession is to live up to its own cherished ideals and to reclaim its reputation as an honourable undertaking, it must challenge each of its present and future members to take this task seriously.

- By *pragmatic*, it is certainly not meant that lawyers should take an expedient or less-than-serious approach to issues of legal ethics and professional responsibility. On the contrary, a pragmatic perspective implies a committed ethical stance and demands a genuine appreciation of what taking responsibility involves. What it does suggest is that no one simple and straightforward account can be given about the legal process which is cogent or valid as an accurate description of what goes on or a reliable prescription of how to change it. The only constant about law, society, and their interaction is their messiness and contingency. Any theoretical attempt to privilege one explanation of the role of the lawyer is doomed to failure.

- There is always the personal ethical challenge of determining whether, because the Rules allow certain conduct, the individual lawyer should reflect on and perhaps refuse to operate in certain ways. The fact that the Rules allow lawyers to ignore the interests of other parties entirely does not mean that this course is a morally unimpeachable one to follow: *can* does not necessarily imply *must*.

- Lawyers must be prepared to answer for the ethical choices they make and the legal practice in which they engage. An explicit and enduring focus on the cultivation of a strong sense of professional purpose and judgment must be pursued and institutionalized. For instance, while there is no more important issue for lawyers than how they are going to select the persons to whom they agree to provide their legal services, this issue is sadly neglected by the institutional norms of professional responsibility. On the pragmatic approach that I encourage, lawyers should treat their clients as a conversational partner who can contribute and be persuaded about particular courses of action and their likely consequences.

- While there are few actual restrictions on lawyers making their services known and available to those who are least able to afford them and most likely to need them, there is no ethical obligation to ensure that such people's needs are met. Again, insofar as lawyers hold a state-backed monopoly over an indispensable social resource, and insofar as many make a handsome living from that privilege, there ought to be more of a collective and personal commitment to sharing access in a more egalitarian and less restrictive way.
- Contrary to the common understanding, lawyers' duty to their clients is only a secondary one; the duty to the court and the profession is primary. Further, lawyers' primary duty to their clients does not automatically justify acting with complete disregard for the interests of opposing parties. Winning on behalf of your client does not mean destroying or humiliating the losing party.

## B. TAKING IT PERSONALLY

My most central recommendation is to urge lawyers to take personal responsibility for what they say and do in their professional capacities. Although it seems a modest proposal, it has traditionally been treated as a radical import and implication. By rejecting the hackneyed and unsustainable notion of an entirely differentiated role, lawyers might begin to gain the respect of the public and themselves. In the same way that "good oratory is a good person speaking well,"[4] so good lawyering is a good person acting well. As trivial and trite as this may seem, it is the best advice that can be given to the fledgling lawyer and the most compelling injunction to the jaded lawyer. It offers no magical guide as to what to do in any specific or conflicted situation, since there is none to be given. It is for each person to arrive at an informed and conscientious decision in accordance with his or her political and moral lights. The objective is not to chastize lawyers simply because they are corporate lawyers or because they represent rapists and bigots: it is to encourage all lawyers to take responsibility for the clients they take, the causes they fight for, and the tactics they use. In doing so, however, the pragmatic lawyer will ensure that those moral and political lights are always brought into play and are themselves open to debate and reconsideration. In the pragmatic play-book, an enforced and impersonal orthodoxy is not the goal; rather, it is a respectful and responsible heterodoxy.

---

4   Quintilian, *The Institutio Oratoria of Quintilian*, trans. H.E. Butler (Cambridge: Harvard University Press, 1958–61) at Book XII, s.1.1.

Owing to the power vested in lawyers as officers of the court and as representatives of ordinary people who may not know their rights or how to defend them, lawyers should have a corresponding degree of (moral) responsibility to their clients and to the institution of law. As these responsibilities are complex and often in conflict, it is imperative that "good judgment" or "moral reasoning" be given more consideration within the curriculum of the law school. It is too simplistic for members of the profession to throw up their hands and say, "such things can't be taught; either you have good judgment and moral reasoning or you don't."

Developmental psychology suggests that moral reasoning does not appear in a vacuum, but is based on a number of variables, most notably that it is a skill that can be developed gradually.[5] As such, morality can be seen as a process of social understanding that can be introduced and refined through constant discussion and debate about ethical dilemmas; moral reasoning skills can be exercised like a mental muscle. As well, students benefit from exposure to people of other groups (cultural, political, and so on) and involvement in social organizations. Whether improved moral reasoning skills lead to the application and exercising of good judgment when encountering real-life ethical dilemmas remains to be proven. There are many variables that will determine whether a person will act in a morally responsible way, but there is some correlation between better-educated adults and reflective ethical judgment. The research generated almost all points to the importance of continuing seminar discussion groups and role-playing situations within (a heterogeneous) law school in order to stimulate the moral reasoning potential of all law students.

The directive to lawyers to take responsibility for what they do (and do not do) ought not to be viewed as an excuse to ignore the needs of clients or to take control of a legal case in the same way as realist critics openly defend and traditionalists covertly effect (see chapter 2). The recommendation is for lawyers to be neither the clients' unquestioning servant nor their know-all master. Instead, lawyers and clients might be persuaded to work towards a non-hierarchical relationship that is premised on the fact that they both have something to contribute — the lawyer's insider knowledge and the client's outsider perspective — to the joint enterprise in which they are both equally, if differently, engaged. An important distinction here is between lawyers' personal set of substantive values and the more general constraints of their moral

---

5   P. Grey, *Psychology*, 2d ed. (New York: Worth Publishers, 1994) at 477–79.

convictions. Pragmatic lawyers will not foist their own values on the client, nor will they work with clients in ways that offend their own moral convictions. Initiated and sustained in this way, the lawyer-client relationship will be mutually respectful and engaged.

Also, in assuming responsibility, it is important that lawyers look beyond their dealings with their own clients. Part of any mature understanding of what amounts to responsible behaviour will include in its moral almanac the belief that one should do as little harm as possible. Although it will make life much more complicated, it is incumbent on pragmatic lawyers to weigh the effects of their actions on other people and the harm that will ensue. Society has a stake in the legal profession's actions, and this fact should be accepted by lawyers themselves. Again, this is a matter in which there is no magic formula to be followed or applied: every lawyer will have different views about the weight to be attached to different considerations and how they are to be weighed against the obligation to their clients and themselves. Contrary to popular misconceptions, the portrait of pragmatic lawyering is not painted exclusively in the familiar shades of moral grey: it is a living tableau that is filmed in bold and bright colours whose edges are constantly blurred and whose contrast is continually shifting.

As with so much else, de Tocqueville was only half-right in his assessment of (American) lawyers at the time he was writing. However, his conclusions remain equally valid and invalid today. While he was surely accurate in his pronouncement that lawyers constituted the new aristocracy of society, he was wide of the mark in believing that such an élite status was warranted because the legal profession functioned as the enlightened and sensible guardians of the public good.[6] Although traditional versions of legal ethics are still defended in the name of public service, there are few lawyers who conduct their daily professional lives in such a spirit. It is unrealistic to imagine or expect that every lawyer will, like Socrates, be guided only by the need to do right rather than wrong: most lawyers are reasonably concerned about their jobs, paying their mortgages, providing for their kids, and enhancing their social standing. Indeed, there is ample evidence to demonstrate that lawyers will hold to ethical principles when it is in their interests to do so, or, more accurately, when their financial considerations coincide with their ethical ones.[7] However, it is neither unreasonable nor unrealistic to

---

6    See A. de Tocqueville, *Democracy in America*, trans. H. Reeve (London: Oxford University Press, 1946).

7    See J.E. Carlin, *Lawyers on Their Own: A Study of Individual Practitioners in Chicago* (New Brunswick, NJ: Rutgers University Press, 1962).

expect that they can be persuaded, collectively and individually, to accept the noble challenge of redeeming the legal profession's moral standing and of fashioning a fresh image of legal ethics and professional responsibility that serves a fragmented society.

At the heart of any efforts to reaffirm the profession in its own and the public's moral esteem must be the commitment to emphasize that lawyers need not and should not spend the bulk of their professional lives doing what they would shy away from in their personal lives. Can it really be appropriate that lawyers should act in wilful disregard of moral considerations that would weigh heavily on them and others in their personal lives? In short, lawyers must stop asking whether a good lawyer can be a bad person and begin providing answers to how good persons and good lawyers can co-exist in the same person. This is a task that all lawyers should relish. Moreover, legal ethics should not be thought of as something that arises in discrete and exceptional circumstances. Everything that lawyers do, from the selection of clients to their involvement in civic affairs, implicates and reflects a lawyer's approach to and understanding of what it means to be an ethical lawyer. A lawyer who appreciates the full import of what is demanded of an ethical lawyer understands that ethical considerations are at the heart of lawyering, not a peripheral or occasional concern. To be a good person and a good lawyer need not be the oxymoron that Plato and more modern pessimists seem to believe it to be: "the lawyer has become keen and shrewed, but his soul is small and righteous."

Of course, the kind of pragmatic and personalized proposals that I have suggested will not sit well with everyone. For example, although directing his comments to those lawyers who use the courts for political activism, the comments of a former Law Society treasurer and judge, George Finlayson, evince the traditional scepticism towards my alternative account of legal ethics and professional responsibility:

> So where are we left? Back to first principles, I would suggest. Please remember that you are not law professors, students of human behaviour, or social or political scientists. You are lawyers, first and last. Your mandate is not to change the world; yours is a much higher calling. You are charged with the defence of the freedom of the Queen's subjects under the law. . . .[S]o long as you choose to practise law in the traditional sense: the representation of a client in any sphere: you must never forget that your duty is to that client alone. He puts his trust in you to advise and represent him in what to him is an unfathomable mystery: the Law. If you confuse your social or political conscience with your duty to that client, you betray his trust; you betray us all.[8]

As I have tried to insist throughout the book, this kind of blinkered thinking is as misconceived as it is misleading. While lawyers are required to place their clients' interest ahead of others', it is simply mistaken to insist that "you must never forget that your duty is to that client alone." Lawyers have duties to the courts, the profession, the community, and, not least of all, to themselves: they fulfill their legal obligations best when they acknowledge and assume ethical responsibility for what they do in the name and service of their clients. Indeed, one of the ways in which they can most effectively do this is to refuse to accept that law is "an unfathomable mystery" and work towards making law more accessible and amenable to their clients' concerns. After all, law is meant to be for the greater good of people, not an arcane resource for lawyers' benefit. Far from acting in a way that will "betray us all," the appropriate incorporation of "social or political conscience" into lawyers' daily routines might allow the legal profession to redeem its reputation and satisfy its higher calling. A pragmatic approach to professional responsibility and legal ethics will better allow lawyers to realize their ethical potential and come good on their social mandate.

## C. FOOD FOR THOUGHT

The promise and failure of prevailing views on legal ethics and professional responsibility can be brought home through a short story. Walking along a city street, a person comes upon three people who are cooking food and selling it for a small price to passers-by. When asked what they are doing, one of them answers, "I am making a living and earning money." The second one states, "I am using my culinary skills." The third one replies, "I am doing the best I can to help society by feeding those who are hungry." Lawyers could do worse than heed the moral of this tale.[9] There is more to being a lawyer than simply earning (often a lot of) money and exercising the legal equivalent of the ability to cook. Neither of these reasons are necessarily bad in themselves: there is nothing wrong with craft or business. It is the fact that they are not encompassed within a more ennobling justification that is the problem. As many lawyers conveniently and selectively choose to forget, their work

---

8    G.D. Finlayson, "The Lawyer as a Professional" (1980) 14 L.S.U.C. Gazette 229 at 235.
9    This is adapted from F. Iacobucci, "The Practice of Law: Business and Professionalism" (1991) 49 Advocate 859 at 864. Justice Iacobucci's tale is about building a cathedral, which is a little too precious and tradition-bound for my taste.

is not simply part of a general craft or business: it is a profession. It has been entrusted with considerable authority and privilege, including the right to regulate its own affairs. In return for such power and status, lawyers must expect and be willing to act for the public's as well as their own benefit.

In matters of legal ethics and professional responsibility (as so much else), there has to be a move from empty rhetoric to meaningful reality. Rather than be content simply to mouth the shibboleths of traditional policy, lawyers must be prepared to break professional ranks and connect their personal values with their professional lives. Such a bold initiative need not be viewed as an abandonment of professional responsibility. On the contrary, it is a proud gesture to hold the profession up to its own responsible standards in order that it might fulfill rather than confound its ethical ideals. As such, a concerted effort is required to reclaim legal practice from its presently neglected and desultory state. The example of those many individual lawyers who strive to develop and take responsibility for an ethical professional life must be complemented and reinforced by the legal profession collectively. In a manner of speaking, the challenge that all lawyers must meet is to have the vision, courage, and commitment to "feed society" and be proud of it. There is no higher calling.

# CANADIAN BAR ASSOCIATION: CODE OF PROFESSIONAL CONDUCT

## CHAPTER I: INTEGRITY

### RULE

The lawyer must discharge with integrity all duties owed to clients, the court, other members of the profession and the public.

*Commentary*

### Guiding Principles

1. Integrity is the fundamental quality of any person who seeks to practise as a member of the legal profession. If the client is in any doubt about the lawyer's trustworthiness the essential element in the lawyer-client relationship will be missing. If personal integrity is lacking the lawyer's usefulness to the client and reputation within the profession will be destroyed regardless of how competent the lawyer may be.
2. The principle of integrity is a key element of each rule of the Code.

### Disciplinary Action

3. Dishonourable or questionable conduct on the part of the lawyer in either private life or professional practice will reflect adversely upon the lawyer, the integrity of the legal profession and the administration of justice as a whole. If the conduct, whether within or outside

the professional sphere, is such that knowledge of it would be likely to impair the client's trust in the lawyer as a professional consultant, a governing body may be justified in taking disciplinary action.

### Non-Professional Activities

4. Generally speaking, however, a governing body will not be concerned with the purely private or extra-professional activities of a lawyer that do not bring into question the integrity of the legal profession or the lawyer's professional integrity or competence.

# CHAPTER II: COMPETENCE AND QUALITY OF SERVICE

## RULE

(a) The lawyer owes the client a duty to be competent to perform any legal services undertaken on the client's behalf.
(b) The lawyer should serve the client in a conscientious, diligent and efficient manner so as to provide a quality of service at least equal to that which lawyers generally would expect of a competent lawyer in a like situation.

## Commentary

### Knowledge and Skill

1. Competence in the context of the first branch of this Rule goes beyond formal qualification to practise law. It has to do with the sufficiency of the lawyer's qualifications to deal with the matter in question. It includes knowledge, skill, and the ability to use them effectively in the interests of the client.
2. As members of the legal profession, lawyers hold themselves out as being knowledgeable, skilled and capable in the practice of law. The client is entitled to assume that the lawyer has the ability and capacity to deal adequately with any legal matters undertaken on the client's behalf.
3. The lawyer should not undertake a matter without honestly feeling either competent to handle it, or able to become competent without undue delay, risk or expense to the client. The lawyer who proceeds on any other basis is not being honest with the client. This is an ethical consideration and is to be distinguished from the standard of care that a court would apply for purposes of determining negligence.

4. Competence involves more than an understanding of legal principles: it involves an adequate knowledge of the practice and procedures by which such principles can be effectively applied. To accomplish this the lawyer should keep abreast of developments in all branches of law wherein the lawyer's practice lies.

5. In deciding whether the lawyer has employed the requisite degree of knowledge and skill in a particular matter, relevant factors will include the complexity and specialized nature of the matter, the lawyer's general experience, the lawyer's training and experience in the field in question, the preparation and study the lawyer is able to give the matter and whether it is appropriate or feasible to refer the matter to, or associate or consult with, a lawyer of established competence in the field in question. In some circumstances expertise in a particular field of law may be required; often the necessary degree of proficiency will be that of the general practitioner.

## Seeking Assistance

6. The lawyer must be alert to recognize any lack of competence for a particular task and the disservice that would be done the client by undertaking that task. If consulted in such circumstances, the lawyer should either decline to act or obtain the client's instructions to retain, consult or collaborate with a lawyer who is competent in that field. The lawyer should also recognize that competence for a particular task may sometimes require seeking advice from or collaborating with experts in scientific, accounting or other non-legal fields. In such a situation the lawyer should not hesitate to seek the client's instructions to consult experts.

## Quality of Service

7. Numerous examples could be given of conduct that does not meet the quality of service required by the second branch of the Rule. The list that follows is illustrative, but not by any means exhaustive:
   (a) failure to keep the client reasonably informed;
   (b) failure to answer reasonable requests from the client for information;
   (c) unexplained failure to respond to the client's telephone calls;
   (d) failure to keep appointments with clients without explanation or apology;
   (e) informing the client that something will happen or that some step will be taken by a certain date, then letting the date pass without follow-up information or explanation;

(f)   failure to answer within a reasonable time a communication that requires a reply;

(g)   doing the work in hand but doing it so belatedly that its value to the client is diminished or lost;

(h)   slipshod work, such as mistakes or omissions in statements or documents prepared on behalf of the client;

(i)   failure to maintain office staff and facilities adequate to the lawyer's practice;

(j)   failure to inform the client of proposals of settlement, or to explain them properly;

(k)   withholding information from the client or misleading the client about the position of a matter in order to cover up the fact of neglect or mistakes;

(1)   failure to make a prompt and complete report when the work is finished or, if a final report cannot be made, failure to make an interim report where one might reasonably be expected;

(m)   self-induced disability, for example from the use of intoxicants or drugs, which interferes with or prejudices the lawyer's services to the client.

## Promptness

8. The requirement of conscientious, diligent and efficient service means that the lawyer must make every effort to provide prompt service to the client. If the lawyer can reasonably foresee undue delay in providing advice or services, the client should be so informed.

## Consequences of Incompetence

9. It will be observed that the Rule does not prescribe a standard of perfection. A mistake, even though it might be actionable for damages in negligence, would not necessarily constitute a failure to maintain the standard set by the Rule, but evidence of gross neglect in a particular matter or a pattern of neglect or mistakes in different matters may be evidence of such a failure regardless of tort liability. Where both negligence and incompetence are established, while damages may be awarded for the former, the latter can give rise to the additional sanction of disciplinary action.

10. The lawyer who is incompetent does the client a disservice, brings discredit to the profession, and may bring the administration of justice into disrepute. As well as damaging the lawyer's own reputation and practice, incompetence may also injure the lawyer's associates or dependants.

# CHAPTER III: ADVISING CLIENTS

## RULE

The lawyer must be both honest and candid when advising clients.

## *Commentary*

### Scope of Advice

1. The lawyer's duty to the client who seeks legal advice is to give the client a competent opinion based on sufficient knowledge of the relevant facts, an adequate consideration of the applicable law and the lawyer's own experience and expertise. The advice must be open and undisguised, clearly disclosing what the lawyer honestly thinks about the merits and probable results.
2. Whenever it becomes apparent that the client has misunderstood or misconceived what is really involved, the lawyer should explain as well as advise, so that the client is informed of the true position and fairly advised about the real issues or questions involved.
3. The lawyer should clearly indicate the facts, circumstances and assumptions upon which the lawyer's opinion is based, particularly where the circumstances do not justify an exhaustive investigation with resultant expense to the client. However, unless the client instructs otherwise, the lawyer should investigate the matter in sufficient detail to be able to express an opinion rather than merely make comments with many qualifications.
4. The lawyer should be wary of bold and confident assurances to the client, especially when the lawyer's employment may depend upon advising in a particular way.

### Second Opinion

5. If the client so desires, the lawyer should assist in obtaining a second opinion.

### Compromise or Settlement

6. The lawyer should advise and encourage the client to compromise or settle a dispute whenever possible on a reasonable basis and should discourage the client from commencing or continuing useless legal proceedings.

## Dishonesty or Fraud by Client

7. When advising the client the lawyer must never knowingly assist in or encourage any dishonesty, fraud, crime or illegal conduct, or instruct the client on how to violate the law and avoid punishment. The lawyer should be on guard against becoming the tool or dupe of an unscrupulous client or of persons associated with such a client.

## Test Cases

8. A *bona fide* test case is not necessarily precluded by the preceding paragraph and, so long as no injury to the person or violence is involved, the lawyer may properly advise and represent a client who, in good faith and on reasonable grounds, desires to challenge or test a law and this can most effectively be done by means of a technical breach giving rise to a test case. In all such situations the lawyer should ensure that the client appreciates the consequences of bringing a test case.

## Threatening Criminal Proceedings

9. Apart altogether from the substantive law on the subject, it is improper for the lawyer to advise, threaten or bring a criminal or quasi-criminal prosecution in order to secure some civil advantage for the client, or to advise, seek or procure the withdrawal of a prosecution in consideration of the payment of money, or transfer of property to, or for the benefit of the client.

## Advice on Non-Legal Matters

10. In addition to opinions on legal questions, the lawyer may be asked for or expected to give advice on non-legal matters such as the business, policy or social implications involved in a question, or the course the client should choose. In many instances the lawyer's experience will be such that the lawyer's views on non-legal matters will be of real benefit to the client. The lawyer who advises on such matters should, where and to the extent necessary, point out the lawyer's lack of experience or other qualification in the particular field and should clearly distinguish legal advice from such other advice.

## Errors and Omissions

11. The duty to give honest and candid advice requires the lawyer to inform the client promptly of the facts, but without admitting liability, upon discovering that an error or omission has occurred in a

matter for which the lawyer was engaged and that is or may be damaging to the client and cannot readily be rectified. When so informing the client the lawyer should be careful not to prejudice any rights of indemnity that either of them may have under any insurance, client's protection or indemnity plan, or otherwise. At the same time the lawyer should recommend that the client obtain legal advice elsewhere about any rights the client may have arising from such error or omission and whether it is appropriate for the lawyer to continue to act in the matter. The lawyer should also give prompt notice of any potential claim to the lawyer's insurer and any other indemnitor so that any protection from that source will not be prejudiced and, unless the client objects, should assist and cooperate with the insurer or other indemnitor to the extent necessary to enable any claim that is made to be dealt with promptly. If the lawyer is not so indemnified, or to the extent that the indemnity may not fully cover the claim, the lawyer should expeditiously deal with any claim that may be made and must not, under any circumstances, take unfair advantage that might defeat or impair the client's claim. In cases where liability is clear and the insurer or other indemnitor is prepared to pay its portion of the claim, the lawyer is under a duty to arrange for payment of the balance.

### Giving Independent Advice

12. Where the lawyer is asked to provide independent advice or independent representation to another lawyer's client in a situation where a conflict exists, the provision of such advice or representation is an undertaking to be taken seriously and not lightly assumed or perfunctorily discharged. It involves a duty to the client for whom the independent advice or representation is provided that is the same as in any other lawyer and client relationship and ordinarily extends to the nature and result of the transaction.

# CHAPTER IV: CONFIDENTIAL INFORMATION

## RULE

The lawyer has a duty to hold in strict confidence all information concerning the business and affairs of the client acquired in the course of the professional relationship, and should not divulge such information unless disclosure is expressly or impliedly authorized by the client, required by law or otherwise permitted or required by this Code.

## Commentary

### Guiding Principles

1. The lawyer cannot render effective professional service to the client unless there is full and unreserved communication between them. At the same time the client must feel completely secure and entitled to proceed on the basis that without any express request or stipulation on the client's part, matters disclosed to or discussed with the lawyer will be held secret and confidential.

2. This ethical rule must be distinguished from the evidentiary rule of lawyer and client privilege with respect to oral or written communications passing between the client and the lawyer. The ethical rule is wider and applies without regard to the nature or source of the information or to the fact that others may share the knowledge.

3. As a general rule, the lawyer should not disclose having been consulted or retained by a person unless the nature of the matter requires such disclosure.

4. The lawyer owes a duty of secrecy to every client without exception, regardless of whether it be a continuing or casual client. The duty survives the professional relationship and continues indefinitely after the lawyer has ceased to act for the client, whether or not differences have arisen between them.

### Confidential Information Not to Be Used

5. The fiduciary relationship between lawyer and client forbids the lawyer to use any confidential information covered by the ethical rule for the benefit of the lawyer or a third person, or to the disadvantage of the client. The lawyer who engages in literary works, such as an autobiography, memoirs and the like, should avoid disclosure of confidential information.

6. The lawyer should take care to avoid disclosure to one client of confidential information concerning or received from another client and should decline employment that might require such disclosure.

7. The lawyer should avoid indiscreet conversations, even with the lawyer's spouse or family, about a client's affairs and should shun any gossip about such things even though the client is not named or otherwise identified. Likewise the lawyer should not repeat any gossip or information about the client's business or affairs that may be overheard by or recounted to the lawyer. Apart altogether from ethical considerations or questions of good taste, indiscreet shop-talk between lawyers, if overheard by third parties able to identify

the matter being discussed, could result in prejudice to the client. Moreover, the respect of the listener for the lawyers concerned and the legal profession generally will probably be lessened.

8. Although the Rule may not apply to facts that are public knowledge, the lawyer should guard against participating in or commenting upon speculation concerning the client's affairs or business.

## Disclosure Authorized by Client

9. Confidential information may be divulged with the express authority of the client concerned and, in some situations, the authority of the client to divulge may be implied. For example, some disclosure may be necessary in a pleading or other document delivered in litigation being conducted for the client. Again, the lawyer may (unless the client directs otherwise) disclose the client's affairs to partners and associates in the firm and, to the extent necessary, to non-legal staff such as secretaries and filing clerks. This implied authority to disclose places the lawyer under a duty to impress upon associates, students and employees the importance of nondisclosure (both during their employment and afterwards) and requires the lawyer to take reasonable care to prevent their disclosing or using any information that the lawyer is bound to keep in confidence.

## Disclosure Where Lawyer's Conduct in Issue

10. Disclosure may also be justified in order to establish or collect a fee, or to defend the lawyer or the lawyer's associates or employees against any allegation of malpractice or misconduct, but only to the extent necessary for such purposes. (As to potential claims for negligence, see Commentary 10 of the Rule relating to Advising Clients.)

## Disclosure to Prevent a Crime

11. Disclosure of information necessary to prevent a crime will be justified if the lawyer has reasonable grounds for believing that a crime is likely to be committed and will be mandatory when the anticipated crime is one involving violence.

12. The lawyer who has reasonable grounds for believing that a dangerous situation is likely to develop at a court facility shall inform the person having responsibility for security at the facility and give particulars. Where possible the lawyer should suggest solutions to the anticipated problem such as:

    (a)  the need for further security;
    (b)  that judgement be reserved;
    (c)  such other measures as may seem advisable.

**Disclosure Required by Law**

13.  When disclosure is required by law or by order of a court of competent jurisdiction, the lawyer should always be careful not to divulge more information than is required.

14.  The lawyer who has information known to be confidential government information about a person, acquired when the lawyer was a public officer or employee, shall not represent a client (other than the agency of which the lawyer was a public officer or employee) whose interests are adverse to that person in a matter in which the information could be used to the material disadvantage of that person.

# CHAPTER V: IMPARTIALITY AND CONFLICT OF INTEREST BETWEEN CLIENTS

## RULE

The lawyer shall not advise or represent both sides of a dispute and, save after adequate disclosure to and with the consent of the clients or prospective clients concerned, shall not act or continue to act in a matter when there is or is likely to be a conflicting interest.

*Commentary*

**Guiding Principles**

1.  A conflicting interest is one that would be likely to affect adversely the lawyer's judgement or advice on behalf of, or loyalty to, a client or prospective client.

2.  The reason for the Rule is self-evident. The client or the client's affairs may be seriously prejudiced unless the lawyer's judgement and freedom of action on the client's behalf are as free as possible from compromising influences.

3.  Conflicting interests include, but are not limited to, the duties and loyalties of the lawyer or a partner or professional associate of the lawyer to any other client, whether involved in the particular transaction or not, including the obligation to communicate information.

## Disclosure of Conflicting Interest

4. The Rule requires adequate disclosure to enable the client to make an informed decision about whether to have the lawyer act despite the existence or possibility of a conflicting interest. As important as it is to the client that the lawyer's judgement and freedom of action on the client's behalf should not be subject to other interests, duties or obligations, in practice this factor may not always be decisive. Instead it may be only one of several factors that the client will weigh when deciding whether to give the consent referred to in the Rule. Other factors might include, for example, the availability of another lawyer of comparable expertise and experience, the extra cost, delay and inconvenience involved in engaging another lawyer and the latter's unfamiliarity with the client and the client's affairs. In the result, the client's interests may sometimes be better served by not engaging another lawyer. An example of this sort of situation is when the client and another party to a commercial transaction are continuing clients of the same law firm but are regularly represented by different lawyers in that firm.

5. Before the lawyer accepts employment from more than one client in the same matter, the lawyer must advise the clients that the lawyer has been asked to act for both or all of them, that no information received in connection with the matter from one can be treated as confidential so far as any of the others is concerned and that, if a dispute develops that cannot be resolved, the lawyer cannot continue to act for both or all of them and may have to withdraw completely. If one of the clients is a person with whom the lawyer has a continuing relationship and for whom the lawyer acts regularly, this fact should be revealed to the other or others at the outset with a recommendation that they obtain independent representation. If, following such disclosure, all parties are content that the lawyer act for them, the lawyer should obtain their consent, preferably in writing, or record their consent in a separate letter to each. The lawyer should, however, guard against acting for more than one client where, despite the fact that all parties concerned consent, it is reasonably obvious that an issue contentious between them may arise or their interests, rights or obligations will diverge as the matter progresses.

6. If, after the clients involved have consented, an issue contentious between them or some of them arises, the lawyer, although not necessarily precluded from advising them on other non-contentious matters, would be in breach of the Rule if the lawyer attempted to advise them on the contentious issue. In such circumstances the

lawyer should ordinarily refer the clients to other lawyers. However, if the issue is one that involves little or no legal advice, for example a business rather than a legal question in a proposed business transaction, and the clients are sophisticated, they may be permitted to settle the issue by direct negotiation in which the lawyer does not participate. Alternatively, the lawyer may refer one client to another lawyer and continue to advise the other if it was agreed at the outset that this course would be followed in the event of a conflict arising.

### Lawyer as Arbitrator

7. The Rule will not prevent a lawyer from arbitrating or settling, or attempting to arbitrate or settle, a dispute between two or more clients or former clients who are *sui juris* and who wish to submit the dispute to the lawyer.

### Acting against Former Client

8. A lawyer who has acted for a client in a matter should not thereafter act against the client (or against persons who were involved in or associated with the client in that matter) in the same or any related matter, or take a position where the lawyer might be tempted or appear to be tempted to breach the Rule relating to confidential information. It is not, however, improper for the lawyer to act against a former client in a fresh and independent matter wholly unrelated to any work the lawyer has previously done for that person.

9. For the sake of clarity the foregoing paragraphs are expressed in terms of the individual lawyer and client. However, the term "client" includes a client of the law firm of which the lawyer is a partner or associate, whether or not the lawyer handles the client's work. It also includes the client of a lawyer who is associated with the lawyer in such a manner as to be perceived as practising in partnership or association with the first lawyer, even though in fact no such partnership or association exists.

### Acting for More Than One Client

10. In practice, there are many situations where even though no actual dispute exists between the parties their interests are in conflict. Common examples in a conveyancing practice are vendor and purchaser, or mortgagor and mortgagee. In cases where the lawyer is asked to act for more than one client in such a transaction, the lawyer should recommend that each party be separately represented.

In all such transactions the lawyer must observe the rules prescribed by the governing body.

11. There are also many situations where more than one person may wish to retain the lawyer to handle a transaction and, although their interests appear to coincide, in fact a potential conflict of interest exists. Examples are co-purchasers of real property and persons forming a partnership or corporation. Such cases will be governed by Commentaries 4 and 5 of this Rule.

12. A lawyer who is employed or retained by an organization represents that organization acting through its duly authorized constituents. In dealing with the organization's directors, officers, employees, members, shareholders or other constituents, the lawyer shall make clear that it is the organization that is the client when it becomes apparent that the organization's interests are adverse to those of the constituents with whom the lawyer is dealing. The lawyer representing an organization may also represent any of the directors, officers, employees, members, shareholders or other constituents, subject to the provisions of this Rule dealing with conflicts of interest.

### Burden of Proof

13. Generally speaking, in disciplinary proceedings arising from a breach of this Rule the lawyer has the burden of showing good faith and that adequate disclosure was made in the matter and the client's consent was obtained.

# CHAPTER VI: CONFLICT OF INTEREST BETWEEN LAWYER AND CLIENT

## RULE

(a) The lawyer should not enter into a business transaction with the client or knowingly give to or acquire from the client an ownership, security or other pecuniary interest unless:

(i) the transaction is a fair and reasonable one and its terms are fully disclosed to the client in writing in a manner that is reasonably understood by the client;

(ii) the client is given a reasonable opportunity to seek independent legal advice about the transaction, the onus being on the lawyer to prove that the client's interests were protected by such independent advice; and

(iii) the client consents in writing to the transaction.

(b)  The lawyer shall not enter into or continue a business transaction with the client if:
  (i)   the client expects or might reasonably be assumed to expect that the lawyer is protecting the client's interests;
  (ii)  there is a significant risk that the interests of the lawyer and the client may differ.
(c)  The lawyer shall not act for the client where the lawyer's duty to the client and the personal interests of the lawyer or an associate are in conflict.
(d)  The lawyer shall not prepare an instrument giving the lawyer or an associate a substantial gift from the client, including a testamentary gift.

## Commentary

### Guiding Principles

1.  The principles enunciated in the Rule relating to impartiality and conflict of interest between clients apply *mutatis mutandis* to this Rule.
2.  A conflict of interest between lawyer and client exists in all cases where the lawyer gives property to or acquires it from the client by way of purchase, gift, testamentary disposition or otherwise. When they are contemplated, the prudent course is to insist that the client either be independently represented or have independent legal advice.
3.  This Rule applies also to situations involving associates of the lawyer. Associates of the lawyer within the meaning of the Rule include the lawyer's spouse, children, any relative of the lawyer (or of the lawyer's spouse) living under the same roof, any partner or associate of the lawyer in the practice of law, a trust or estate in which the lawyer has a substantial beneficial interest or for which the lawyer acts as a trustee or in a similar capacity, and a corporation of which the lawyer is a director or in which the lawyer or an associate owns or controls, directly or indirectly, a significant number of shares.

### Debtor-Creditor Relationship to Be Avoided

4.  The lawyer should avoid entering into a debtor-creditor relationship with the client. The lawyer should not borrow money from a client who is not in the business of lending money. It is undesirable that the lawyer lend money to the client except by way of advancing necessary expenses in a legal matter that the lawyer is handling for the client.

## Joint Ventures

5. The lawyer who has a personal interest in a joint business venture with others may represent or advise the business venture in legal matters between it and third parties, but should not represent or advise either the joint business venture or the joint venturers in respect of legal matters as between them.

## When Person to Be Considered a Client

6. The question of whether a person is to be considered a client of the lawyer when such person is lending money to the lawyer, or buying, selling, making a loan to or investment in, or assuming an obligation in respect of a business, security or property in which the lawyer or an associate of the lawyer has an interest, or in respect of any other transaction, is to be determined having regard to all the circumstances. A person who is not otherwise a client may be deemed to be a client for purposes of this Rule if such person might reasonably feel entitled to look to the lawyer for guidance and advice in respect of the transaction. In those circumstances the lawyer must consider such person to be a client and will be bound by the same fiduciary obligations that attach to a lawyer in dealings with a client. The onus shall be on the lawyer to establish that such a person was not in fact looking to the lawyer for guidance and advice.

# CHAPTER VII: OUTSIDE INTERESTS AND THE PRACTICE OF LAW

## RULE

The lawyer who engages in another profession, business or occupation concurrently with the practice of law must not allow such outside interest to jeopardize the lawyer's professional integrity, independence or competence.

*Commentary*

### Guiding Principles

1. The term "outside interest" covers the widest possible range and includes activities that may overlap or be connected with the practice of law, such as engaging in the mortgage business, acting as a director of a client corporation, or writing on legal subjects, as well

as activities not so connected such as a career in business, politics, broadcasting or the performing arts. In each case the question of whether the lawyer may properly engage in the outside interest and to what extent the lawyer will be subject to any applicable law or rule of the governing body.

2.  Whenever an overriding social, political, economic or other consideration arising from the outside interest might influence the lawyer's judgement, the lawyer should be governed by the considerations declared in the Rule relating to conflict of interest between lawyer and client.

3.  Where the outside interest is in no way related to the legal services being performed for clients, ethical considerations will usually not arise unless the lawyer's conduct brings either the lawyer or the profession into disrepute, or impairs the lawyer's competence as, for example, where the outside interest occupies so much time that clients suffer because of the lawyer's lack of attention or preparation.

4.  The lawyer must not carry on, manage or be involved in any outside business, investment, property or occupation in such a way that makes it difficult to distinguish in which capacity the lawyer is acting in a particular transaction, or that would give rise to a conflict of interest or duty to a client. When acting or dealing in respect of a transaction involving an outside interest in a business, investment, property or occupation, the lawyer must disclose any personal interest, must declare to all parties in the transaction or to their solicitors whether the lawyer is acting on the lawyer's own behalf or in a professional capacity or otherwise, and must adhere throughout the transaction to standards of conduct as high as those that this Code requires of a lawyer engaged in the practice of law.

5.  The lawyer who has an outside interest in a business, investment, property or occupation:
    (a)  must not be identified as a lawyer when carrying on, managing or being involved in such outside interest; and
    (b)  must ensure that monies received in respect of the day-to-day carrying on, operation and management of such outside interest are deposited in an account other than the lawyer's trust account, unless such monies are received by the lawyer when acting in a professional capacity as a lawyer on behalf of the outside interest.

6.  In order to be compatible with the practice of law the other profession, business or occupation:
    (a)  must be an honourable one that does not detract from the status of the lawyer or the legal profession generally; and

(b) must not be such as would likely result in a conflict of interest between the lawyer and a client.

# CHAPTER VIII: PRESERVATION OF CLIENT'S PROPERTY

## RULE

The lawyer owes a duty to the client to observe all relevant laws and rules respecting the preservation and safekeeping of the client's property entrusted to the lawyer. Where there are no such laws or rules, or the lawyer is in any doubt, the lawyer should take the same care of such property as a careful and prudent owner would when dealing with property of like description.

*Commentary*

**Guiding Principles**

1. The lawyer's duties with respect to safekeeping, preserving and accounting for the clients' monies and other property are generally the subject of special rules. In the absence of such rules the lawyer should adhere to the minimum standards set out in the note. "Property", apart from clients' monies, includes securities such as mortgages, negotiable instruments, stocks, bonds, etc., original documents such as wills, title deeds, minute books, licences, certificates, etc., other papers such as clients' correspondence files, reports, invoices, etc., as well as chattels such as jewelry, silver, etc.

2. The lawyer should promptly notify the client upon receiving any property of or relating to the client unless satisfied that the client knows that it has come into the lawyer's custody.

3. The lawyer should clearly label and identify the client's property and place it in safekeeping separate and apart from the lawyer's own property.

4. The lawyer should maintain adequate records of clients' property in the lawyer's custody so that it may be promptly accounted for, or delivered to, or to the order of, the client upon request. The lawyer should ensure that such property is delivered to the right person and, in case of dispute as to the person entitled, may have recourse to the courts.

5. The duties here expressed are closely related to those concerning confidential information. The lawyer should keep clients' papers

and other property out of sight as well as out of reach of those not entitled to see them and should, subject to any right of lien, return them promptly to the clients upon request or at the conclusion of the lawyer's retainer.

## Privilege

6. The lawyer should be alert to claim on behalf of clients any lawful privilege respecting information about their affairs, including their files and property if seized or attempted to be seized by a third party. In this regard the lawyer should be familiar with the nature of clients' privilege, and with relevant statutory provisions such as those in the *Income Tax Act*, the *Criminal Code*, the *Canadian Charter of Rights and Freedoms* and other statutes.

# CHAPTER IX: THE LAWYER AS ADVOCATE

## RULE

When acting as an advocate, the lawyer must treat the tribunal with courtesy and respect and must represent the client resolutely, honourably and within the limits of the law.

*Commentary*

### Guiding Principles

1. The advocate's duty to the client "fearlessly to raise every issue, advance every argument, and ask every question, however distasteful, which he thinks will help his client's case" and to endeavour "to obtain for his client the benefit of any and every remedy and defence which is authorized by law" must always be discharged by fair and honourable means, without illegality and in a manner consistent with the lawyer's duty to treat the court with candour, fairness, courtesy and respect.

### Prohibited Conduct

2. The lawyer must not, for example:
   (a) abuse the process of the tribunal by instituting or prosecuting proceedings that, although legal in themselves, are clearly motivated by malice on the part of the client and are brought solely for the purpose of injuring another party;

(b) knowingly assist or permit the client to do anything that the lawyer considers to be dishonest or dishonourable;

(c) appear before a judicial officer when the lawyer, the lawyer's associates or the client have business or personal relationships with such officer that give rise to real or apparent pressure, influence or inducement affecting the impartiality of such officer;

(d) attempt or allow anyone else to attempt, directly or indirectly, to influence the decision or actions of a tribunal or any of its officials by any means except open persuasion as an advocate;

(e) knowingly attempt to deceive or participate in the deception of a tribunal or influence the course of justice by offering false evidence, misstating facts or law, presenting or relying upon a false or deceptive affidavit, suppressing what ought to be disclosed or otherwise assisting in any fraud, crime or illegal conduct;

(f) knowingly misstate the contents of a document, the testimony of a witness, the substance of an argument or the provisions of a statute or like authority;

(g) knowingly assert something for which there is no reasonable basis in evidence, or the admissibility of which must first be established;

(h) deliberately refrain from informing the tribunal of any pertinent adverse authority that the lawyer considers to be directly in point and that has not been mentioned by an opponent;

(i) dissuade a material witness from giving evidence, or advise such a witness to be absent;

(j) knowingly permit a witness to be presented in a false or misleading way or to impersonate another;

(k) needlessly abuse, hector or harass a witness;

(l) needlessly inconvenience a witness.

## Errors and Omissions

3. The lawyer who has unknowingly done or failed to do something that, if done or omitted knowingly, would have been in breach of this Rule and discovers it, has a duty to the court, subject to the Rule relating to confidential information, to disclose the error or omission and do all that can reasonably be done in the circumstances to rectify it.

## Duty to Withdraw

4. If the client wishes to adopt a course that would involve a breach of this Rule, the lawyer must refuse and do everything reasonably pos-

sible to prevent it. If the client persists in such a course the lawyer should, subject to the Rule relating to withdrawal, withdraw or seek leave of the court to do so.

## The Lawyer as Witness

5. The lawyer who appears as an advocate should not submit the lawyer's own affidavit to or testify before a tribunal save as permitted by local rule or practice, or as to purely formal or uncontroverted matters. This also applies to the lawyer's partners and associates; generally speaking, they should not testify in such proceedings except as to merely formal matters. The lawyer should not express personal opinions or beliefs, or assert as fact anything that is properly subject to legal proof, cross-examination or challenge. The lawyer must not in effect become an unsworn witness or put the lawyer's own credibility in issue. The lawyer who is a necessary witness should testify and entrust the conduct of the case to someone else. Similarly, the lawyer who was a witness in the proceedings should not appear as advocate in any appeal from the decision in those proceedings. There are no restrictions upon the advocate's right to cross-examine another lawyer, and the lawyer who does appear as a witness should not expect to receive special treatment by reason of professional status.

## Interviewing Witnesses

6. The lawyer may properly seek information from any potential witness (whether under subpoena or not) but should disclose the lawyer's interest and take care not to subvert or suppress any evidence or procure the witness to stay out of the way. The lawyer shall not approach or deal with an opposite party who is professionally represented save through or with the consent of that party's lawyer.

## Unmeritorious Proceedings

7. The lawyer should never waive or abandon the client's legal rights (for example an available defence under a statute of limitations) without the client's informed consent. In civil matters it is desirable that the lawyer should avoid and discourage the client from resorting to frivolous or vexatious objections or attempts to gain advantage from slips or oversights not going to the real merits, or tactics that will merely delay or harass the other side. Such practices can readily bring the administration of justice and the legal profession into disrepute.

## Encouraging Settlements

8. Whenever the case can be settled fairly, the lawyer should advise and encourage the client to do so rather than commence or continue legal proceedings.

## Duties of Prosecutor

9. When engaged as a prosecutor, the lawyer's prime duty is not to seek a conviction, but to present before the trial court all available credible evidence relevant to the alleged crime in order that justice may be done through a fair trial upon the merits. The prosecutor exercises a public function involving much discretion and power and must act fairly and dispassionately. The prosecutor should not do anything that might prevent the accused from being represented by counsel or communicating with counsel and, to the extent required by law and accepted practice, should make timely disclosure to the accused or defence counsel (or to the court if the accused is not represented) of all relevant facts and known witnesses, whether tending to show guilt or innocence, or that would affect the punishment of the accused.

## Duties of Defence Counsel

10. When defending an accused person, the lawyer's duty is to protect the client as far as possible from being convicted except by a court of competent jurisdiction and upon legal evidence sufficient to support a conviction for the offence charged. Accordingly, and notwithstanding the lawyer's private opinion as to credibility or merits, the lawyer may properly rely upon all available evidence or defences including so-called technicalities not known to be false or fraudulent.

11. Admissions made by the accused to the lawyer may impose strict limitations on the conduct of the defence and the accused should be made aware of this. For example, if the accused clearly admits to the lawyer the factual and mental elements necessary to constitute the offence, the lawyer, if convinced that the admissions are true and voluntary, may properly take objection to the jurisdiction of the court, or to the form of the indictment, or to the admissibility or sufficiency of the evidence, but must not suggest that some other person committed the offence, or call any evidence that, by reason of the admissions, the lawyer believes to be false. Nor may the lawyer set up an affirmative case inconsistent with such admissions, for

example, by calling evidence in support of an alibi intended to show that the accused could not have done, or in fact had not done, the act. Such admissions will also impose a limit upon the extent to which the lawyer may attack the evidence for the prosecution. The lawyer is entitled to test the evidence given by each individual witness for the prosecution and argue that the evidence taken as a whole is insufficient to amount to proof that the accused is guilty of the offence charged, but the lawyer should go no further than that.

## Agreement on Guilty Plea

12. Where, following investigation,
    (a) the defence lawyer *bona fide* concludes and advises the accused client that an acquittal of the offence charged is uncertain or unlikely,
    (b) the client is prepared to admit the necessary factual and mental elements,
    (c) the lawyer fully advises the client of the implications and possible consequences of a guilty plea and that the matter of sentence is solely in the discretion of the trial judge, and
    (d) the client so instructs the lawyer, preferably in writing,
    it is proper for the lawyer to discuss and agree tentatively with the prosecutor to enter a plea of guilty on behalf of the client to the offence charged or to a lesser or included offence or to another offence appropriate to the admissions, and also on a disposition or sentence to be proposed to the court. The public interest and the client's interests must not, however, be compromised by agreeing to a guilty plea.

## Undertakings

13. An undertaking given by the lawyer to the court or to another lawyer in the course of litigation or other adversary proceedings must be strictly and scrupulously carried out. Unless clearly qualified in writing, the lawyer's undertaking is a personal promise and responsibility.

## Courtesy

14. The lawyer should at all times be courteous and civil to the court and to those engaged on the other side. Legal contempt of court and the professional obligation outlined here are not identical, and a consistent pattern of rude, provocative or disruptive conduct by the lawyer, even though unpunished as contempt, might well merit disciplinary action.

## Role in Adversary Proceedings

15. In adversary proceedings, the lawyer's function as advocate is openly and necessarily partisan. Accordingly, the lawyer is not obliged (save as required by law or under paragraphs 2(h) or 7 above) to assist an adversary or advance matters derogatory to the client's case. When opposing interests are not represented, for example in ex parte or uncontested matters, or in other situations where the full proof and argument inherent in the adversary system cannot be obtained, the lawyer must take particular care to be accurate, candid and comprehensive in presenting the client's case so as to ensure that the court is not misled.

## Communicating with Witnesses

16. When in court the lawyer should observe local rules and practices concerning communication with a witness about the witness's evidence or any issue in the proceeding. Generally, it is considered improper for counsel who called a witness to communicate with that witness without leave of the court while such witness is under cross-examination.

## Agreements Guaranteeing Recovery

17. In civil proceedings the lawyer has a duty not to mislead the court about the position of the client in the adversary process. Thus, where a lawyer representing a client in litigation has made or is party to an agreement made before or during the trial whereby a plaintiff is guaranteed recovery by one or more parties notwithstanding the judgement of the court, the lawyer shall disclose full particulars of the agreement to the court and all other parties.

## Scope of the Rule

18. The principles of this Rule apply generally to the lawyer as advocate and therefore extend not only to court proceedings but also to appearances and proceedings before boards, administrative tribunals and other bodies, regardless of their function or the informality of their procedures.

# CHAPTER X: THE LAWYER IN PUBLIC OFFICE

## RULE

The lawyer who holds public office should, in the discharge of official duties, adhere to standards of conduct as high as those that these rules require of a lawyer engaged in the practice of law.

*Commentary*

### Guiding Principles

1. The Rule applies to the lawyer who is elected or appointed to legislative or administrative office at any level of government, regardless of whether the lawyer attained such office because of professional qualifications. Because such a lawyer is in the public eye, the legal profession can more readily be brought into disrepute by failure on the lawyer's part to observe its professional standards of conduct.

### Conflicts of Interest

2. The lawyer who holds public office must not allow personal or other interests to conflict with the proper discharge of official duties. The lawyer holding part-time public office must not accept any private legal business where duty to the client will or may conflict with official duties. If some unforeseen conflict arises, the lawyer should terminate the professional relationship, explaining to the client that official duties must prevail. The lawyer who holds a full-time public office will not be faced with this sort of conflict, but must nevertheless guard against allowing the lawyer's independent judgement in the discharge of official duties to be influenced by the lawyer's own interest, or by the interests of persons closely related to or associated with the lawyer, or of former or prospective clients, or of former or prospective partners or associates.

3. In the context of the preceding paragraph, persons closely related to or associated with the lawyer include a spouse, child, or any relative of the lawyer (or of the lawyer's spouse) living under the same roof, a trust or estate in which the lawyer has a substantial beneficial interest or for which the lawyer acts as a trustee or in a similar capacity, and a corporation of which the lawyer is a director or in which the lawyer or some closely related or associated person holds or controls, directly or indirectly, a significant number of shares.

4. Subject to any special rules applicable to a particular public office, the lawyer holding such office who sees the possibility of a conflict

of interest should declare such interest at the earliest opportunity and take no part in any consideration, discussion or vote with respect to the matter in question.

## Appearances before Official Bodies

5. When the lawyer or any of the lawyer's partners or associates is a member of an official body such as, for example, a school board, municipal council or governing body, the lawyer should not appear professionally before that body. However, subject to the rules of the official body it would not be improper for the lawyer to appear professionally before a committee of such body if such partner or associate is not a member of that committee.
6. The lawyer should not represent in the same or any related matter any persons or interests that the lawyer has been concerned with in an official capacity. Similarly, the lawyer should avoid advising upon a ruling of an official body of which the lawyer either is a member or was a member at the time the ruling was made.

## Disclosure of Confidential Information

7. By way of corollary to the Rule relating to confidential information, the lawyer who has acquired confidential information by virtue of holding public office should keep such information confidential and not divulge or use it even though the lawyer has ceased to hold such office. (As to the taking of employment in connection with any matter in respect of which the lawyer had substantial responsibility or confidential information, see Commentary 3 of the Rule relating to avoiding questionable conduct.)

## Disciplinary Action

8. Generally speaking, a governing body will not be concerned with the way in which a lawyer holding public office carries out official responsibilities, but conduct in office that reflects adversely upon the lawyer's integrity or professional competence may subject the lawyer to disciplinary action.

# CHAPTER XI: FEES

## RULE

The lawyer shall not
(a) stipulate for, charge or accept any fee that is not fully disclosed, fair and reasonable;
(b) appropriate any funds of the client held in trust or otherwise under the lawyer's control for or on account of fees without the express authority of the client, save as permitted by the rules of the governing body.

## Commentary

### Factors to Be Considered

1. A fair and reasonable fee will depend on and reflect such factors as:
   (a) the time and effort required and spent;
   (b) the difficulty and importance of the matter;
   (c) whether special skill or service has been required and provided;
   (d) the customary charges of other lawyers of equal standing in the locality in like matters and circumstances;
   (e) in civil cases the amount involved, or the value of the subject matter;
   (f) in criminal cases the exposure and risk to the client;
   (g) the results obtained;
   (h) tariffs or scales authorized by local law;
   (i) such special circumstances as loss of other employment, urgency and uncertainty of reward;
   (j) any relevant agreement between the lawyer and the client.
   A fee will not be fair and reasonable and may subject the lawyer to disciplinary proceedings if it is one that cannot be justified in the light of all pertinent circumstances, including the factors mentioned, or is so disproportionate to the services rendered as to introduce the element of fraud or dishonesty, or undue profit.
2. It is in keeping with the best traditions of the legal profession to reduce or waive a fee in cases of hardship or poverty, or where the client or prospective client would otherwise effectively be deprived of legal advice or representation.

### Avoidance of Controversy

3. Breaches of this Rule and misunderstandings about fees and financial matters bring the legal profession into disrepute and reflect adversely upon the administration of justice. The lawyer should try

to avoid controversy with the client over fees and should be ready to explain the basis for charges, especially if the client is unsophisticated or uninformed about the proper basis and measurements for fees. The lawyer should give the client an early and fair estimate of fees and disbursements, pointing out any uncertainties involved, so that the client may be able to make an informed decision. When something unusual or unforeseen occurs that may substantially affect the amount of the fee, the lawyer should forestall misunderstandings or disputes by explaining this to the client.

## Interest on Overdue Accounts

4. Save where permitted by law or local practice, the lawyer should not charge interest on an overdue account except by prior agreement with the client and then only at a reasonable rate.

## Apportionment and Division of Fees

5. The lawyer who acts for two or more clients in the same matter is under a duty to apportion the fees and disbursements equitably among them in the absence of agreement otherwise.
6. A fee will not be a fair one within the meaning of the Rule if it is divided with another lawyer who is not a partner or associate unless (a) the client consents, either expressly or impliedly, to the employment of the other lawyer and (b) the fee is divided in proportion to the work done and responsibility assumed.

## Hidden Fees

7. The fiduciary relationship that exists between lawyer and client requires full disclosure in all financial matters between them and prohibits the lawyer from accepting any hidden fees. No fee, reward, costs, commission, interest, rebate, agency or forwarding allowance or other compensation whatsoever related to the professional employment may be taken by the lawyer from anyone other than the client without full disclosure to and consent of the client. Where the lawyer's fees are being paid by someone other than the client, such as a legal aid agency, a borrower, or a personal representative, the consent of such other person will be required. So far as disbursements are concerned, only *bona fide* and specified payments to others may be included. If the lawyer is financially interested in the person to whom the disbursements are made, such as an investigating, brokerage or copying agency, the lawyer shall expressly disclose this fact to the client.

## Sharing Fees with Non-Lawyers

8. Any arrangement whereby the lawyer directly or indirectly shares, splits or divides fees with notaries public, law students, clerks, or other non-lawyers who bring or refer business to the lawyer's office is improper and constitutes professional misconduct. It is also improper for the lawyer to give any financial or other reward to such persons for referring business.
9. The lawyer shall not enter into a lease or other arrangement whereby a landlord or other person directly or indirectly shares in the fees or revenues generated by the law practice.

## Contingent Fees

10. Except where prohibited by the laws of the jurisdiction in which the lawyer practises, it is not improper for the lawyer to enter into an arrangement with the client for a contingent fee, provided such fee is fair and reasonable and the lawyer adheres to any rules of court or local practice relating to such an arrangement.

# CHAPTER XII: WITHDRAWAL

## RULE

The lawyer owes a duty to the client not to withdraw services except for good cause and upon notice appropriate in the circumstances.

## *Commentary*

### Guiding Principles

1. Although the client has a right to terminate the lawyer-client relationship at will, the lawyer does not enjoy the same freedom of action. Having once accepted professional employment, the lawyer should complete the task as ably as possible unless there is justifiable cause for terminating the relationship.
2. The lawyer who withdraws from employment should act so as to minimize expense and avoid prejudice to the client, doing everything reasonably possible to facilitate the expeditious and orderly transfer of the matter to the successor lawyer.
3. Where withdrawal is required or permitted by this Rule, the lawyer must comply with all applicable rules of court as well as local rules and practice.

## Obligatory Withdrawal

4. In some circumstances, the lawyer will be under a duty to withdraw. The obvious example is following discharge by the client. Other examples are (a) if the lawyer is instructed by the client to do something inconsistent with the lawyer's duty to the court and, following explanation, the client persists in such instructions; (b) if the client is guilty of dishonourable conduct in the proceedings or is taking a position solely to harass or maliciously injure another; (c) if it becomes clear that the lawyer's continued employment will lead to a breach of these Rules such as, for example, a breach of the Rules relating to conflict of interest; or (d) if it develops that the lawyer is not competent to handle the matter. In all these situations there is a duty to inform the client that the lawyer must withdraw.

## Optional Withdrawal

5. Situations where a lawyer would be entitled to withdraw, although not under a positive duty to do so, will as a rule arise only where there has been a serious loss of confidence between lawyer and client. Such a loss of confidence goes to the very basis of the relationship. Thus, the lawyer who is deceived by the client will have justifiable cause for withdrawal. Again, the refusal of the client to accept and act upon the lawyer's advice on a significant point might indicate such a loss of confidence. At the same time, the lawyer should not use the threat of withdrawal as a device to force the client into making a hasty decision on a difficult question. The lawyer may withdraw if unable to obtain instructions from the client.

## Non-Payment of Fees

6. Failure on the part of the client after reasonable notice to provide funds on account of disbursements or fees will justify withdrawal by the lawyer unless serious prejudice to the client would result.

## Notice to Client

7. No hard and fast rules can be laid down as to what will constitute reasonable notice prior to withdrawal. Where the matter is covered by statutory provisions or rules of court, these will govern. In other situations the governing principle is that the lawyer should protect the client's interests so far as possible and should not desert the client at a critical stage of a matter or at a time when withdrawal would put the client in a position of disadvantage or peril.

## Duty Following Withdrawal

8. Upon discharge or withdrawal the lawyer should:
   (a) deliver in an orderly and expeditious manner to or to the order of the client all papers and property to which the client is entitled;
   (b) give the client all information that may be required about the case or matter;
   (c) account for all funds of the client on hand or previously dealt with and refund any remuneration not earned during the employment;
   (d) promptly render an account for outstanding fees and disbursements;
   (e) co-operate with the successor lawyer for the purposes outlined in paragraph 2.

   The obligation in clause (a) to deliver papers and property is subject to the lawyer's right of lien referred to in paragraph 11. In the event of conflicting claims to such papers and property, the lawyer should make every effort to have the claimants settle the dispute.

9. Co-operation with the successor lawyer will normally include providing any memoranda of fact and law that have been prepared by the lawyer in connection with the matter, but confidential information not clearly related to the matter should not be divulged without the express consent of the client.

10. The lawyer acting for several clients in a case or matter who ceases to act for one or more of them should co-operate with the successor lawyer or lawyers to the extent permitted by this Code, and should seek to avoid any unseemly rivalry, whether real or apparent.

## Lien for Unpaid Fees

11. Where upon the discharge or withdrawal of the lawyer the question of a right of lien for unpaid fees and disbursements arises, the lawyer should have due regard to the effect of its enforcement upon the client's position. Generally speaking, the lawyer should not enforce such a lien if the result would be to prejudice materially the client's position in any uncompleted matter.

## Duty of Successor Lawyer

12. Before accepting employment, the successor lawyer should be satisfied that the former lawyer approves, or has withdrawn or been discharged by the client. It is quite proper for the successor lawyer to urge the client to settle or take reasonable steps toward settling or securing any account owed to the former lawyer, especially if the latter withdrew for good cause or was capriciously discharged. But

if a trial or hearing is in progress or imminent, or if the client would otherwise be prejudiced, the existence of an outstanding account should not be allowed to interfere with the successor lawyer acting for the client.

### Dissolution of Law Firm

13. When a law firm is dissolved, this will usually result in the termination of the lawyer-client relationship as between a particular client and one or more of the lawyers involved. In such cases, most clients will prefer to retain the services of the lawyer whom they regarded as being in charge of their business prior to the dissolution. However, the final decision rests in each case with the client, and the lawyers who are no longer retained by the client should act in accordance with the principles here set out, and in particular Commentary 2.

# CHAPTER XIII: THE LAWYER AND THE ADMINISTRATION OF JUSTICE

## RULE

The lawyer should encourage public respect for and try to improve the administration of justice.

*Commentary*

### Guiding Principles

1. The admission to and continuance in the practice of law imply a basic commitment by the lawyer to the concept of equal justice for all within an open, ordered and impartial system. However, judicial institutions will not function effectively unless they command the respect of the public. Because of changes in human affairs and the imperfection of human institutions, constant efforts must be made to improve the administration of justice and thereby maintain public respect for it.

2. The lawyer, by training, opportunity and experience, is in a position to observe the workings and discover the strengths and weaknesses of laws, legal institutions and public authorities. The lawyer should, therefore, lead in seeking improvements in the legal system, but any criticisms and proposals should be *bona fide* and reasoned.

## Scope of the Rule

3. The obligation outlined in the Rule is not restricted to the lawyer's professional activities but is a general responsibility resulting from the lawyer's position in the community. The lawyer's responsibilities are greater than those of a private citizen. The lawyer must not subvert the law by counselling or assisting in activities that are in defiance of it and must do nothing to lessen the respect and confidence of the public in the legal system of which the lawyer is a part. The lawyer should take care not to weaken or destroy public confidence in legal institutions or authorities by broad irresponsible allegations of corruption or partiality. The lawyer in public life must be particularly careful in this regard because the mere fact of being a lawyer will lend weight and credibility to any public statements. For the same reason, the lawyer should not hesitate to speak out against an injustice. (As to test cases, see Commentary 8 of the Rule relating to advising clients.)

## Criticism of the Tribunal

4. Although proceedings and decisions of tribunals are properly subject to scrutiny and criticism by all members of the public, including lawyers, members of tribunals are often prohibited by law or custom from defending themselves. Their inability to do so imposes special responsibilities upon lawyers. Firstly, the lawyer should avoid criticism that is petty, intemperate or unsupported by a *bona fide* belief in its real merit, bearing in mind that in the eyes of the public, professional knowledge lends weight to the lawyer's judgements or criticism. Secondly, if the lawyer has been involved in the proceedings, there is the risk that any criticism may be, or may appear to be, partisan rather than objective. Thirdly, where a tribunal is the object of unjust criticism, the lawyer, as a participant in the administration of justice, is uniquely able to and should support the tribunal, both because its members cannot defend themselves and because the lawyer is thereby contributing to greater public understanding of and therefore respect for the legal system.

## Improving the Administration of Justice

5. The lawyer who seeks legislative or administrative changes should disclose whose interest is being advanced, whether it be the lawyer's interest, that of a client, or the public interest. The lawyer may advocate such changes on behalf of a client without personally agreeing with them, but the lawyer who purports to act in the pub-

lic interest should espouse only those changes that the lawyer conscientiously believes to be in the public interest.

# CHAPTER XIV: ADVERTISING, SOLICITATION AND MAKING LEGAL SERVICES AVAILABLE

## RULE

Lawyers should make legal services available to the public in an efficient and convenient manner that will command respect and confidence, and by means that are compatible with the integrity, independence and effectiveness of the profession.

*Commentary*

### Guiding Principles

1.  It is essential that a person requiring legal services be able to find a qualified lawyer with a minimum of difficulty or delay. In a relatively small community where lawyers are well known, the person will usually be able to make an informed choice and select a qualified lawyer in whom to have confidence. However, in larger centres these conditions will often not obtain. As the practice of law becomes increasingly complex and many individual lawyers restrict their activities to particular fields of law, the reputations of lawyers and their competence or qualification in particular fields may not be sufficiently well known to enable a person to make an informed choice. Thus one who has had little or no contact with lawyers or who is a stranger in the community may have difficulty finding a lawyer with the special skill required for a particular task. Telephone directories, legal directories and referral services may help find a lawyer, but not necessarily the right one for the work involved. Advertising of legal services by the lawyer may assist members of the public and thereby result in increased access to the legal system. Where local rules permit, the lawyer may, therefore, advertise legal services to the general public.

2.  When considering whether advertising in a particular area meets the public need, consideration must be given to the clientele to be served. For example, in a small community with a stable population a person requiring a lawyer for a particular purpose will not have the same difficulty in selecting one as someone in a newly established community or a large city. Thus the governing body

must have freedom of action in determining the nature and content of advertising that will best meet the community need.

3. Despite the lawyer's economic interest in earning a living, advertising, direct solicitation or any other means by which the lawyer seeks to make legal services more readily available to the public must comply with any rules prescribed by the governing body, must be consistent with the public interest and must not detract from the integrity, independence or effectiveness of the legal profession. They must not mislead the uninformed or arouse unattainable hopes and expectations, because this could result in distrust of legal institutions and lawyers. They must not adversely affect the quality of legal services, nor must they be so undignified, in bad taste or otherwise offensive as to be prejudicial to the interests of the public or the legal profession.

## Finding a Lawyer

4. The lawyer who is consulted by a prospective client should be ready to assist in finding the right lawyer to deal with the problem. If unable to act, for example because of lack of qualification in the particular field, the lawyer should assist in finding a practitioner who is qualified and able to act. Such assistance should be given willingly and, except in very special circumstances, without charge.

5. The lawyer may also assist in making legal services available by participating in legal aid plans and referral services, by engaging in programs of public information, education or advice concerning legal matters, and by being considerate of those who seek advice but are inexperienced in legal matters or cannot readily explain their problems.

6. The lawyer has a general right to decline particular employment (except when assigned as counsel by a court) but it is a right the lawyer should be slow to exercise if the probable result would be to make it very difficult for a person to obtain legal advice or representation. Generally speaking, the lawyer should not exercise the right merely because the person seeking legal services or that person's cause is unpopular or notorious, or because powerful interests or allegations of misconduct or malfeasance are involved, or because of the lawyer's private opinion about the guilt of the accused. As stated in Commentary 4, the lawyer who declines employment should assist the person to obtain the services of another lawyer competent in the particular field and able to act.

### Enforcement of Restrictive Rules

7. The lawyer should adhere to rules made by the governing body with respect to making legal services available and respecting advertising, but rigid adherence to restrictive rules should be enforced with discretion where the lawyer who may have infringed such rules acted in good faith in trying to make legal services available more efficiently, economically and conveniently than they would otherwise have been.

# CHAPTER XV: RESPONSIBILITY TO THE PROFESSION GENERALLY

## RULE

The lawyer should assist in maintaining the integrity of the profession and should participate in its activities.

### *Commentary*

### Guiding Principles

1. Unless the lawyer who tends to depart from proper professional conduct is checked at an early stage, loss or damage to clients or others may ensue. Evidence of minor breaches may, on investigation, disclose a more serious situation or may indicate the beginning of a course of conduct that would lead to serious breaches in the future. It is, therefore, proper (unless it be privileged or otherwise unlawful) for a lawyer to report to a governing body any occurrences involving a breach of this Code. Where, however, there is a reasonable likelihood that someone will suffer serious damage as a consequence of an apparent breach, for example where a shortage of trust funds is involved, the lawyer has an obligation to the profession to report the matter unless it is privileged or otherwise unlawful to do so. In all cases, the report must be made *bona fide* without malice or ulterior motive. Further, subject to local rules, the lawyer must not act on a client's instructions to recover from another lawyer funds allegedly misappropriated by that other lawyer unless the client authorizes disclosure to the governing body and the lawyer makes such disclosure.
2. The lawyer has a duty to reply promptly to any communication from the governing body.

3.  The lawyer should not in the course of a professional practice write letters, whether to a client, another lawyer or any other person, that are abusive, offensive or otherwise totally inconsistent with the proper tone of a professional communication from a lawyer.

### Participation in Professional Activities

4.  In order that the profession may discharge its public responsibility of providing independent and competent legal services, the individual lawyer should do everything possible to assist the profession to function properly and effectively. In this regard, participation in such activities as law reform, continuing legal education, tutorials, legal aid programs, community legal services, professional conduct and discipline, liaison with other professions and other activities of the governing body or local, provincial or national associations, although often time-consuming and without tangible reward, is essential to the maintenance of a strong, independent and useful profession.

# CHAPTER XVI:  RESPONSIBILITY TO LAWYERS INDIVIDUALLY

## RULE

The lawyer's conduct toward other lawyers should be characterized by courtesy and good faith.

*Commentary*

### Guiding Principles

1.  Public interest demands that matters entrusted to the lawyer be dealt with effectively and expeditiously. Fair and courteous dealing on the part of each lawyer engaged in a matter will contribute materially to this end. The lawyer who behaves otherwise does a disservice to the client, and neglect of the Rule will impair the ability of lawyers to perform their function properly.
2.  Any ill feeling that may exist or be engendered between clients, particularly during litigation, should never be allowed to influence lawyers in their conduct and demeanour toward each other or the parties. The presence of personal animosity between lawyers involved in a matter may cause their judgement to be clouded by emotional factors and hinder the proper resolution of the matter.

Personal remarks or references between them should be avoided. Haranguing or offensive tactics interfere with the orderly administration of justice and have no place in our legal system.

3. The lawyer should accede to reasonable requests for trial dates, adjournments, waivers of procedural formalities and similar matters that do not prejudice the rights of the client. The lawyer who knows that another lawyer has been consulted in a matter should not proceed by default in the matter without enquiry and warning.

## Avoidance of Sharp Practices

4. The lawyer should avoid sharp practice and not take advantage of or act without fair warning upon slips, irregularities or mistakes on the part of other lawyers not going to the merits or involving any sacrifice of the client's rights. The lawyer should not, unless required by the transaction, impose on other lawyers impossible, impractical or manifestly unfair conditions of trust, including those with respect to time restraints and the payment of penalty interest.

5. The lawyer should not use a tape-recorder or other device to record a conversation, whether with a client, another lawyer or anyone else, even if lawful, without first informing the other person of the intention to do so.

6. The lawyer should answer with reasonable promptness all professional letters and communications from other lawyers that require an answer and should be punctual in fulfilling all commitments.

## Undertakings

7. The lawyer should give no undertaking that cannot be fulfilled, should fulfill every undertaking given, and should scrupulously honour any trust condition once accepted. Undertakings and trust conditions should be written or confirmed in writing and should be absolutely unambiguous in their terms. If the lawyer giving an undertaking does not intend to accept personal responsibility, this should be stated clearly in the undertaking itself. In the absence of such a statement, the person to whom the undertaking is given is entitled to expect that the lawyer giving it will honour it personally. If the lawyer is unable or unwilling to honour a trust condition imposed by someone else, the subject of the trust condition should be immediately returned to the person imposing the trust condition unless its terms can be forthwith amended in writing on a mutually agreeable basis.

8. The lawyer should not communicate upon or attempt to negotiate or compromise a matter directly with any party who is represented by a lawyer except through or with the consent of that lawyer.

**Acting against Another Lawyer**

9. The lawyer should avoid ill-considered or uninformed criticism of the competence, conduct, advice or charges of other lawyers, but should be prepared, when requested, to advise and represent a client in a complaint involving another lawyer.
10. The same courtesy and good faith should characterize the lawyer's conduct toward lay persons lawfully representing others or themselves.
11. The lawyer who is retained by another lawyer as counsel or adviser in a particular matter should act only as counsel or adviser and respect the relationship between the other lawyer and the client.

# CHAPTER XVII: PRACTICE BY UNAUTHORIZED PERSONS

## RULE

The lawyer should assist in preventing the unauthorized practice of law.

## Commentary

### Guiding Principles

1. Statutory provisions against the practice of law by unauthorized persons are for the protection of the public. Unauthorized persons may have technical, or personal ability, but they are immune from control, regulation and, in the case of misconduct, from discipline by any governing body. Their competence and integrity have not been vouched for by an independent body representative of the legal profession. Moreover, the client of a lawyer who is authorized to practise has the protection and benefit of the lawyer-client privilege, the lawyer's duty of secrecy, the professional standards of care that the law requires of lawyers, as well as the authority that the courts exercise over them. Other safeguards include group professional liability insurance, rights with respect to the taxation of bills, rules respecting trust monies, and requirements for the maintenance of compensation funds.

### Suspended or Disbarred Persons

2. The lawyer should not, without the approval of the governing body, employ in any capacity having to do with the practice of law (a) a lawyer who is under suspension as a result of disciplinary proceedings, or (b) a person who has been disbarred as a lawyer or has

been permitted to resign while facing disciplinary proceedings and has not been reinstated.

## Supervision of Employees

3. The lawyer must assume complete professional responsibility for all business entrusted to the lawyer, maintaining direct supervision over staff and assistants such as students, clerks and legal assistants to whom particular tasks and functions may be delegated. The lawyer who practices alone or operates a branch or part-time office should ensure that all matters requiring a lawyer's professional skill and judgement are dealt with by a lawyer qualified to do the work and that legal advice is not given by unauthorized persons, whether in the lawyer's name or otherwise. Furthermore, the lawyer should approve the amount of any fee to be charged to a client.

## Legal Assistants

4. There are many tasks that can be performed by a legal assistant working under the supervision of a lawyer. It is in the interests of the profession and the public for the delivery of more efficient, comprehensive and better quality legal services that the training and employment of legal assistants be encouraged.

5. Subject to general and specific restrictions that may be established by local rules and practice, a legal assistant may perform any task delegated and supervised by a lawyer so long as the lawyer maintains a direct relationship with the client and assumes full professional responsibility for the work. Legal assistants shall not perform any of the duties that lawyers only may perform or do things that lawyers themselves may not do. Generally speaking, the question of what the lawyer may delegate to a legal assistant turns on the distinction between the special knowledge of the legal assistant and the professional legal judgement of the lawyer, which must be exercised whenever it is required.

6. A legal assistant should be permitted to act only under the supervision of a lawyer. Adequacy of supervision will depend on the type of legal matter, including the degree of standardization and repetitiveness of the matter as well as the experience of the legal assistant, both generally and with regard to the particular matter. The burden rests on the lawyer who employs a legal assistant to educate the latter about the duties to which the legal assistant may be assigned and also to supervise on a continuing basis the way in which the legal assistant carries them out so that the work of the legal assistant will be shaped by the lawyer's judgement.

# CHAPTER XVIII:  PUBLIC APPEARANCES AND PUBLIC STATEMENTS BY LAWYERS

## RULE

The lawyer who engages in public appearances and public statements should do so in conformity with the principles of the Code.

### *Commentary*

### Guiding Principles

1. The lawyer who makes public appearances and public statements should behave in the same way as when dealing with clients, fellow practitioners and the courts. Dealings with the media are simply an extension of the lawyer's conduct in a professional capacity. The fact that an appearance is outside a courtroom or law office does not excuse conduct that would be considered improper in those contexts.

### Public Statements Concerning Clients

2. The lawyer's duty to the client demands that before making a public statement concerning the client's affairs, the lawyer must first be satisfied that any communication is in the best interests of the client and within the scope of the retainer. The lawyer owes a duty to the client to be qualified to represent the client effectively before the public and not to permit any personal interest or other cause to conflict with the client's interests.

3. When acting as an advocate, the lawyer should refrain from expressing personal opinions about the merits of the client's case.

### Standard of Conduct

4. The lawyer should, where possible, encourage public respect for and try to improve the administration of justice. In particular, the lawyer should treat fellow practitioners, the courts and tribunals with respect, integrity and courtesy. Lawyers are subject to a separate and higher standard of conduct than that which might incur the sanction of the court.

5. The lawyer who makes public appearances and public statements must comply with the requirements of Commentary 3 of the Rule relating to advertising, solicitation and making legal services available.

## Contacts with the Media

6. The media have recently shown greater interest in legal matters than they did formerly. This is reflected in more coverage of the passage of legislation at national and provincial levels, as well as of cases before the courts that may have social, economic or political significance. This interest has been heightened by the enactment of the *Canadian Charter of Rights and Freedoms*. As a result, media reporters regularly seek out the views not only of lawyers directly involved in particular court proceedings but also of lawyers who represent special interest groups or have recognized expertise in a given field in order to obtain information or provide commentary.

7. Where the lawyer, by reason of professional involvement or otherwise, is able to assist the media in conveying accurate information to the public, it is proper for the lawyer to do so, provided that there is no infringement of the lawyer's obligations to the client, the profession, the courts or the administration of justice, and provided also that the lawyer's comments are made *bona fide* and without malice or ulterior motive.

8. The lawyer may make contact with the media in a non-legal setting to publicize such things as fund-raising, expansion of hospitals or universities, promoting public institutions or political organizations, or speaking on behalf of organizations that represent various racial, religious or other special interest groups. This is a well-established and completely proper role for the lawyer to play in view of the obvious contribution it makes to the community.

9. The lawyer is often called upon to comment publicly on the effectiveness of existing statutory or legal remedies, on the effect of particular legislation or decided cases, or to offer an opinion on causes that have been or are about to be instituted. It is permissible to do this in order to assist the public to understand the legal issues involved.

10. The lawyer may also be involved as an advocate for special interest groups whose objective is to bring about changes in legislation, government policy or even a heightened public awareness about certain issues, and the lawyer may properly comment publicly about such changes.

11. Given the variety of cases that can arise in the legal system, whether in civil, criminal or administrative matters, it is not feasible to set down guidelines that would anticipate every possible situation. In some circumstances, the lawyer should have no contact at all with the media; in others, there may be a positive duty to contact the media in order to serve the client properly. The latter situation will arise more often when dealing with administrative

boards and tribunals that are instruments of government policy and hence susceptible to public opinion.

12. The lawyer should bear in mind when making a public appearance or giving a statement that ordinarily the lawyer will have no control over any editing that may follow, or the context in which the appearance or statement may be used.

13. This Rule should not be construed in such a way as to discourage constructive comment or criticism.

# CHAPTER XIX: AVOIDING QUESTIONABLE CONDUCT

## RULE

The lawyer should observe the rules of professional conduct set out in the Code in the spirit as well as in the letter.

*Commentary*

### Guiding Principles

1. Public confidence in the administration of justice and the legal profession may be eroded by irresponsible conduct on the part of the individual lawyer. For that reason, even the appearance of impropriety should be avoided.

2. Our justice system is designed to try issues in an impartial manner and decide them upon the merits. Statements or suggestions that the lawyer could or would try to circumvent the system should be avoided because they might bring the lawyer, the legal profession and the administration of justice into disrepute.

### Duty after Leaving Public Employment

3. After leaving public employment, the lawyer should not accept employment in connection with any matter in which the lawyer had substantial responsibility or confidential information prior to leaving, because to do so would give the appearance of impropriety even if none existed. However, it would not be improper for the lawyer to act professionally in such a matter on behalf of the particular public body or authority by which the lawyer had formerly been employed. As to confidential government information acquired when the lawyer was a public officer or employee, see Commentary 14 of the Rule relating to confidential information.

## Retired Judges

4. A judge who returns to practice after retiring or resigning from the bench should not (without the approval of the governing body) appear as a lawyer before the court of which the former judge was a member or before courts of inferior jurisdiction thereto in the province where the judge exercised judicial functions. If in a given case the former judge should be in a preferred position by reason of having held judicial office, the administration of justice would suffer; if the reverse were true, the client might suffer. There may, however, be cases where a governing body would consider that no preference or appearance of preference would result, for example, where the judge resigned for good reason after only a very short time on the bench. In this paragraph "judge" refers to one who was appointed as such under provincial legislation or section 96 of the *Constitution Act, 1982* and "courts" include chambers and administrative boards and tribunals.

5. Conversely, although it may be unavoidable in some circumstances or areas, generally speaking the lawyer should not appear before a judge if by reason of relationship or past association, the lawyer would appear to be in a preferred position.

## Inserting Retainer in Client's Will

6. Without express instructions from the client, it is improper for the lawyer to insert in the client's will a clause directing the executor to retain the lawyer's services in the administration of the estate.

## Duty to Meet Financial Obligations

7. The lawyer has a professional duty, quite apart from any legal liability, to meet financial obligations incurred or assumed in the course of practice when called upon to do so. Examples are agency accounts, obligations to members of the profession, fees or charges of witnesses, sheriffs, special examiners, registrars, reporters and public officials as well as the deductible under a governing body's errors and omissions insurance policy.

## Dealings with Unrepresented Persons

8. The lawyer should not undertake to advise an unrepresented person, but should urge such a person to obtain independent legal advice and, if the unrepresented person does not do so, the lawyer must take care to see that such person is not proceeding under the

impression that the lawyer is protecting such person's interests. If the unrepresented person requests the lawyer to advise or act in the matter, the lawyer should be governed by the considerations outlined in the Rule relating to impartiality and conflict of interest between clients. The lawyer may have an obligation to a person whom the lawyer does not represent, whether or not such person is represented by a lawyer.

### Bail

9. The lawyer shall not stand bail for an accused person for whom the lawyer or a partner or associate is acting, except where there is a family relationship with the accused in which case the person should not be represented by the lawyer but may be represented by a partner or associate.

### Standard of Care

10. The lawyer should try at all times to observe a standard of conduct that reflects credit on the legal profession and the administration of justice generally and inspires the confidence, respect and trust of both clients and the community.

# CHAPTER XX: NON-DISCRIMINATION

## RULE

The lawyer shall respect the requirements of human rights and constitutional laws in force in Canada, and in the respective provinces and territories thereof, and shall not discriminate on grounds, including, but not limited to, of race, language, national or ethnic origin, colour, religion, age, sex, sexual orientation, marital status, family status, or disability.

*Commentary*

### Duty of Non-Discrimination

1. The lawyer has a duty to respect the dignity and worth of all persons and to treat persons equally, without discrimination. Discrimination is defined as any distinction that disproportionately and negatively impacts on an individual or group identifiable by the grounds listed in the Rule, in a way that does not impact on others. This duty includes, but is not limited to:

(a) the requirement that the lawyer does not deny services or provide inferior services on the basis of the grounds noted in the Rule;

(b) the requirement that the lawyer not discriminate against another lawyer in any professional dealings;

(c) the requirement that the lawyer act in accordance with the legal duty to accommodate and not engage in discriminatory employment practices; and

(d) the requirement that the lawyer prohibit partners, co-workers and employees and agents subject to the lawyer's discretion and control from engaging in discriminatory practices.

## Extent of Duty of Non-Discrimination

2. As a member of the legal profession, the lawyer must ensure that he or she is at all times acting in compliance with the law. The law applicable in this context is human rights legislation. According to the law, discrimination can be constituted by the effect of action or omission.

   Intent to discriminate is not a prerequisite to a finding of discrimination. Discrimination can also arise through the adverse impact of neutral practices on the basis of the grounds noted in the Rule. Failure by the lawyer to take reasonable steps to prevent or stop discrimination by the lawyer's partner, co-worker or by any employee or agent also violates the duty of non-discrimination.

## Special Programs

3. Discrimination does not include special programs designed to relieve disadvantage for individuals or groups on the grounds noted in the Rule.

## Responsibility

4. Discriminatory attitudes on the part of partners, employees, agents or clients do not diminish the responsibility of the lawyer to refrain from discrimination in the provision of service or employment.

## Discrimination in Employment

5. The Rule applies to discrimination by the lawyers in any aspect of employment and working conditions, including recruitment, promotion, training, allocation of work, compensation, receipt of benefits, dismissal, lay-offs, discipline, performance appraisal and hours of work.

It applies to all discrimination with repercussions for employment and workplace conditions including physical work sites, washrooms, conferences, business travel and social events. Examples of discrimination in employment include:

(a) setting unnecessary or unfair hiring criteria that tend to exclude applications on prohibited grounds;

(b) asking questions during an employment or promotion interview that are not logically related to the essential requirements of the job;

(c) assigning work on the basis of factors or assumptions other than individual ability or denying work to lawyers on the basis of prohibited grounds;

(d) failing to provide appropriate maternity and parental leave thereby discriminating on the basis of sex or family status;

(e) failing to accommodate religious holidays or religious practices thereby discriminating on the basis of religion;

(f) requiring billable hour targets or workload expectations which effectively exclude those who have child care responsibilities and adversely affect such persons on the basis of family status or sex.

It is not considered discrimination when distinctions are made as a result of a reasonable and *bona fide* occupational qualification or requirement. For example, if an applicant for a position is not sufficiently proficient in the language(s) required for the competent performance of the essential duties and responsibilities required in that position, it would not constitute discrimination to deny the applicant employment solely on the ground of language. Where facility in a particular language is clearly an essential requirement for the position, the employer is not prevented from demanding the necessary proficiency.

## Duty of Accommodation

6. One aspect of the duty of non-discrimination is the duty to accommodate the diverse needs of lawyers on the basis of grounds noted in the Rule. Such accommodation is required unless it would cause undue hardship to the lawyer. Examples of this type of accommodation include

(a) the provision of flexible hours to accommodate family responsibilities or to accommodate transportation difficulties for persons with disabilities;

(b) the modification of the physical workplace to include wheel-chair access, modified furniture and assistive devices;

(c) a benefits policy that includes same sex couples;

(d) adjusting the billable hour or workload expectations to accommodate family responsibilities;

(e) accommodation of religious holidays or religious practices.

## Sexual Harassment and Harassment

7. Sexual harassment and harassment are forms of discrimination. The lawyer should refrain from engaging in vexatious comment or conduct that is known or reasonably ought to be known to constitute sexual harassment or harassment in all areas of professional conduct.

   (a) Sexual harassment includes the use of a position of power to import sexual requirements into the workplace thereby negatively altering the working conditions of employees;

   (b) Harassment includes all conduct which has the effect of eroding the dignity and equality of opportunity of the victim, particularly based on the grounds noted in the Rule.

## Discriminatory Activities

8. The lawyer must refrain from participating in discriminatory activities in his or her professional life.

# CANADIAN BAR ASSOCIATION: ONTARIO ADR SECTION MODEL CODE OF CONDUCT FOR MEDIATORS

(Note: This model code of conduct has been developed by the ADR section of the Canadian Bar Association Ontario Branch and has received approval by the Ontario Branch. It has gone forward to the national ADR section for discussion and development of a national code of conduct for mediators.)

## I. OBJECTIVES FOR MODEL CODE OF CONDUCT FOR MEDIATORS

The main objectives of this Model Code of Conduct for mediators are as follows:
(a)  to provide guiding principles for mediators' conduct;
(b)  to provide a means of protection for the public; and
(c)  to promote confidence in mediation as a process for resolving disputes.

## II. DEFINITIONS

In this Model Code of Conduct:

"mediation" means a process in which an impartial person, a mediator, helps disputing parties to try to reach a voluntary, mutually acceptable resolution of some or all of the issues of their dispute.

"mediator" means an impartial person whose role in mediation is to assist and encourage parties to a dispute:

- to communicate and negotiate in good faith with each other;
- to identify and convey their interests to one another;
- to assess risks;
- to consider possible settlement options; and
- to resolve voluntarily their dispute.

"impartial" means being and being seen as unbiased toward parties to a dispute, toward their interests and toward the options they present for settlement.

"conflict of interest" means direct or indirect financial or personal interest in the outcome of the dispute or any existing or past financial, business, professional, family or social relationship which is likely to affect impartiality or reasonably create an appearance of partiality or bias.

## III. PRINCIPLE OF SELF-DETERMINATION

1. Self-determination is the right of parties in a mediation to make their own voluntary and non-coerced decisions regarding the possible resolution of any issue in dispute. It is a fundamental principle of mediation which mediators shall respect and encourage.
2. Mediators shall provide information about their role in the mediation before mediation commences, including the fact that authority for decision-making rests with the parties, not mediators.
3. Mediators shall not provide legal advice to the parties.
4. Mediators have the responsibility to advise unrepresented parties to obtain independent legal advice, where appropriate. Mediators also have the responsibility to advise parties of the need to consult other professionals to help parties make informed decisions.

## IV. IMPARTIALITY

1. Mediators shall serve only in those matters in which they can remain impartial.
2. Mediators have a duty to remain impartial throughout the course of the mediation process.
3. If mediators become aware of their lack of impartiality, they shall immediately disclose to the parties that they can no longer remain impartial and shall withdraw from the mediation.

# V. CONFLICT OF INTEREST

1. Mediators have a responsibility to disclose to the parties in dispute any conflict of interest reasonably known to the mediator, as soon as possible.
2. Mediators who have disclosed a conflict of interest to the parties shall withdraw as mediator, unless the parties consent to retain the mediator.
3. Mediators or their associates or partners shall not establish a professional relationship with any of the parties in a matter related to the mediation which could give rise to a conflict of interest, without the consent of all parties.
4. Mediators' commitment is to the parties and the process and they shall not allow pressure or influence from third parties (persons, service providers, mediation facilities, organizations, or agencies) to compromise the independence of the mediator.

# VI. CONFIDENTIALITY

1. Mediators shall inform the parties of the confidential nature of mediation.
2. Mediators shall not disclose to anyone who is not a party to the mediation any information or documents that are exchanged for or during the mediation process except:
   (a) with the mediating parties' written consent;
   (b) when ordered to do so by a court or otherwise required to do so by law;
   (c) when the information/documentation discloses criminal activities and/or an actual or potential threat to human life;
   (d) any report or summary that is required to be prepared by mediators; or
   (e) when the information/documentation is non-identifiable (unless all of the parties otherwise authorize identification), and is used for research, statistical, accreditation, or educational purposes and is limited only to what is required to achieve these purposes.
3. If mediators hold private sessions (breakout meetings, caucuses) with a party, they shall discuss the nature of such sessions with all parties prior to commencing such sessions. Mediators shall not disclose anything that is said or given to him or her in confidence, during private meetings, unless the party authorizes the mediator to do so.
4. Mediators shall maintain confidentiality in the storage and disposal of mediation notes, records and files.

# VII. QUALITY OF THE PROCESS

1. Mediators shall make reasonable efforts to ensure the parties understand the mediation process before mediation commences.
2. Mediators have a duty to ensure that they conduct a process which provides parties with the opportunity to participate in the mediation and which encourages respect among the parties.
3. Mediators shall inform parties to a dispute that mediation is most effective when the parties with authority to settle are in attendance and when they are willing to consider options for settlement.
4. Mediators who are lawyers shall not represent any party(ies) to the mediation.
5. Mediators have an obligation to acquire and maintain professional skills and abilities required to uphold the quality of the mediation process.

# VIII. ADVERTISING

In advertising or offering services to clients or potential clients:
1. Mediators shall refrain from guaranteeing settlement or promising specific results.
2. Mediators shall provide accurate information about their education, background, mediation training and experience in any representation, biographical or promotional material and in any oral explanation of same.

# IX. FEES

1. If mediators or service providers charge fees, they shall provide parties with the fee structure, likely expenses and any and all payment or retainer requirements, before mediation commences.
2. Mediators shall not base their fees on the outcome of mediation, whether there is a settlement or what the settlement is.
3. Mediators may charge a cancellation or a late/delay fee within the mediator's discretion, provided the mediator advises the parties in advance of this practice and the amount of the fee.

# X. AGREEMENT TO MEDIATE

Mediators shall ensure before the mediation commences that the parties understand the terms of mediation whether or not they are contained in an agreement/contract to mediate, which terms shall include but not be limited to the following:

(a) confidentiality of communications and documents;

(b) the right of the mediator and parties to terminate or suspend mediation;

(c) fee expenses, retainer, method of payment and what, if any, fee there is for cancellation, lateness or delay; and

(d) the fact that the mediator is not compellable as a witness in court proceedings by any parties to the mediation.

# XI. TERMINATION OR SUSPENSION OF MEDIATION

1. Mediators shall withdraw from mediation for the reasons referred to in paragraphs IV.3 and V.2.

2. Mediators may suspend or terminate mediation if requested by one or more of the parties;

3. Mediators may suspend or terminate mediation if in their opinion:

   (a) the process is likely to prejudice one or more of the parties;

   (b) one or more of the parties is using the process inappropriately;

   (c) one or more of the parties is delaying the process to the detriment of another party or parties;

   (d) the mediation process is detrimental to one or more of the parties or the mediator;

   (e) it appears that a party is not acting in good faith; or

   (f) there are other reasons that are or appear to be counterproductive to the process.

4. Members shall terminate mediation if the conditions referred to in XI.3. (a)-(f) are not rectified.

# XII. OTHER CONDUCT OBLIGATIONS

Nothing in this Model Code of Conduct replaces, supersedes or alienates ethical standards and codes which may be imposed or additionally imposed upon any mediator by virtue of the mediator's professional calling.

# CONCORDANCE TABLE FOR THE CBA, LSUC, AND BC CODES OF PROFESSIONAL CONDUCT

The following table correlates the professional codes of conduct of the law societies of Ontario and British Columbia with that of the Canadian Bar Association (CBA), which serves as the table's point of reference. Exact symmetry between the codes was not required for their correlation. Rather, if the rules/commentaries (or parts of them) as between the CBA and the province spoke to a similar point within a shared subject matter, they were correlated. An attempt was made to be as specific as possible in correlating the rules by including their subsections and the various places where portions of the CBA code (on a particular rule) appear in the provincial code. This appendix was compiled in July 1998.

It should be noted that the CBA code of conduct is composed of several chapters, each one having a general rule at the beginning with commentaries that follow (hence the designation "c"). The Law Society of Ontario's code of conduct is composed of several general rules that also have associated commentaries. The Law Society of British Columbia's code of conduct does not have commentaries, nor (usually) a statement of a general rule. Instead, each chapter is composed of specific and numbered rules. Finally, for the Ontario code of conduct, there are places in the table where numbers are indicated alone, without a "c." in front of them. This connotes a numbered point that is part of the rule itself, not the commentary associated with the rule. Furthermore, rules/commentaries were noted as correlated if there was overlap between some of their parts; for example, a BC rule and a CBA rule may be noted as correlated, even though only part of the CBA rule may be present in the BC rule. Many of the provincial law societies' rules seem composed of portions of CBA rules, which are often mixed and matched.

| CBA | Ontario | British Columbia |
|---|---|---|
| Chapter I, Rule | Rule 1 | Chapter 1, introduction and rule 5(1); Chapter 2, rule 1 |
| c.1 | c.1 | Chapter 1, introduction and rule 5(1), (3), (6) |
| c.2 | — | — |
| c.3 | c.2 | — |
| c.4 | c.3 | — |
| | | |
| Chapter II, Rule  (a) | Rule 2  (a) | Chapter 3, rule 2 |
| (b) | (b) | Chapter 3, introductory text; Chapter 3, rule 3 |
| c.1 | c.1 | Chapter 3, rule 1 |
| c.2 | c.2 | — |
| c.3 | c.3 | Chapter 3, rule 2, rule 4(a) |
| c.4 | c.4, c.5 | Chapter 3, rule 1 |
| c.5 | — | — |
| c.6 | c.6 | Chapter 3, rule 4 |
| c.7  (a) | c.8  (a) | Chapter 3, rule 3  (a) |
| (b) | (b) | (b) |
| (c) | (c) | (c) |
| (d) | (d) | (d) |
| (e) | (e) | (e) |
| (f) | (f) | (f) |
| (g) | (g) | (g) |
| (h) | (h) | (h) |
| (i) | (i) | (i) |
| (j) | (j) | (j) |
| (k) | (k) | (k) |
| (l) | (n) | (l) |
| (m) | (o) | (m) |
| c.8 | c.7 | Chapter 3, rule 5 |
| c.9 | c.9 | — |
| c.10 | c.10 | — |
| | | |
| Chapter III, Rule | Rule 3 | — |
| c.1 | c.1 | Chapter 1, rule 3(1) |
| c.2 | c.2 | — |
| c.3 | c.3 | — |
| c.4 | c.4 | Chapter 1, rule 3(1) |
| c.5 | — | — |
| c.6 | c.5 | Chapter 1, rule 3(3) |

| c.7 | c.6 | Chapter 1, rule 1(1); Chapter 1, rule 3(5) |
|---|---|---|
| c.8 | c.7 | — |
| c.9 | c.8 | Chapter 4, rule 2 |
| c.10 | c.9 | — |
| c.11 | c.10 | Chapter 4, rule 5.1 |
| c.12 | Rule 5, c.9 (a), (c) | — |
| | | |
| Chapter IV, Rule | Rule 4 | Chapter 5, rule 1 |
| c.1 | c.1 | Chapter 5, rule 2 |
| c.2 | c.2 | — |
| c.3 | c.3 | Chapter 5, rule 3 |
| c.4 | c.4 | Chapter 5, rule 4 |
| c.5 | c.5 | Chapter 5, rules 5 and 6 |
| c.6 | c.6 | Chapter 5, rule 7 |
| c.7 | c.7 | Chapter 5, rule 8 |
| c.8 | c.8 | — |
| c.9 | c.9 | Chapter 5, rule 11 |
| c.10 | c.12 | — |
| c.11 | c.11 | Chapter 5, rule 12 |
| c.12 | — | — |
| c.13 | c.10 | Chapter 5, rule 13 |
| c.14 | — | Chapter 5, rule 10 |
| | | |
| Chapter V, Rule | Rule 5 | Chapter 1, rule 3(2); Chapter 6, rules 1–3 |
| c.1 | c.1 | — |
| c.2 | c.2 | — |
| c.3 | c.3 | — |
| c.4 | c.4 | Chapter 1, rule 3(2) |
| c.5 | c.5 | Chapter 6, rule 4 |
| c.6 | c.6 | Chapter 6, rule 5 |
| c.7 | c.11 | — |
| c.8 | c.13 | Chapter 1, rule 3(7); Chapter 6, rule 7 |
| c.9 | c.16 | — |
| c.10 | — | — |
| c.11 | — | — |
| c.12 | — | — |
| c.13 | c.17 | — |

| | | | |
|---|---|---|---|
| Chapter VI, Rule (a) | | — | Chapter 1, rule (3)7 |
| | (i) | — | |
| | (ii) | — | Chapter 7, rule 5(b) |
| | (iii) | — | — |
| | (b) | — | — |
| | (i) | — | Chapter 7, rule 5(b) |
| | (ii) | — | — |
| | (c) | Rule 5, c.7, c.8 | Chapter 7, rules 1 and 2 |
| | (d) | — | — |
| c.1 | | Rule 5, c.7 | — |
| c.2 | | — | — |
| c.3 | | Rule 5, c.7 | — |
| c.4 | | Rule 7, 1. (a) | Chapter 7, rule 4 |
| c.5 | | — | — |
| c.6 | | — | — |
| | | | |
| Chapter VII, Rule | | Rule 17 | — |
| c.1 | | c.1 | — |
| c.2 | | c.2 | Chapter 7, rule 6 |
| c.3 | | c.3 | — |
| c.4 | | — | Chapter 7, rule 6 |
| c.5 (a) | | — | — |
| (b) | | — | — |
| c.6 (a) | | — | — |
| (b) | | — | — |
| | | | |
| Chapter VIII, Rule | | Rule 6 | Chapter 7.1, rule 3 |
| c.1 | | c.1 | — |
| c.2 | | c.2 | Chapter 1, rule 3(8); Chapter 7.1, rule 4 |
| c.3 | | c.3 | Chapter 1, rule 3(8); Chapter 7.1, rule 5 (a) and (b) |
| c.4 | | c.4 | Chapter 1, rule 3(8); Chapter 7.1, rule 5 (c) |
| c.5 | | c.5 | Chapter 7, rule 6 |
| c.6 | | c.6 | Chapter 5, rule 14 |
| | | | |
| Chapter IX, Rule | | Rule 10 | Chapter 1, rule 2(1) |
| c.1 | | c.2 | Chapter 1, rule 3(5) |
| c.2 (a) | | c.2 (a) | Chapter 8, rule 1 (a) |
| (b) | | (b) | (b) |
| (c) | | (c) | (c) |

| | | |
|---|---|---|
| (d) | (d) | (d) |
| (e) | (e) | Chapter 1, rule 2(3) |
| (f) | (f) | — |
| (g) | (g) | Chapter 8, rule 1  (e) |
| (h) | (h) | (f) |
| (i) | (i) | (g) |
| (j) | (j) | (h) |
| (k) | (k) | Chapter 1, rule 3(4) |
| (l) | (l) | Chapter 1, rule 3(4) |
| c.3 | 3. (a) | Chapter 4, rule 5.1 |
| c.4 | 3. (b) | Chapter 8, rules 7 and 8 |
| c.5 | c.16 (a), (b) | Chapter 1, rule 3(11); Chapter 8, rules 9 and 10 |
| c.6 | c.14 | Chapter 1, rule 4(2); Chapter 8, rules 12, 12.1, 12.2, 12.3 |
| c.7 | c.5 | — |
| c.8 | c.6 | Chapter 1, rule 3(3) |
| c.9 | c.9 | Chapter 1, rule 1(2); Chapter 8, rule 18 |
| c.10 | c.10 | Chapter 1, rule 3(6) |
| c.11 | c.11 | — |
| c.12  (a) | c.12  (a) | — |
| (b) | (b) | Chapter 8, rule 20 (a) |
| (c) | (c) | — |
| (d) | (d) | Chapter 8, rule 20 (b) |
| c.13 | c.8 | Chapter 1, rule 4(2) |
| c.14 | c.7 | Chapter 1, rules 2(1) and 4(1) |
| c.15 | c.13 | Chapter 8, rule 21 |
| c.16 | c.15 | — |
| c.17 | — | — |
| c.18 | c.1 | — |
| | | |
| Chapter X, Rule | Rule 18 | — |
| c.1 | c.1 | — |
| c.2 | c.3 | — |
| c.3 | — | — |
| c.4 | c.4 | — |
| c.5 | c.6 | — |
| c.6 | c.5 | Chapter 5, rule 9 |
| c.7 | c.8 | — |
| c.8 | c.2 | — |

| | | |
|---|---|---|
| Chapter XI, Rule (a) | Rule 9 (a) | Chapter 1, rule 3(9); Chapter 9, rules 1 and 7 |
| (b) | (d) | Chapter 1, rule 3(8) |
| c.1 (a) | c.1 (a) | — |
| (b) | (b) | — |
| (c) | (c) | — |
| (d) | — | — |
| (e) | (d) | — |
| (f) | — | — |
| (g) | (e) | — |
| (h) | (f) | — |
| (i) | (g) | — |
| (j) | — | — |
| c.2 | c.2 | Chapter 1, rule 3(9) |
| c.3 | c.5 | Chapter 1, rule 3(10) |
| c.4 | c.6 | — |
| c.5 | c.3 | Chapter 9, rule 5 |
| c.6 | Rule 9 (b) | — |
| c.7 | c.8 | Chapter 9, rules 7–9 |
| c.8 | c.7 | Chapter 9, rule 2(a); Chapter 9, rule 6 |
| c.9 | c.7 | — |
| c.10 | c.10 | — |
| Chapter XII, Rule | Rule 8 | — |
| c.1 | c.1 | Chapter 10, rule 3(b), rule 5 |
| c.2 | c.2 | Chapter 10, rule 3 (a), rule 4 |
| c.3 | — | — |
| c.4 | c.3 | Chapter 10, rule 1 |
| c.5 | c.4 | Chapter 10, rule 2 |
| c.6 | c.5 | Chapter 10, rule 7 |
| c.7 | c.7 | — |
| c.8 (a) | c.8 (a) | Chapter 10, rule 8 (d) (ii) and (e) |
| (b) | (b) | Chapter 10, rule 8 (e) |
| (c) | (c) | Chapter 10, rule 8 (d) (i) |
| (d) | (d) | — |
| (e) | (e) | Chapter 10, rule 8 (e) |
| c.9 | — | — |
| c.10 | c.9 | — |
| c.11 | c.10 | — |
| c.12 | c.11 | — |
| c.13 | c.12 | — |

| Chapter XIII, Rule | Rule 11 | Chapter 1, introduction |
|---|---|---|
| c.1 | c.2 | Canons, introduction; Chapter 1, rule 5(1) |
| c.2 | c.3 | — |
| c.3 | c.1 | Chapter 1, introduction; Chapter 1, rule 1(1) and rule 5(1), (4) |
| c.4 | c.5 | Chapter 1, rule 2(2) |
| c.5 | c.4 | — |
| | | |
| Chapter XIV, Rule | Rule 12, 1. | Chapter 14, rule 3 |
| c.1 | c.1 | — |
| c.2 | — | — |
| c.3 | 2. (a), (b); c.4 | Chapter 14, rule 4 |
| c.4 | c.2 | — |
| c.5 | c.3 | — |
| c.6 | c.5 | — |
| c.7 | — | — |
| | | |
| Chapter XV, Rule | Rule 13 | Chapter 1, rule 5(1) |
| c.1 | c.1 | Chapter 1, rule 5(1); Chapter 13, rules 1 and 2 |
| c.2 | c.3 | Chapter 13, rule 3 |
| c.3 | c.4 | — |
| c.4 | — | — |
| | | |
| Chapter XVI, Rule | Rule 14 | Chapter 1, rule 4(1) |
| c.1 | c.1 | Chapter 1, rule 5(3) |
| c.2 | c.2 | Chapter 1, rule 4(1) |
| c.3 | c.3 | Chapter 11, rule 12; Chapter 1, rule 4(3) |
| c.4 | c.4 | Chapter 1, rule 4(3) |
| c.5 | c.4 | Chapter 11, rule 14 |
| c.6 | c.5 | Chapter 11, rules 5 and 6 |
| c.7 | c.6 | Chapter 1, rule 4(2); Chapter 11, rules 7, 7.1 |
| c.8 | c.7 | Chapter 1, rule 4(2) |
| c.9 | c.8 | Chapter 11, rule 13 |
| c.10 | c.9 | — |
| c.11 | — | — |

| | | |
|---|---|---|
| Chapter XVII, Rule | Rule 19 | — |
| c.1 | Rule 19, c.1 | — |
| c.2 | Rule 20 | Chapter 13, rule 5 (a), (b) |
| c.3 | Rule 19, c.2 | Chapter 12, rule 1 |
| c.4 | Rule 16, 1. | Chapter 12, rule 4 |
| c.5 | Rule 16, 2. | Chapter 12, rule 5 |
| c.6 | Rule 16, 3. | Chapter 12, rule 7 |
| | | |
| Chapter XVIII, Rule | Rule 21 | — |
| c.1 | 1. | — |
| c.2 | 2. | Chapter 14, rule 6.1 |
| c.3 | 3. | Chapter 14, rule 6(a) |
| c.4 | 4. | Chapter 1, introduction; Chapter 1, rules 2(1) and 4(1) |
| c.5 | 5. | — |
| c.6 | c.1 | — |
| c.7 | c.1 | — |
| c.8 | c.2 | — |
| c.9 | c.3 | — |
| c.10 | c.4 | — |
| c.11 | c.5 | — |
| c.12 | c.6 | — |
| c.13 | — | — |
| | | |
| Chapter XIX, Rule | Foreword, paragraph 1 | Chapter 2, rule 1 |
| c.1 | Foreword, paragraph 2 | — |
| c.2 | — | — |
| c.3 | Rule 18, c.7 | Chapter 5, rules 9 and 10 |
| c.4 | Rule 15, 1. and 2. | — |
| c.5 | — | Chapter 8, rule 1 (c) |
| c.6 | Rule 12, c.6 | — |
| c.7 | Rule 13, c.6 | Chapter 2, rule 2 |
| c.8 | Rule 5, c.14 | Chapter 4, rule 1 |
| c.9 | — | Chapter 8, rule 19 |
| c.10 | Foreword, paragraph 2 | Chapter 2, rule 1 |
| | | |
| Chapter XX, Rule | Rule 28, c.1 | Chapter 2, rule 3 |

# TABLE OF CASES

# INDEX

# ABOUT THE AUTHOR

Allan Hutchinson is professor of law at Osgoode Hall Law School at York University and one of Canada's leading experts in legal theory. He is the author of numerous scholarly books and articles in critical legal studies and a regular contributor on legal issues in the popular media both in Canada and abroad. Professor Hutchinson has been invited to lecture in Australia, New Zealand, the United Kingdom, and the United States. He served as Associate Dean of Law at Osgoode Hall from 1993 to 1997. He is co-author of *The Law School Book* (Irwin Law, 1996).